Listening to Idries Shah

Listening to Idries Shah

How understanding can grow

Memoirs

IVAN TYRRELL

PUBLISHING

PUBLISHING

First published in Great Britain 2016
Copyright © Ivan Tyrrell 2016

The right of Ivan Tyrrell to be identified as the author of this work
has been asserted in accordance with sections 77 and 78 of the
Copyright Designs and Patents Act 1988.
Published by HG Publishing an imprint of
Human Givens Publishing Ltd, Chalvington,
East Sussex, BN27 3TD, United Kingdom.
www.humangivens.com

A catalogue record for this book is available from the British Library.
ISBN - 10: 1-899398-08-2
ISBN - 13: 978-1-899398-08-9

Typeset in Minion Pro and Gotham
Printed and bound in Great Britain

Born: *"Where do we come from?"*
Live: *"What for?"*
Die: *"Where do we go to?"*

CONTENTS   Page No

*Surely you know that pleasures and pains
evaporate into thin air
and all we are left with is stories?*

Hanan Al-Shaykh

A personal account

I was born on 18th October 1943 in a house opposite the main entrance to Hampton Court Palace (on the outside looking in right from the start). My first passport gave my place of birth as 'Hampton Court', which I was rather pleased with. When I applied for a new one some years later it came back with my place of birth changed to 'Staines', which put me back in my place.

MY FATHER, Frederick Tyrrell, deeply regretted not writing about his life until four years before he left us. He had wanted to record his memories much earlier, in his late 70s, and I offered to help him turn them into a proper book as a present for his 80th birthday. But my mother, Gladys, wouldn't let him devote time to it. She could be a bit of an emotional tyrant at times and wanted all his attention and couldn't stand the thought of him spending long hours telling his stories into my tape recorder and mocked the idea even more when I suggested that she could be involved too. In the end she nagged Dad so much about it that we reluctantly abandoned the project. It wasn't until she later became senile and her resulting disposition gentle enough for her to forget her selfish objections that he was able to start. She slept a lot by then and was unaware that he was writing when he was sitting at his 100 year old bureau. But by then it was almost too late: he was 91, could hardly see and only managed to write a few sentences a day with the aid of a large magnifying glass. Every paragraph he wrote was a struggle for him and, before he died, he sadly confided that he had only written a tiny fraction of what he had wanted to. Nevertheless what he produced was a beautifully written document describing a world long gone. He died in his 96th year.

Learning from this, I am writing down a few observations and highlights from my own life by beginning the process 25 years earlier than my father did; whilst my mind, eyes and typing fingers are still functioning.

Writing is helpful for developing an ability to reflect and attempt to extract the meaning behind events so as to set them into a context of interconnectedness: everything is connected in mysterious ways after all, so, ultimately, all is one. Each of us is an individual window on the

Universe and, in line with a fundamental principle of quantum mechanics, the information of our lives is never lost. I infer from this that our experiences and the information we gather is absorbed into the universal mind when we leave this material realm.

Another reason for writing a memoir is that I have had the good fortune to meet and work with an interesting range of individuals, the most notable of these being the author Idries Shah (who incidentally recommended memoir writing), and Joe Griffin, the Irish psychologist who discovered why we evolved to dream and with whom I helped create the Human Givens approach to psychotherapy, education, management and conflict resolution. Joe and I met through a mutual interest in hypnosis that eventually led us to having insights beyond the realm of psychotherapy; into time, consciousness and how the Universe maintains itself. In our book, *Godhead: The Brain's Big Bang – The Explosive Origin of Creativity, Mysticism and Mental Illness* we attempted to present these in a way we felt might be compatible with both modern science and mystical intuition.

It is for these reasons that the following pages of my recollections and thoughts may be of interest beyond my immediate family.

CHAPTER 1

Why do we die daddy?

THREE months into the chaotic Iran-Iraq war that killed more than a million people, I was part of a small group of Europeans running down a dusty backstreet in Baghdad being chased by angry Iraqis yelling fierce threats whilst manically waving meat cleavers and large knives at us like demented puppets. Emotions were running high in Iraq in 1980. The city had suffered bombing from Iranian planes in the previous weeks and it was quite feasible, in the heat of that moment, that we would suffer a severe beating or be killed. Fuelled by adrenalin my legs took me away whilst my dissociated mind asked the question: surely being hacked to pieces in Baghdad wasn't how my life was meant to end?

My predicament arose because of a project instigated by the writer Idries Shah, an extraordinary man, a Sufi guide who never described himself as such but nevertheless had already impacted in myriad ways on countless lives, including mine. One thing he taught was that we only learn something new when our expectations aren't fulfilled, that is to say, when something interrupts our habitual responses. It's only when we leave our comfort zone, involve ourselves in the world and make sufficient effort to understand what's happening to us that we really learn: an insight summed up by the lines of the 13th century Persian poet, Saadi of Shiraz: 'Deep in the sea are riches beyond compare, but if you seek safety, it is on the shore.'

At home in Sussex a few days earlier my expectations certainly hadn't included a visit to Mesopotamia and I was unprepared for a melodramatic death in Baghdad (or any other kind of death for that matter). I had quite forgotten Shah's words: 'As soon as we are born we become moving targets for the world.'

Prior to my trip Baghdad was a place of romance in my mind: an ancient city, gateway to Central Asia and once the largest and wealthiest capital in the world. I thought of it as one of those nodes of civilization on the Silk Road, the setting for numerous stories from *One Thousand and One Nights*, home of saints and mystics and Caliph Harun al-Rashid's House of Wisdom, the learned institution created for the vital role of rescuing and collating profound pagan knowledge that had all but been destroyed by Christian and Arab fanatics, the fundamentalists of their day. Seeing Baghdad's contemporary face displaced the more romantic notions I held about Eastern cultures. But it was exciting to be there nonetheless.

Sadly the subsequent collapse of order in that region, brought about by the hubristic, illegal Western invasion, the subsequent civil wars and massive corruption, means that I am unlikely to visit that once great city again – or Mosul, Damascus, Aleppo, and countless other destinations I once hoped to see.

That occasion in Baghdad was only the second time in my life that I was directly threatened in a country at war. The first was in 1944 in London when I was nearly one year old and the very first of Hitler's 13 tonne V2 rockets landed on a house in Stavely Road a few streets away from where we lived, killing the occupants. There was no warning because the rocket, travelling at over 3,000 miles per hour, arrived faster than the speed of sound: survivors only heard the approach and sonic boom *after* the blast. My parents told me that I slept peacefully through the explosion, unaware that it represented the gruesome endpoint of Mankind's first sub-orbital spaceflight.

Over the next six months 1,400 V2 rockets were launched at Britain killing about 3,000 civilians. More than 500 landed on London. In the same period Hitler's 'doodle bugs', the forerunner of today's drones, added to the death toll, killing over 6,000 and destroying half a million homes. It was terrorism on an industrial scale and, being a toddler at the time, I lived through it all oblivious.

During the blitz earlier in the war my father, a manager for the London Electricity Board, was kept constantly busy repairing the bomb damaged electricity supply network. His was a 'reserved occupation', which meant his work was regarded as vital to the war effort and he was not allowed to join the military forces, apart from the Home Guard (Dad's Army). Nevertheless the violence of the war deeply affected him. He witnessed horrendous scenes as a result of the bombing – smashed and burnt corpses, appalling injuries, homes and businesses destroyed – and he saw at close hand the despair of distraught families suddenly made homeless. He told me that one night at the height of the blitz he walked across Chiswick Bridge and stared downriver towards the centre of London. It seemed to him as if the whole city was ablaze – the Thames itself appeared on fire. At that moment he was overcome by a wave of hopelessness because he felt that Britain could not possibly survive such an onslaught. However, he and everyone else just carried on. What else could they do? Later, an explosion in a damaged electricity substation severely burned and hospitalised him for months, but he returned to work as soon as his skin started healing.

As I was growing up I became aware of my father's hatred for America because of the way Americans had financed and supplied Hitler's war machine. The depths of chicanery in this regard by powerful American industrialists and financial institutions, has only recently been fully unravelled by historians, but, in my teens, I thought Dad's attitude was a bit extreme and couldn't bring myself to despise all American culture. However he did have a beautiful deep voice and thought of the black American singer, Paul Robeson, as some kind of saintly figure and sang his songs at family gatherings. Robeson's singing was all he could concede of as being a good to have come out of America.

Like many working class boys of my age born to left-wing parents, I was named Ivan in honour of the Russians who had suddenly become wartime allies after Germany broke its pact with the Soviet Union and attacked it. The Russians were the first to inflict major defeats on Hitler's armies. (In the 1930s my parents had taken part in anti-fascist demonstrations, including the infamous Battle of Cable Street that prevented a mass march of Mosley's Blackshirts from going through the Jewish East End of London.) For the first few decades of my life I had to politely endure the supposed humour of people who, when I was introduced, grinned back at me, 'Oh, Ivan the Terrible!' – expecting me to think they were the first person to make the connection. I've noticed that younger people today don't make that response, no doubt because history is so poorly taught now that they have never heard of the first Tsar to rule all of Russia.

Forgetting is easier than remembering. Memories come and go, drifting like mist through shafts of sunlight on a warm autumn morning: one moment sharp and clear, the next hazy and confused. This makes writing memoirs difficult, especially since every time we recall something we transform it slightly, perhaps to paint ourselves in a better light, or bring structure and coherence to what seem like random events, or, as some believe, make the story more 'true'. Being a war baby back then, no detailed memory of that time stayed with me. How could it? But the psychological and physical effects of the war on our parents and the wrecked environment coloured the lives of all children in the years after it ended. Throughout the 1940s and 50s we played amid ruins, bomb craters and bomb shelters.

How we make and store memories is little understood and my early ones, like everyone else's, are only those 'snapshot' images attached to strong emotions concerning innate emotional needs being satisfied or frustrated: intense pleasure, feeling safe and loved, or being angry or afraid. My earliest recollection, for example, is of taking my first independent steps through sunbeams walking diagonally on a green carpet across a room, with Mum and Dad laughing and shouting encouragement. This was in 1944 when I was about one year old. As an adult I described to my parents the details of this glorious moment of happiness at learning to walk and they confirmed that they were true. They were amazed that my description was identical to how they remembered it.

Although we don't have proper narrative memories of events from much before the age of five or six (when our self-concept begins to form), our emotional life in our early years affects us deeply. It shapes our personality and how we later relate to others. The insecurity and periods of intense stress while living through the wartime bombing of London affected my parents so it indirectly affected me – and likewise most of my generation.

Many of my happiest childhood moments involve my father, but unfortunately less so my mother. I know she loved us all in her own way and worked hard and did her best. She was as great a mum as she was capable of being, but somehow I never felt close to her. My sister, Jennifer, was born in 1945; she was blonde like Lilian, mother's sister.

I often heard people refer to Dad as 'one of nature's gentlemen'. He always seemed considerate of others, was kind and thoughtful and had more patience with Jenny and me than Mum did; he had the imagination to act on his knowledge of what a child needs. I now think he knew about this because of his own upbringing. He remembered both his parents as being depressed: his mother by the deaths of his two sisters who died from childhood diseases, and his father by what he had witnessed in the trenches during the First World War. This, coupled with his natural intelligence, meant that he had learnt what children needed. He never once hit, shouted or swore at us. His usual way of disciplining me was to adopt an air of disappointment about any behaviour of which he disapproved. That was how I knew he was cross and, because I loved him, it worked a treat with me (such a method doesn't work when you don't love and respect the person disciplining you).

In contrast, my mother's reaction to what she disapproved of was always highly emotional. In her attempt to control us she was prone to shouting a lot and slapping legs, particularly mine. That didn't work so well with me, especially as I often felt that the slapping was unfair. It seemed to me that my sister, being innately more in tune with the emotional female way of doing things, instinctively knew how to manipulate my mother to ensure it was me who got the slapping.

Until I was nearly ten we lived in a two story upstairs flat at 1 Elm Road, East Sheen. After the war Grandfather Tyrrell, by then a sad widower lost in sorrow, came to live in the attic rooms above us. He kept to himself so we didn't see much of him. My parents had rented the flat after spending several years in the 1930s living a left-wing Bohemian existence on a houseboat that Dad had converted from a lifeboat hull and moored at Eel Pie Island on the Thames. They sold it during the Blitz and moved away from the river to Elm Road because they felt they would be safer from German bombs if they lived in a house rather than a wooden boat that offered no protection. They were right. A week after the sale went through a direct hit blasted the beloved houseboat to smithereens. Fortunately the new owners were not on it at the time.

Although we lived on the top floor with two attic rooms above, we also had access to a back garden. This was little more than a yard where washing was dried, chickens kept, vegetables grown and where we children played. Onions were stored in a woodshed that had enough space high up on some planks where I could hide, read and daydream. At the end of the garden was an Anderson shelter left over from the time when we took refuge with our neighbours during the nightly bombing raids. It must have been grim.

As children, when it was too cold or wet to stay in the garden, we played indoors. To keep us quiet Mum used to turn the kitchen table upside down so it could become a raft, or, with a blanket draped over it, a cave and we amused ourselves in fantasy games for what seemed like hours. Sometimes she gave us our meals to suit whatever form the adventure took: raft, ship, cave, or castle. These creative games based around the kitchen table, plus other free amusements undoubtedly stimulated our imaginations – Jenny and I enjoyed them enormously. It's difficult for us older people not to feel sorry for children today whose parents bury them with plastic toys or allow them to become hypnotised by screen-fed techno trash unaware that many of California's Silicon Valley billionaires don't let their own children interact with screens and send them to schools that don't use computers.

Post war austerities meant that for poorer families toys were usually hand-made and few and far between. One Christmas, for example, my parents gave me just three presents. Dad carved me a toy aeroplane and painted it blue and Mum gave me a picture book and an orange (how she got hold of the fruit still mystifies me). In those days Christmas was not the long, drawn-out and unpleasant celebration of consumerism it is now. Although atheists, Mum and Dad made the three-day festival a magical time for Jenny and me, decorating the rooms in the flat with paper chains, cheap ornaments and Christmas lights from Woolworths. For several years on Christmas Eve a large colourful Victorian print of Father Christmas on a snow-covered roof was ceremoniously placed on the mantelpiece. Though now considered corny, I still find Victorian festive images arouse warm and comforting feelings due to my memory pattern-matching back to my childhood, which I remember as a mostly happy time.

* * * * *

I learnt to read early and devoured books as a child. Reading was exciting and it is astonishing to me that, thanks to the UK adopting absurd teaching methods and the inability of head teachers to sack bad teachers, today nearly 17% of pupils leave school functionally illiterate, making them unemployable and driving some of them into lives of criminality. My father told me that when he was a boy nearly everyone could read and write.

At about six I read a version of *The Magic Porridge Pot* and it frightened me. I couldn't get the story out of my head. It was about a starving girl living with her poor parents at a time of great hardship. She went into the cold forest to find berries to eat and among the trees she met a strange old travelling man with whom, despite her hunger and without thought for herself, she shared some of what little she had collected. She told him about how poor and hungry the people in her village were. Because she had shown him kindness, he gave her a magic pot together with two spells, one to start the pot producing a supply of nutritious porridge and another to stop it.

She took the pot home and found that what the kindly old man had said was true. As soon as she spoke the first spell, it produced porridge. Whenever the pot was full she stopped it with the second spell. With the pot she was able to feed not only her family but also the whole village. This wonderful food put hope in people's hearts that they could survive this terrible time and soon the villagers began to prosper again.

But then a terrible thing happened. One day, when the little girl and her parents were asleep, a greedy man from the other side of the village who had overheard the spell crept into their home and stole the pot. Back in his house he commanded the magic pot to produce porridge, and it did so. But then, in a moment of pure horror, as he was enjoying his breakfast, he realised he didn't know how to stop it cooking. The porridge started flowing from the pot onto the floor and throughout his house. It then flooded into the surrounding streets, filling houses and fields and growing deeper and deeper. Soon everyone was afraid. Panicking villagers began climbing up trees and onto roofs to escape. There seemed no end to it: eventually the whole world would drown in the thick, sticky porridge.

Eventually the little girl woke up and realised what had happened. At the top of her voice she shouted the magic word that would stop the pot from producing porridge. Fortunately the pot heard her and that was how she saved the world.

The metaphors in the story resonate with me still (try substituting 'red-tape', 'corruption' or 'welfare state' for 'porridge', for example) and cast a long shadow. I have always felt the world in danger of being over-run by mindless folly.

Both my parents were born before the First World War. In those times any law-abiding person could pass through life and hardly notice the existence of the state, beyond the post office and the policeman. Now we cannot do anything without bureaucracy intervening and constantly undermining our innate need for control. Like many older people I have a longing for minimal state interference in human affairs believing personal freedom and taking responsibility for oneself to be of para-mount importance.

Richmond Park was a short walk away up Sheen Lane and a great outdoor extension to our backyard playground. Mum and her friend Peggy (whose son, David, was about my age) were always taking us there to let off steam, picnic, play hide-and-seek and fish for frogs and tiddlers in Pen Ponds. A favourite pastime of ours' was to creep up as close as we could get to the deer and rabbits without startling them. I loved being there and felt connected to everything in the way Shakespeare expressed it, 'One touch of nature makes the whole world kin.' To my boyhood self Richmond Park seemed vast, its grassy open spaces made for ranging across and its woods and fern filled valleys full of secret places waiting to be explored – until it was time to go home for tea. Even though it was only a London park it fostered a love of the natural world in me and being there was a great relief after the confines of school classrooms and pavements.

The direct vision that children have, and sometimes adults get, when looking at something wondrous: a butterfly, a flower, a sunset, a beautiful person – anything in the natural world – has always intrigued me. Why do so many of us want to paint or photograph such visions? Is it because, without realising it, we ourselves are an aspect of universal consciousness witnessing creation and that, somehow, we intuit this and paint a picture or take a photograph as a way of participating in the process. Is there an innate drive to do something with our experience, even though there is never ever going to be a painting that captures that initial enchantment a child has when he or she first stares at a raindrop or a flower? I can remember those intense feelings of connection to Nature when looking at something in that fresh, childlike way. No painting or photograph can recapture that feeling exactly and I have concluded that we are moved by images in a different way.

Today Richmond Park is a noisy rat run for cars.

* * * * *

Other walks we did back then were along the Thames footpath. And every year that we lived in Elm Road we would go down to Chiswick Bridge to watch the finish of the Oxford-Cambridge boat race. For some reason my parents always wanted Oxford to win, I think because they were viewed as the underdogs. For decades before and after the war Oxford lost almost every race. That was my first experience of crowds. Another treat was to visit Kew Gardens, which was a short bus ride away. Admission was free for children and only one penny for adults. We also went to London Zoo, the big London museums and, in 1951, we visited The Festival of Britain on the South Bank of the river, all of which we enjoyed.

My parents were not churchgoers and so it was at the age of six or seven at Mortlake Infants School that I was introduced to the curious world of religion. In a green and brown painted classroom, whose only decoration I remember was a large map of the British Empire, a teacher of spindly aspect told us a dramatic tale involving Jesus walking on water to rescue his disciples, who were at sea in a boat when a storm blew up. You may remember that, in the story, when the disciples saw him gliding across the waves, they were frightened because they thought he was a ghost. But Jesus told them not to be afraid. He climbed aboard the boat, calmed the storm and thus they survived.

I enjoyed the story but in the school playground afterwards I was earnestly discussing it with another little boy and saying that it couldn't possibly be true because no one could walk on water. Suddenly there was an excruciating pain in my right ear. The Christian pedagogue who had told us the story had crept up and overheard us and yanked my ear so hard she pulled me off balance, which really hurt. She then angrily dragged me at high speed through the school to the headmistress and repeated what she had overheard me say. This led to a vigorous telling off from both of them: I was a wicked little boy for suggesting the story wasn't true. My effrontery was swiftly dealt with by a caning, three strokes on each hand, in order to teach me 'not to take the Lord's words in vain'. Never having experienced such bigotry and cruelty from an adult before it shocked and confused me and I was too ashamed to tell my parents about it. I didn't even know what 'Lord's words' or 'vain' meant. Thus was my interest in religions sparked.

Naturally I became wary of schoolteachers after that. My default position became not to trust what they said. As an adult I have often noticed that a dulling effect seems to happen to many children when they start attending school. In the first few years of life before then the world is totally fascinating and then school changes everything. It begins to degrade children's consciousness. Wordsworth clearly meant this when he wrote; 'Heaven lies about us in our infancy! But shades of the prison-house begin to close upon the growing boy.' From then on I remember most of my schooling as a confinement, something to endure, not enjoy, and so I am largely self-educated. Throughout my childhood I created projects for myself – read continually and liked making models, drawing and devising mischief with friends. I suppose that makes me an autodidact.

Because my father worked as a manager at the London Electricity Board we had a telephone. He was often called out to emergency explosions at crackling substations and to sort out power cuts and, if it wasn't a night-time callout, he used to let me accompany him. That was educational.

It was also because of his job that we had a car, one of only two in our street back then. It must be hard for young people today to imagine how different life in London was in the 1940s and 50s. It was rare, for example, for working class families to have a phone at home, which meant the iconic red public phone boxes were everywhere (mobile phones only featured in science fiction comics). There were few cars: no yellow lines in the roads, no parking meters and streetlights were turned off at 10 o'clock to save electricity. Some horse-drawn carts and vans were still used for delivering coal, milk and other staples. I sometimes followed them round the streets with my mother's father, Grandfather Cheshire, helping him collect bucket loads of horse manure to fertilize his garden.

Late one moonless night, when I was quite small, we were driving back from Ealing where the Cheshires lived. It was late and dark; the streetlights were off and there was no thick London smog to slow us down. By the time we arrived home my sister and I were sound asleep. Mum carried Jenny indoors and Dad lifted me out of the car to do the same with me. But, when we reached the front door, he turned round and stepped back into the middle of the road urging me to wake up. He then lifted me to shoulder height saying, 'Look up there!' With one arm holding me and the other pointing upwards he showed me the stars for the first time explaining that each twinkling light was a sun like ours but so far away that they looked small.

It was a magical moment – and suddenly I was wide-awake. 'Keep looking,' he said. 'The more you look, the more you'll see.' And it was true. As I stared into the night sky and my eyes adjusted, more and more stars came into view and a sense of wonder at what his words meant about the size of the Universe and the immensity of creation flooded my burgeoning mind. Of course the knowledge that the stars we see are only some of hundreds of billions of suns in our own galaxy, that in turn is only one galaxy among about one hundred billion others was not known then, but I never forgot that lesson: the more you look, the more you see. He fostered my curiosity and I loved it when he showed me things. He inspired me in a way schoolteachers never did. Education was always more real for me when it came naturally like that, or when books stimulated my imagination.

Memories, however, are not always reliable. For example I had a strong one of Grandfather Tyrrell appearing on the stairs dishevelled and covered in white plaster as a result of the ceiling of his attic room crashing down on him. Decades later I mentioned this incident to my parents and was surprised when they insisted that it never happened. I was shocked because for me it was an actual event in my past. In fact I would have bet money that it *had* happened. But it seems it was an illusory memory, a confabulation of my imagination, perhaps influenced by watching Mr Pastry – the comedian, whose slapstick children's TV shows always seemed to end up with him falling down stairs covered in flour. (I still find Mr Pastry dancing The Lancers one of the funniest black and white clips on YouTube.)

Thus I experienced for myself the reality of illusory memories, a topic that was to play a part later in my life.

* * * * *

History is a story of what historians decide is important, just as autobiography is the tale of what an individual found most meaningful about his or her life.

One day in the flat there were a lot of people milling about all dressed in black: Grandfather Tyrrell had died. I didn't know what this meant at first but over the following days the absolute reality of the inevitability of death sunk home deeply. None of us gets out of this world alive! In bed every night for weeks I would cry about it and my father would come to my little room to comfort me.

'Will you die too Daddy?' I asked.

'Yes, but not for a long time.'

'Will Mummy?'

'Yes, but don't worry about it. All of us die when we are very old.'

'But I don't want to die,' I cried. 'Why do we die Daddy? Why?!'

My mother on the other hand had no sympathy with my disorientation at discovering the unavoidability of death. As Dad tried to reassure me she would bark orders from the living room, 'Fred! Tell him not to be silly. Leave him alone! For goodness sake tell him to be quiet. Give him an aspirin! Tell him to go to sleep!' Being a kind man however, Dad ignored her and would stay with me. But he had no answers to my questions; all he could do was cuddle up in mutual sadness until I fell asleep. And to comfort me he had kindly told me a white lie. I eventually found out that it was not true that we only die when we are very old. Many years later he told me of the death of his elder sister who was four years older than him. She'd been like a second mother to him and he adored her. When she died of scarlet fever at the age of twelve he was heartbroken. He also talked about his other sister whom he had never met because she had died before he was born. I think my distress reminded him of his own pain when, as a boy, he realised death can come to anyone at any time. It was then, I think, that he decided there was no God. And no doubt his own childhood suffering was the reason he felt my childish cries should not be dismissed as silly.

Dad was generally thought of as a quiet man, but he was a great storyteller when Mum allowed him to be. He was funny in a dry way that often had me in stitches, though my mother and sister rarely knew why we were laughing. I've experienced the most tears of laughter, the belly aching kind that well up from deep down, when Dad and I shared ridiculous experiences or described eccentric behaviour of people we both knew. Once on the hills near Inkpen, where he and mum had retired to, he and I went out walking and he told me we should make for a pub he had heard served good food. We arrived and looked at the menu, which offered two pages of extravagantly described dishes – a generous choice we thought. However, when it came to ordering our meal everything we asked for was 'off that day'. Everything! Time after time this happened. Then with a smile Dad suddenly said to the patron, 'This is a *wonderful* lesson. I've just realised you can have the best menu in the world if you don't have to produce the actual dishes!' The earnest, apologetic, strained look on the publican's face that this observation produced started us laughing, and we never really stopped for the rest of the day. Everything seemed to have a comical aspect, as indeed most things do if you tune your sense of humour to them.

* * * * *

The UK is a small island and whenever Dad spoke about his childhood he was describing a country that was even then overcrowded – home to some 38 million people. But by the time I was born the population had grown to 48 million. Now it is over 65 million and growing ever more rapidly. England is the most crowded major country in Europe and in ten years' time is expected to hold twice the population than it did when Dad was a boy.

Out of the blue, a couple of years before he died, he told me that when he was about eleven years old he was so unhappy that he ran away from home. This surprised me because he had never mentioned it before; so naturally I asked him why. And he told me the following story, which is about expectation.

He said that his home was a sad place, especially after his eldest sister died. His mother was depressed at the loss of two daughters and he couldn't remember her ever smiling, which was hardly surprising because when his father came home from the trenches he hardly ever spoke to her or his children. 'It was as if he never knew us', Dad said. He told me that he now realised his father, my paternal grandfather, was just one bit of living debris from the 'Great' War and was probably suffering from what today we call post-traumatic stress disorder due to the terrible things he had seen in the trenches in France. The unpleasant and oppressive atmosphere made Dad so fed up he decided to run away and find a better life.

So, early one summer morning, before his parents were up, he quietly packed some cheese, bread, biscuits and a bottle of water into a knapsack, crept out of the door and set off to the bus terminal with a few pennies he had saved and a little puppy dog he had somehow acquired. He left behind a polite note on the kitchen table:

Dear Father and Mother,
When you read this I will be gone. I am travelling to seek my fortune in the West Country. Please don't worry about me. I'll be back within a twelvemonth.
Your loving son,
Fred.

At the bus station he caught the first ride of the day heading out into the countryside and got off in a little village at the end of the route. With tears of happy recollection in his eyes Dad described to me the wonderful feeling of freedom he had striding down rolling country lanes with the sunshine at his back accompanied by the puppy darting in and out of the hedgerows, joyfully alarming the bird life and tracing the scent of rabbits back to their burrows.

By midmorning however, both he and the puppy needed a rest so he left the lane and climbed up a hillside to sit down at a spot where he could eat one of his apples, enjoy the view and contemplate the adventures he felt sure were about to begin. The puppy curled up and slept. As he listened to the song of skylarks and the chattering of rooks and jackdaws, the warm sun gradually made Dad feel dreamy and he too lay back to doze in the embrace of the sweet smelling summer grass.

When he woke up it was lunchtime, but he felt compelled to make more progress before eating. So he jollied the puppy back onto the lane and they set off, but this time at a slower pace – the puppy was more tired than Dad had expected it to be. After a mile or so the little dog made it known that it was determined to stop again. They did so and Dad ate his bread and cheese and the dog had his biscuits. And once more the puppy fell asleep. Thereafter, each time they walked on, the puppy would stop every 100 yards or so and refuse to move until it had another little sleep. Being young it didn't have the staying power required for a long trek into the unknown and gradually Dad's resolve faltered until, regretfully but with some relief, he decided to return home.

By now, however, the only way he could make it back the several miles to the village and bus route was if he carried the puppy most of the time. On the way he started to worry about the punishment his father would inflict on him. Eventually he got there with his arms and legs aching and his feet sore. He was just in time to catch the last bus back to town. It was long after dark when he arrived home and his was the only house with any light on in the street. His parents were waiting up in the hopes for news from the police whom they had alerted. As he stood outside he could hear his mother crying and moaning to his father, of whom he was wary. It was common for boys in those times to get a beating for serious misdemeanours and his father wore a big leather belt with a brass buckle.

Bucking up courage he pushed open the door and let the puppy down on the floor to await the onslaught. His mother screeched and rushed over, alternatively slapping and hugging him whilst angrily shouting about what a terrible thing he'd done and crying with relief. Dad said he didn't mind this so much – it's what he expected mums to do, being such emotional creatures. But all the time he couldn't take his anxious eyes off his father who, ominously, said nothing. He just stood in the shadowy corner staring at the scene with his thumbs hooked into his belt.

My Dad was sure he was about to get a beating. Then his father stepped out of the shadows, told his mother to calm down and sympathetically patted him on the head and said, 'Run along to bed son. At least you told the truth. You were back within a twelvemonth'.

I now believe that Dad spent much of his life seeking to experience again that feeling of release and freedom he felt when he first escaped into the English countryside on that sunny morning. Certainly he was always encouraging us to develop a love of the outdoors and natural wonders. At every opportunity we used to drive into the country on Fridays to go camping or stay the weekend on farms with friends of my parents.

As a member of the Home Guard during the war he had acquired a couple of guns: a .303 rifle and a .22. He was a champion shot and had won prizes on training exercises at Bisley. After the war ended he gave back the .303 but kept the .22 and he sometimes took me along when hunting rabbits for the pot. He would always shoot them in the head, which impressed the farmers.

Early one morning we went out at sunrise and crawled up a large hillock. When we peered over we found we were looking down into a green dewy dell where many rabbits were nibbling grass. It was a peaceful scene and I sensed Dad didn't want to spoil it by shooting. Suddenly to our amazement a fox strolled into the dell among the rabbits. The fox took no notice of them, and the rabbits seemed not the slightest bit alarmed. Presumably he had already eaten and the rabbits somehow knew this.

One old farm we stayed at was in a remote part of Cambridgeshire and across the yard was a pond bordering a spinney. A slatted wooden footbridge, faded silver with age, crossed the pond to a little island. One hot sunny day, left to my own devices, I was lying flat out on the warm wood dreamily gazing through the slats down into the clear water, spying on the fish, looking for frogs and contemplating the water boatmen. I was fascinated by the way they skated on the water's surface. My parents and all the other adults were indoors in the large farmhouse kitchen drinking tea and nattering.

Relaxing with the warm sun on my back while listening to birdsong, the buzzing of bees and the swishing sound of dragonfly wings was a joyous moment of idyllic boyish recreation. Bliss! Such moments - when every sense seems open and unencumbered by thought and one is intensely connected to the natural world - often occur in childhood and are hard to convey in words. Although Wordsworth came close when he wrote;

'There was a time when meadow, grove and stream,
the earth and every common sight,
to me did seem apparell'd in celestial light,
the glory and the freshness of a dream'.

It seemed to me then that Nature responded to my attention directly, as it did at other times, as when I lay on my back in long grass looking up at the changing shapes of summer clouds slowly passing across blue sky, or when hiding high up among the leaves of a tree I'd perched in, or while gazing at the moon. Watching birds, insects and other creatures going about their lives felt intimately involving because a strong instinct in me knew their world was my world too. Any observant child, when calm, knows that everything is interconnected. That feeling goes of course when we submit to civilization's obsession: naming creatures and things and collecting data. So back then in my ignorance there was no barrier between nature and myself. I just absorbed it all. It was in that kind of charmed state that I lay daydreaming on the sun-drenched wooden bridge.

Then the mood changed.

To my shock, unexpectedly, a snake swam right underneath me. It seemed large because my face was so close to it. In my surprise I jumped up yelling, 'SNAKE! Snake! SNAKE!' And darted back across the bridge towards the farmhouse. 'SNAKE!' Thus alerted, all the adults tumbled out into the sunshine. As they ran towards me the men grabbed sticks and shovels and asked me where it was. I pointed to the island. They ran across the bridge and started beating about looking for it.

Then my father asked me, 'Where *exactly* did you see it?' I showed him the spot where I had lain on my tummy and said, 'It swam across right underneath me. I was just here.'

And at once I knew he didn't believe me.

I wiggled my arm to illustrate how it swam … but to no avail. Neither my parents nor any of the country folk thought that snakes could swim. They'd never heard of such a thing. And the harder I insisted I'd seen it the more they denied it. 'It must have been a fish,' they said. 'You've got a good imagination young'un.' Once the collective denial kicked in and the momentary excitement was over the search was called off. But I couldn't deny the reality of my own experience. I *had* seen it. From that moment on I knew for sure that all adults, even my parents, were not always right about everything.

Strangely, and to his credit, my father reminded me of this incident when I was in my forties. He had seen a nature documentary on TV that included a scene of adders swimming across a pond, just as I had described. He was so surprised that at the first opportunity he phoned to apologise for not believing me all those years ago. For my part, looking back on such incidents, I value them. They made me less inclined to follow the herd and taught me to trust more in my own lived experiences rather than just accepting the characteristic conventional customs and beliefs of the people around me. Because of TV nature programmes it is, of course, now common knowledge that snakes swim.

* * * * *

When I was little Dad took us a few times to see his elderly Aunt Polly who had never married. She lived in an old cottage next to a village hall in a small village in woodland to the west of Uxbridge. The hall was never locked and I used to play under the stage and among the props and faded stage curtains. The place had a musty woody smell that I rather liked. As a young woman Polly had worked in a big house for £15 a year. Dad told me that when she came to London in the 1940s after the war had ended he had handed a phone to her so she could talk to a relative she hadn't seen for years. Not having used one before she was in awe of the modern instrument but, after exchanging a few stilted words down the line, thrust the phone back at him with the memorable line, 'It's like talking to the dead!'

We had holidays in Devon too, staying in a house opposite the old chain ferry on the river Dart at Dartmouth. I learned to swim in a little bay in Kingswear. One year I befriended another boy who lived nearby and who was always happy to join me in mischief, which on one occasion led to us having a nasty fright. We had noticed that, when the tide went out on the opposite bank by the railway line that ran alongside the river, beached war-damaged landing craft appeared near the ferry. We decided to have a close look at them so we smuggled our way onto the ferry without anyone seeing us and set off along the railway track to the spot where the craft were. Naturally enough we wanted to climb in, which we did easily enough despite every surface being coated with wet mud. At first it was exciting, an adventure – nobody knew we were there. But then we saw the water was rising quickly as the tide came in. And when we tried to climb out we couldn't because the inside was so slippery. We panicked for a while, thinking we were going to drown. When we calmed down and reason kicked in, we realised that eventually the water would rise high enough so we could float up. And that's how we escaped, clambering out and splashing our way to the shore. We crossed back on the ferry somehow and arrived filthy and wet to a much-deserved telling off.

Some of my happiest times as a boy were spent at Kimcote House in the tiny Leicestershire village of Seagrave, where we went to relax away from London. My father's uncle, George, had been a butler to a number of great families and had risen to become a 'gentleman's gentleman' and had travelled all over the world with a wealthy family. Along the way he met and married a head housekeeper, Gertie. When Auntie Gertie and Uncle George retired, the family they worked for rewarded them for their long and faithful service by giving them an income for life and Kimcote House, together with a wonderful Bentley car in the garage whose luxurious leather and oiled wood interior evoked an age of aristocratic motoring comfort. Kimcote was the largest house in the village with a huge lawn, vegetable garden, orchard and paddock. The pleasure of waking up to the distant sound of church bells, crowing cockerels and lowing cows seeped into my being. The ticking grandfather clock in the hall added to the reassuring sense that all was well with the world and when we came down to breakfast in the Aga-warmed kitchen the wholesome smell of homemade food being prepared reliably brought contented smiles of anticipation to every face.

The grounds were big enough to hold the annual village fete and flower show on the lawn, which they did – one year I nearly won a pig! We went to Seagrave at least once every year for many years and that was where I learned to catch a ball, ride a bike and, at the age of seven, drive *Little Grey Fergie*, which was what the farmworkers called the Ferguson tractor.

I roamed the fields and woods with Phillip Hardy, a boy of my own age who was the son of the owner of the largest farm in the area. We went on picnics in the fields with Auntie Aida, one of Gertie's sisters. She would tell us stories and let us make camps in the stooks. On Sundays there was always a large formal lunch at Kimcote with silver cutlery and Gertie's sisters cooking and serving. It was like a scene out of Downton Abbey.

On one occasion my father drove us from Seagrave on a trip to a nearby town and on the way we saw a sign offering 'Aeroplane rides'. Of course Philip and I pleaded for a ride. A little Auster three-seater stood in a field by a farm and Dad drove over to it to arrange a flight. It turned out we could go up straight away: all three of us for ten shillings. It was one of those planes that you had to start by swinging the propeller. We climbed in, Philip and I on one seat and Dad and the pilot on the others. The Auster bumped across the field until it got up speed and we took off across the rolling Leicestershire countryside. It was noisy, everything rattled. The pilot said we flew about 100 miles but I couldn't see much through the dirty Perspex windows. Nevertheless it was exciting.

About a month later, back home in East Sheen, our little plane made the national news. There was a picture in the newspaper of the very same pilot proudly standing next to it. It was taken prior to the day he had swung the propeller for the last time when, before he could get in, his little Auster had accelerated over the field, took off and flown south, pilotless, until, running out of fuel, it finally glided down and crash-landed in some trees. The plane was wrecked.

* * * * *

Shortly after the Queen's coronation in March 1953, which we watched on a tiny black-and-white television in our neighbours flat, we moved to Aultone Way in Sutton, Surrey – a big step up for us. It had what seemed to me at the time a large garden. There were two lawns separated by a pond, a Victoria Plum tree to one side, a group of oak trees at the far end and a field beyond that, all promising many happy hours of play (although to my disappointment within a couple of years the field was sold and became a housing estate). I was sent to Tweedale Primary School about a mile away on the other side of Rosehill Park. It was surrounded by estates made up largely of prefabs whose children were mostly from families that had moved out from the East End of London because of the devastation caused by German bombing. Some of them were smelly and malnourished; many were illiterate.

I spent ten months at Tweedale but, because I could read well and lived in a middle class street on what most of the children thought of as the posh side of the park, I was mocked and bullied. I particularly remember the feeling of dread I had on my way home when one young thug and his gang appeared in the park coming after me shouting my name and taunting me. Instead of running ahead, which I could have done, I stubbornly walked on until they caught up and surrounded me. The tubby leader of the gang told everyone, 'Now you're going to see a one punch fight,' a phrase designed to intimidate that he had heard from his equally obnoxious elder brothers. Being outnumbered I took a few hits, refused to cry and continued walking until they got bored and left me alone.

The only good thing I remember about Tweedale was a couple of books I found in the school library there; *Cache Lake Country*, by John J Rowlands, and *Robin Hood and the Men of Greenwood* by Henry Gilbert. These influenced me a lot at the time, both being about escape and living in harmony with nature and, in the case of Robin Hood, about fearlessly fighting injustice – themes I could relate to.

Cache Lake Country told the story of how the author left the city and set out by canoe into the wilds of Maine to survey land for a timber company. After paddling alone for several days he came upon the lake of his boyhood dreams. He never left. He named it Cache Lake because it was a hidden paradise where the best that the north had to offer was stored – timber for a cabin, fish, game and berries to live on; and the peace and contentment he felt he could not live without. He made friends with other wood dwellers and a Native American who helped him survive the cold winters. Living in remote woods seemed to my boyish mind something to aim for since the book exemplified the idea that what is most worth finding lies far from the tracks of civilization, and that what is most worth doing demands resourcefulness and wit. The folklore, philosophy and wisdom about self-reliance appealed enormously, as did the numerous pen and ink drawings illustrating wildlife and woodcraft skills. It was about that time that Peter Pauly, a draughtsman friend of my father, showed me his wonderful pen and scraperboard illustrations of animals. When he realised I was fascinated by how he produced them he gave me a pen and ink set so I could learn to produce black and white drawings myself. My father, who could also draw well, then taught me about perspective.

Some years ago my storyteller friend, Pat Williams, who is as fascinated by yarns as I am, asked me out of the blue what story I most remembered from childhood that had had the biggest impact on my life. Without thinking I knew instantly – it was Robin Hood. Pat had a theory that she had tried out on many people and found to be true, that any major story that captured our imagination in childhood had what she called a 'forward shadow effect' and influenced how a person's life panned out. And she said that, 'without you realising it Ivan, you're a Robin Hood type with a deep mistrust of authority, a supporter of underdogs who was prone to taking risks and interested in ideas that overturn conventional thought.' Pat was, of course, referring to me taking on the psychotherapy establishment. I had to agree: if a crowd moves in one direction my instinct is to go in another.

I recently reread both books when they were reissued in paperback. Gilbert's was first published in 1912 and I was amazed to find I had read such rich language and vocabulary at so young an age. And it was still a page-turner. Rereading it reminded me how, as a boy, I had cried myself to sleep on realising that such a romantic life of adventure and freedom in the forest was no longer possible. *The Adventures of Robin Hood* starring Errol Flynn was the first film my father took me to see – and we both loved it. In 1951 we saw Kim at the local cinema too, as well as the Tarzan films. These colourful Technicolor treats were magical to a small boy and I was sucked into the stories and the worlds they depicted. That was fiction of course, and real life isn't. At that age I had yet to be clear of the difference or discover that, though stories can provide inspiration and nutriment for our development, we cannot live in a Walter Mitty world.

Throughout childhood I devoured fiction of all kinds: Enid Blyton's *Famous Five* and *Secret Seven* adventures; W. E. Johns exiting tales of the pilot *Biggles;* Richmal Crompton's hilarious *Just William* stories, and the comical novels of Anthony Buckeridge's schoolboy heroes Jennings and Derbyshire (when he was an old man Buckeridge became a patient of mine). I read everything by Arthur Ransom, the science fiction of H.G. Wells and Jules Verne, and loved *Tom Sawyer* and *Huckleberry Finn* by Mark Twain. I was also swept along by the westerns of Zane Grey and a series of swashbuckling adventures set in the 18th century about *Dr Syn* by Russell Thorndike.

When I was fifteen the elder sister of Michael Cooke, a school friend of mine, introduced us to J.R.R. Tolkien's *Lord of The Rings*. She was up at Oxford and said that all the students there were raving about it because Tolkien was a professor there. I found it in Sutton library and read all three volumes. In the mid-1960s when it became hugely popular and was required counterculture reading among hippies it was already part of my hinterland.

Years later I heard Idries Shah's sister, Amina, talking about the Tolkien books, saying that she thought the reason they were such a runaway success was because our own traditions were not fulfilling our innate hunger for otherworldly stories: ones that hint at a hidden reality beyond the banal lives most of us were leading. She said that the West didn't have a rich enough heritage of approachable magical tales that could provide us with the inspirational metaphorical templates that we need in order to build sufficient psychological resilience to overcome life's obstacles and see beyond them. (She went on to publish volumes of stories that helped correct that situation and I produced the book jackets for some of them.)

Throughout the 1960s, 70s and 80s I read a great amount of science fiction. I believe that the best of these – such as *Way Station, Dune, Ringworld*, and *Shikasta* – were performing the role Amina described as necessary. Reading them made it easier for aficionados of the genre to think about, appreciate and cope with the rapid changes society was about to undergo: the Internet; terrorism; globalisation of industry; media manipulation; federalisation of Europe; dumbing down of populations; loss of freedoms; information overload; gross pollution; global corruption; planetary changes – and so on. Such stories help create a cast of mind inclined to think about the bigger picture.

CHAPTER TWO

Beinn Nibheis and French Pirates

ON THE first evening when my wife Véronique and I stayed at Zalánpatak, a remote Transylvanian estate in the Carpathian foothills owned by Prince Charles, we gathered with other holiday guests round a large rustic table for dinner in an open sided shed. As we chatted and introduced ourselves on that balmy evening one woman asked me if I had been at Charterhouse (a 400 year old Independent school) because, she said, I spoke like someone she knew who had – which of course was nonsense as my south London accent showed. I obviously didn't cut the mustard with her so I smiled and told her I was a grammar school boy. 'Oh well,' she said, rather too loudly, 'there's nothing wrong with that I suppose,' thus indicating to everyone around the table by her not so subtle put down that she thought there was. She was obviously insecure and spent the rest of the evening name-dropping. After a day or two in our company though, she relaxed and we got on well enough. But I digress.

While at Tweedale I took the eleven plus exam and was one of only two pupils from the school that year who passed, gaining a place at Wallington County Grammar School for Boys. My parents were so pleased that, as was then the fashion among the aspiring class, they rewarded me with a bicycle bought from the world's oldest bike shop: Pearson in Sutton High Street. From that moment I was free to cycle anywhere out into the Surrey and Kent countryside. It was liberating.

I also cycled the three and a half miles to Carew Manor every day, a Tudor building resonating with history that had a large orangery in the grounds and, from 1351 to 1859, had been home to the noble Carew family: hence its name. Due to the lack of accommodation in the main building we first year boys had our morning lessons at the Manor then walked or cycled at lunchtime through Beddington Park to the main school.

Although I'm an 'Old Walcountian' I can't say I enjoyed my time there. Only one of all the teachers, the art master Mr Pepper, showed any interest in our interior lives – in what and how we thought. He had served in the RAF and sported a handlebar moustache favoured by wartime pilots. The Second World War was still fresh in the minds of these adults, most of whom had active service records, and more than one had published a book about their exploits. The school itself had been badly damaged by a bomb in the summer of 1944. All the windows were blown out and the roof of the school hall collapsed. However, it continued to function with prefects, teachers and students working to rebuild it. By the time the war ended it was business as usual again. When I was there a memorial in the school hall commemorated the 52 old boys from the school who were killed in action.

The headmaster, Mr Hutchins, had been in place since the school was founded in 1927 and had known all those poor lads who died. Perhaps because of this he generated a sense of connection to the past and a reverence for tradition, which I picked up. For example, like public schools, we were divided into 'houses' to foster a spirit of competition. Each house was given the name of a famous distinguished family such as Ruskin, Woodcote, Carew or Radcliffe. I was put in 'Mandeville', named after Sir Geoffrey de Mandeville, a resident and landholder after the Norman Conquest who was mentioned in the Domesday Book. While I was there Mr Hutchins retired and was superseded by a similarly named Mr Hitchins, who was more of an authoritarian.

Whilst at school I enjoyed few of the lessons and spent as much time reading under the desk and daydreaming as I could fit in without being reprimanded. It was history, geography and English that most appealed to me – and especially art lessons, which I enjoyed the most. At the time I was producing drawings and paintings of birds (I'd become a fan of the renowned naturalistic painter, C. F. Tunnicliffe). As we moved up the school I was put in a class of misfits: those non-academic individuals, roughnecks, eccentrics and arty types that struggle in tightly disciplined environments and that all schools have to scoop up and try to deal with. Mr Pepper was our form master. He also taught pottery and seemed to like us oddballs, probably because he was one himself. The school handed out timetables to each boy setting out the lessons we had to attend. One year my art classes were swapped with mechanical drawing lessons. This upset me so much that in the first mechanical drawing class I attended, which was supposed to be all about calculating angles and how to use setsquares, compasses and protractors, I produced a surrealistic image of a mechanical swan held together with nuts and bolts in protest. The teacher was not pleased and my insolence was referred up to the headmaster. It was with the sympathetic support of Mr Pepper that I was allowed to drop mechanical drawing and go back to art classes.

A timid weakling with the unfortunate name of Wally lived near me and I often found myself talking with him as we cycled to and from school. Because of this he began to regard me as a friend – and indeed I was in some ways. I sometimes rescued him from being bullied.

One day Wally was late for school. When he did finally arrive he, who always seemed sad at the best of times, couldn't stop crying in class for some reason. The teacher, Mr Evans, a straight backed, sharp tongued disciplinarian who was rumoured among us boys to have been a Nazi interrogator during the war, shouted at him several times: 'Stop snivelling boy!' But he wouldn't. Eventually, out of frustration, Evans loudly snapped, 'Why are you crying boy?' And Wally just quietly whimpered, 'Please sir, my tortoise died.' It was so unexpected that the whole class, including Evans, started laughing. To my eternal shame I joined in. At our display of hilarity Wally cried more openly and softened the stony heart of Evans who gently sent him home.

We never saw him again. That weekend he jumped from a bridge in front of a train. That was my first encounter with suicide.

Despite my lack of conventional academic success at school the years spent there were not uneventful. I read an enormous amount and always had a book or two on the go from many genres including: fiction (especially science fiction and westerns), history, poetry, biographies, and books about explorers and man-eating tiger hunters, (my parents didn't get a TV until I was about fifteen and, at first, they rationed the time spent watching it, for which I am eternally grateful). By earning money doing a newspaper delivery round every morning I saved up enough to buy a Spanish guitar and pay for lessons with a wonderful teacher called Freddie Phillips who lived in Ewell. Once a week I cycled over to his house with my guitar on my back. It was Freddie Phillips who later composed and played the music for children's television programmes such as *Camberwick Green, Trumpton and Chigley.*

Two events interfered with my development as a guitarist. The first occurred when everyone in my year was vaccinated (I think it was for smallpox). Because of my blood group, what should have ended up as a small scar became a hole in my arm that a half crown could easily be dropped in (though I never tried that experiment). To protect me from infection I had to wear a sling that held a cage over the raw flesh since skin was not growing over the hole. This was quite a handicap and stopped me playing the guitar, swimming and mucking about. It was also uncomfortable at night. Doctors at the local clinic said my only chance of the skin growing again was ultra violet light therapy. So, twice a week, I had permission to leave school and walk across Beddington Park to the clinic where I had to expose the hole in my arm for treatment. No progress was made for months and I got quite miserable about it.

One day on my way through the park to the clinic three boys from the local secondary modern school mugged me. Despite my sling one of them held me round the neck with a sheath knife at my throat while the others went through my pockets stealing the little money I had on me. Funnily enough, after that event, my skin began to grow back and after a couple of weeks the cage and sling was removed.

* * * * *

The person in charge of our physical wellbeing at school was a red faced, kilt wearing, ginger haired Scottish PE teacher known to us as Jock. His method of torture was to enforce Scottish sword dancing lessons on us. This was part of our exercise regime. Reluctantly in the school gym we had to jig about above crossed swords to the sound of bagpipe music that he played on a wind-up gramophone. Jock was shorter than many of the boys but he had a Genghis Khan approach to asserting authority: if any one of us misbehaved we were all made to suffer. We would have to stand in a circle and bend over, whereupon he would walk round rapidly thwacking each one of us on the backside with a flat bat, which stung like hell. He seamed to enjoy it though.

Another strand to my life began when a new vaulting horse appeared in the gym. As soon as it was set up and in place, I stupidly took a run at it unsupervised. Although I was a good jumper it was considerably bigger than the one I was used to jumping over and I caught my foot on top of it and fell heavily to one side, breaking my left elbow badly. It was now bent at a weird angle and bits of bone were sticking out. When I put my good arm up and said, 'Please sir, I've broken my arm,' Jock turned white at the sight and began to carefully lead me out of the gym leaving a trail of fainting boys behind us in the hall, adding further to Jock's nightmare moment. He shouted instructions at those still standing, telling them to inform the headmaster about what had happened and ask him to contact my parents because he was taking me straight to hospital.

Every disaster begets a story however. As Jock drove me in his little car to Saint Helier, I remember feeling sick and faint. After being admitted, a tall surgeon took one look at the damage and said he would like to operate straight away. He and a nurse led me to an operating theatre, leaving Jock in a waiting room. It turned out that there was no anaesthetist available so the surgeon asked me, as if it was the most normal thing in the world, if I would mind him using hypnosis instead. He assured me that I would feel no pain during the operation and would recover more quickly.

My arm was badly dislocated as well as broken and he said that during the operation I could choose to have my eyes open if I wished and watch. Being a curious fifteen-year-old in a state of shock I chose to look. Because of that I am one of the relatively few people to have had direct sight of some of my own bones and muscles. He hypnotised me with a swinging fob watch, deepening the trance of shock that I was already in, and continued to talk gently while he worked. I felt pressure but no pain as he relocated the elbow joint back in its shattered socket and began working on the broken bits.

My mother arrived at the hospital, having been alerted by the headmaster, and was allowed by a nurse to look into the theatre while my arm was still being worked on. She had quite a shock when I looked her in the eyes and smiled. I thought she was going to pass out as Jock ushered her away to the waiting room.

By the time the surgeon finished my father had also arrived. The surgeon and his assistant had a word with my parents, after which they took me home. I slept soundly that night. The next morning he rang my parents to ask how I was and find out if I had slept well. He told them about the healing suggestions he had given, including for me to sleep well, and said he was very pleased with the result.

So that was my introduction to hypnosis. Back at school, a couple of weeks later with my arm in a sling, I was telling my classmates about the operation and the hypnosis when a teacher strongly challenged my account. He didn't believe in hypnosis and said I'd made it all up. I was outraged because I knew what had happened – as did my parents. This was the start of my interest in hypnosis and psychology. Later, I went off to Sutton Library and found a book on the subject, which I read assiduously. Few then would have guessed that decades later I would write up and publish Joe Griffin's explanation of hypnotic phenomena and become a leading exponent of the use of hypnosis in psychotherapy.

So that was the second event that interfered with my guitar playing. It took a couple of years before I could bend my arm enough to hold down chords and I never made much progress after that.

It's funny how contrariness plays a role in our lives. Just as my being caned as a six year old for saying Jesus couldn't have walked on water stimulated my interest in religion, the teacher who didn't believe in hypnosis, stimulated my interest in the mysteries of the mind.

* * * * *

During those years my school reports were not good. That didn't bother me in the least, but it worried my parents. For them grammar school represented a route for me into career opportunities that they never had. Meanwhile, I just concentrated on learning what I wanted to, such as building miniature sailing ships in bottles, playing truant as often as I could get away with, riding out into the countryside on my bike, and getting up to the usual boyhood mischief. I did sometimes enjoy history, geography, English and art – depending on the teachers. To be fair my reports were pretty good for those topics. But I loathed maths, the sciences, religious studies and French, largely I now believe because they were so badly taught. They also seemed to me to waste time that could be better spent at home reading in my tree house or wandering around in the great outdoors.

I became a bird watcher, discovered how to develop photographs, and made small bombs and rockets with my friends using weedkiller and sugar (a formula the IRA were later to use to devastating effect). I also built a beautifully crafted matchlock rifle after reading *Bevis* by Richard Jeffries and following his instructions. It worked very well at first, firing ball bearings over a long distance. But when we ran out of gunpowder and substituted weed killer and sugar, the molten sugar gradually clogged up the barrel, which eventually blew up in my face, nearly killing me.

My adventures 'poaching', which mostly involved creeping about private estates in Surrey and being chased, meant I was quite a good runner. My companions in crime and I were once shot at by two game-keepers who were understandably annoyed when we came across their pheasant rearing pens in a clearing in a wood. I can still conjure up the sound of shotgun pellets ripping through the leaves all around us as we made our escape.

Sport, particularly team sports held little interest for me, largely I think because we were always being dragooned into it and I instinctively disliked the group enthusiasm it was supposed to automatically engender. I never ran with the pack. After being forced to play rugby for one term I chose to switch to cross-country running: you got to leave school more than an hour earlier than the rugby players and I felt it was a safer option than hurling oneself at the boots of running opponents in the obligatory tackles the game required. We were told that rugby originated in the early 19th century and I was definitely one of those that wish it had stayed there. (I only started to appreciate it recently when watching the Six Nations Championship on television.) I did come second in a Surrey all School's Swimming Championship Race at Epsom Baths however, and that resulted in my one and only favourable mention in the school assembly one morning. The only good thing one sports teacher felt he could write about me in my school report was, 'Tyrrell is well built physically.' In my late twenties I took to playing badminton and enjoyed it, and, because I had quick reactions, became quite a good player, keeping it up until I snapped a hamstring when I was about 45.

The best thing about school was escaping from it – whether by playing truant during term time or enjoying the holidays away from it. On holiday Dad made sure we had adventurous experiences. On one occasion he drove us up to Scotland, which took two days with a stop in the Lake District (this was before motorways reduced the romance of motoring in the UK). We finally arrived at a campsite near Fort William. Before leaving home he and I had built a crossbow and we took it up there to test – firing bolts over the road and into Loch Linnhe. I'm sure that we would be arrested for doing such a thing today. One day we went from there to Mallaig and caught a boat to the Isle of Skye. We were dropped off on a barren shore and made our way to a viewpoint above Loch Coruisk where we picnicked, looking up into the wild Cuillin Mountains – a magnificent landscape devoid of roads and habitation.

During the second week Dad decided we should climb Ben Nevis, leaving Mum and Jenny in Fort William, which was in those days a much smaller town than it is today. We set off in fine weather. It was a stiff walk and, with a number of short rest stops, it took about four hours to reach the summit where we nourished ourselves with the distant views, sandwiches and hot tea from our flasks.

The name, 'Ben Nevis,' derives from the Gaelic, '*Beinn Nibheis.*' Apparently Beinn is a common Gaelic word for mountain and *nibheis* translates as 'malicious.' I nearly died horribly on the way down 'malicious mountain.' After we started our descent we somehow lost the path and started down a narrow animal track instead. I was overconfident and strode down too quickly. But it was so steep that I began to run. I couldn't stop. Every time I tried, gravity pulled me down faster and faster. I came to the edge of a 2,000-foot drop and went head over heals over it. A woman further up the mountain saw me disappear and began screaming, which added an unwanted dramatic effect to what was happening. But I had landed on my back on a ledge about six feet below the cliff top. I was so winded, however, that I couldn't shout or do anything. I also thought I'd badly injured myself because I could feel liquid running down my spine. As I became aware of the long drop below me my knees turned to jelly. Every slight move I made sent me closer to the edge and what I could see would be my final moment.

I could hear Dad calling, but I was so badly winded I couldn't answer. After what seemed like an age his face appeared above me, white as a sheet. He had bravely edged his way down and was expecting to see my body far below as he looked over. He slowly and carefully talked me up towards him. Eventually I reached for his hand and he pulled me up. It was then I discovered that the liquid I could feel was not blood, as I had feared, but the remains of the tea. My flask had smashed when I landed on my back. We carefully picked our way over to the proper path and set off down the mountain, both of us in a state of shock and me with a badly bruised back. Hundreds have died on Ben Nevis and I had narrowly missed enlarging the statistic.

During the Easter holidays in 1958 we went on a two-week skiing holiday, staying in a little village called Tschagguns in Austria. It was my first trip abroad. We flew in a turboprop from Heathrow to Geneva airport and took a long slow train ride across Switzerland and into the mountains across the border. The Alpine scenery, crisp clean air and distant views entranced us all. I took to skiing like a duck to water, or so I thought. I loved the speed, but was twice pulled out of deep snowdrifts where in my exhilarated and inexperienced state I had pitched headfirst. And in the second week half way up the mountain I slipped off the chair lift into deep soft snow as I was attempting to make the time pass more interestingly by reaching down with my feet to kick snow from the top branches of the pine trees as my chair passed over them. My poor mother, who was on the chair coming up behind me saw me disappear in to deep snow and screamed. I can still bring to mind the falling sensation and the long struggle with painful breath through the snow to find a high tree I could climb so I could leap out to grab a passing empty chair and cling to it for dear life until reaching the top.

One morning, while waiting for Mum and Jenny to get ready, Dad and I took a stroll up a steep lane near our little hotel to look at a picturesque snow covered church. When we walked around the side of it, to our shock, realistically painted on the wall was a twenty-foot high image of a Nazi soldier in full uniform giving the Nazi salute. We can't escape history I thought, all around us in Tschagguns we were surrounded by ex Nazis.

* * * * *

It was at school where my first business experience occurred, though I can't remember what prompted it. With a friend I began collecting cow skulls from the local abattoir. We tied them to our bikes and took them home getting many strange looks on the way. At the bottom of the garden we cut off the horns with a fine bladed hacksaw, boiled them in a cauldron so the marrow would pop out and washed them with DDT. When they were dry we polished them up for sale. The large ones went for three and sixpence and the smaller ones for half a crown. For marketing I persuaded a member of the Boys Brigade band, a lad called Hunnisett, to blow a loud fanfare in the school assembly when the new headmaster entered the hall on a promise that he could have the horn for nothing if he did. When his pure loud notes rang out like a call to arms it took everyone by surprise except our few collaborators. There was a satisfying instant uproar. The disciplinarians among the staff were outraged and ran up and down the lines trying to find the culprit and the offending instrument. Other teachers struggled manfully to look stern but were clearly amused. Miraculously, Hunnisett wasn't identified – he was blessed with an innocent face – and the instrument passed through a chain of us away from the site of the deed never to be found by the school's forces of law and order. It was a triumph! After that my cow horns were in hot demand.

Mr Evans, bluntly told me I would not get to University because I hadn't worked hard enough to get the necessary five 'O' levels to make the 6th form. As it happened, although I did no revision, I passed in enough subjects to do so – but I left school anyway. It had been too rigid a life for me and I assumed university would be a continuation of it. I have some regrets about that now as many of my friends today clearly look back on their time at university with fondness and gained lifelong friendships and valuable contacts from it. However, I also know plenty of people who didn't obtain degrees but nevertheless had interesting lives and successful careers. My son, Mark, for example, like me, never amounted to much at school, apart from as an athlete, and didn't go to university, yet, after a string of dead-end jobs as a young man, he had enough entrepreneurial self-belief to create a successful money generating online community and become wealthy.

* * * * *

Because my desire to leave school was so strong and I enjoyed drawing, my father helped me look for work that would develop that particular talent. A company called F.G. Marshall of Banstead was advertising in the local paper for an apprentice illuminator of manuscripts, and I applied. Shortly before my sixteenth birthday, I was interviewed and accepted – thanks to my folio of pen drawings of birds and landscapes. What followed was an almost medieval period of disciplined apprenticeship, which was to last for three years. I was paid £4 a week, half of which I gave to my mother for my keep.

The main work at Marshall's (a company that still exists, death being a good line to be in) was making beautiful Books of Remembrance for crematoria throughout the country and entering memorial details in them by means of a small team of calligraphers. Some people chose to pay extra to have miniature paintings alongside the entry, and that is what I was taken on to learn how to do. I was taught and encouraged by a brilliant miniaturist called John Haysom. This was my first experience of the apprenticeship system where you gain experience by watching and being in the presence of an experienced person, something Idries Shah pointed out to us much later as being of great value.

John taught me the same skills that Christian monks and Muslim scribes had developed in the Middle Ages: how to prepare vellum for calligraphy and illuminations; and how to grind colours and prepare drawings to trace down and paint in fine detail. I applied and burnished raised gold lettering and painted bunches of flowers, coats-of-arms and military medals. Since I had a talent for it and learned quickly I was soon allowed to work on the books themselves.

There were no other youngsters working at Marshall's however and my social life was somewhat limited. I was getting itchy feet and wanted to see something new, so I resolved to travel round the world to New Zealand, which, being under-populated and beautiful, my imagination convinced me was the ideal country to live in. I began saving and collecting things for the adventure, including a small tent and a large rucksack. When my parents realised that I was serious about leaving home and travelling they suggested my friend Michael Cooke and myself should join the Young Socialists. Their idea was, I think, that this might bind me to a social network that would keep me at home. It was a good move because we both gained pretty girl friends. He, a clever, witty girl called Valerie, and me the elfin-faced Elizabeth, Valerie's equally bright and funny friend.

Elizabeth was the eldest daughter of a nurse and a left-wing social worker and in the Sixth Form of Wallington Grammar School for Girls and, at 17, was a year younger than me. I was quickly besotted and all thoughts of New Zealand went out of my mind and I stayed on at Marshalls. By today's standards, because of my shyness, it was a long courtship. Months went by before I bucked up the courage to hold hands and eventually kiss her.

It's hard when we are young to realise that all experiences (pleasant and unpleasant) and the effort we put into building a life that works, as well as the kind and variety of human contacts we make, are the food needed for spiritual development. I certainly didn't understand then that *anything* that happens is grist to the developmental mill.

* * * * *

My first trip to Ireland occurred that same year when I travelled with a friend from school days, Peter Dale, to visit relatives of his in Belfast. From there his uncle took us climbing in the Mourne Mountains, telling us it was likely to be the last climb he ever did as he was getting old. He was about 50 I recall, which seems young to me now. After we got down he returned to Belfast leaving us to fend for ourselves, the weather being perfect for walking and camping.

On the Friday afternoon after visiting a remote hermitage we happened upon a hidden valley sheltered by rocks and trees. A clear stream ran down it through a string of limpid pools. In this lush green haven from the world we discovered an empty, three-roomed cottage in a grassy clearing. It was unlocked and inside was dry as a bone. One room was full of mattresses, which was odd because we were miles from any road. Such was the ethereal atmosphere that we decided to spend the night there. So we lit a fire in the fireplace to boil up some oxtail soup in our billycan to have with bread and cheese outside in the warm evening air.

Then, as twilight settled over the valley, we heard voices. A group of young people were strolling towards us, all smiles. They looked as if they owned the place. And indeed the mattresses were theirs. It turned out they were university students up from Dublin and this was their bolthole where they invited friends to come and enjoy the peace and quiet – and party. They lit three oil lamps and several candles and over the next hour or so more students arrived until about fifteen boys and girls were gathered. Everyone seemed to regard the cottage as an almost sacred place. Several of them had musical instruments and Peter and I were made welcome in the spirit of carefree Irish student camaraderie of the like we English grammar school boys had never experienced before. We stayed in this otherworldly Celtic hideaway for the weekend enjoying the craic, listening to stories and songs, and when we left we felt we'd made some friends for life – although we never saw any of them again.

Back then, rural Irish roads were primitive by English standards and people were mostly poor so there were few cars or vans from which we could beg a lift. The plus side was that, when one did appear, lifts were freely given. By that method we gradually made our way from the Mourne Mountains via Londonderry to County Donegal, where we arrived one evening at a Youth Hostel beneath the rugged 2,500 foot Mount Errigal, that rose out of the wild and remote bog country.

Next morning, together with a boy from Belfast who was staying at the hostel, we set off in fair weather and sunshine to climb the mountain. Errigal is unusual in that it has two peaks separated by a dangerous narrow track known as 'One Man's Path', a sharp mountain ridge with steep drops on either side. We made our way across to the highest peak but with shocking suddenness the weather turned violent. High winds from the Atlantic swept across the ridge and a fierce gust plucked all three of us off the path, blowing us through the air like autumn leaves in a gale. It was an experience as forceful as when a huge sea wave knocks you over and sweeps you along until it loses power on the shore. We were dropped onto the centre of a great scree slope a hundred yards down. It was terrifying. And our fear did not die away quickly because every move we made also moved the scree slope, which threatened to sweep us down in a landslide. We remained at risk, hearts beating furiously, until we edged our way onto solid ground.

We survived and eventually found our bearings and a path down. Back at the hostel the warden was so relieved to see us safely back that he made us change into dry clothes and sat us in front of his fire, giving us Irish whisky to drink to put some blood back in our cheeks. He told us stories about the mountain and the lives it had claimed. We didn't stop talking over the adventure and the overwhelming power of the wind for days.

In the next week or so we made our way down to Galway. At that point Peter came out in painful boils contracted from bedbugs, so the round trip was aborted and we headed back to the east coast to Dublin and the ferry. All the time in Ireland I was missing Elizabeth and so I did not mind this change of plan.

As soon as I got back to Sutton I went up to Boots in High Street where she had a holiday job. She, thinking I was still in Ireland, was so surprised to see me that she fell backwards into a display of glass products smashing them to pieces on the floor. Thereafter Elizabeth and I were inseparable. We bought two sleeping bags that zipped together to make a double that we shared from then on. She came on Aldermaston marches with me, on weekend boat trips up the Thames with our friends and on trips to youth hostels in Wales and the West Country. In 1962, to our parents' consternation, we announced we were going to hitchhike together around Scandinavia with the aim of spending a glorious couple of summer months away from home before my art college course began.

We caught the ferry across to Bergen in Norway and headed north for the Jotunheimen Mountains. Hitching in Scandinavia was difficult at first until one kind person told us why: 'People think you might be Germans' (resentments about the war and the Nazi occupation were still high). With that extra bit of information we went to great lengths to let people know we were English. Since English seemed to be nearly everyone's second language, the Norwegians, Swedes and Finns – from then on – couldn't do enough for us. Often we camped in the wilderness in our little tent or slept in ancient barns or the homes of generous people who felt we needed some good food and the luxury of a bath.

This holiday marked the end of a two-year period of political activism that began when I joined the Young Socialists. By the age of 19, after marching to Aldermaston twice, being arrested a couple of times on Campaign for Nuclear Disarmament (CND) demonstrations and witnessing police brutality against demonstrators late at night in Trafalgar Square – the deliberate breaking of arms and heads – I realised that authority and the status quo is ultimately backed up by violence. I also become disillusioned by the hypocrisy of some of the so-called 'pacifists' and peace demonstrators after seeing them come to blows with one another. I was beginning to learn about the frailties of human nature and realising how absurd and impractical socialism was in the real world. Needless to say my parents argued endlessly with me about my developing views.

Elizabeth decided not to go away to University but to attend a teachers training college course in South London so we could remain together. I applied to do a Fine Art course at Croydon Art College because my life at Marshall's was no longer satisfying. Having travelled a bit I was still restless and looking for a life that offered more than that found in the closed world of a medieval studio. The Principal accepted me on the strength of my miniature work but warned me that art had moved on since the Middle Ages! He was right about that.

The morning of the first day, after an introductory talk, we new students were all given large sheets of paper, told to spread them on the floor and, with a floppy paint brush and a range of colours in bowls, told to 'Emote!' I think it fair to say that this puzzled most of us. Though some of us somewhat self-consciously pretended to be emotional as we splashed paint around, I immediately saw that, apart from two or three girls, few of us knew how to emote on demand and were not sure what the teachers expected of us. It was odd to say the least. Apparently Jackson Pollock, though dead by then, was all the rage.

* * * * *

Elizabeth and I were married in July 1964. Our frequent youthful lovemaking had led to the conception of our beautiful daughter Jane who was born a week before my 21st birthday. Elizabeth had to abandon her course for a while. We were fortunate to be offered free accommodation by a friend of Elizabeth's uncle, Mrs Burden, who was a trustee of a foreign married students hostel on Peckham Rye, south of the river in

London. We were to act as wardens in return for living rent-free. That's how we started married life together, living in two tiny attic rooms and sharing a bathroom and loo on the floor below. After several months the spacious, self-contained ground floor flat became vacant and we moved into it. It was in our bedroom there, sixteen months after Jane entered the world, that our son Mark was born.

The students in the house were Africans studying law or medicine and we got on well with most of them. We became particularly friendly with a couple whose beautiful baby boy had the unusual name of Hyacinth and who became a favourite playmate of Jane. When I asked why they had given him that unusual name his father told us that back in Africa his best friend was named Hyacinth. But he had been murdered, so every time he looked at his son he was honouring his friend's memory. Another couple were African royalty whose family owned slaves. Their behaviour was somewhat different and they tried to treat Elizabeth and I as menials, barking orders at us and expecting their every wish to be satisfied immediately and getting angry when it wasn't. They were obnoxious and unpopular with all the other residents.

An unusual crisis arose when a single young man living in the hostel stopped drinking and eating. His friends kept coming round and were very worried. He was fading away fast, nearing death. They said a witchdoctor had put a spell on him because he wanted to marry someone his tribal elders didn't approve of. He was convinced he would die and seemed profoundly resigned (despite the GP declaring there was nothing physically wrong with him). He was only saved when another student found a more powerful witchdoctor to provide a stronger spell that lifted the effect of the previous one. It worked!

I also experienced racialism in Peckham. I had bought a Triumph 650 Thunderbird motorbike with a large sidecar to carry my young family around in. Sometimes as a favour I would give these serious and dignified young black men a lift on the pillion. We would be spat at and obscenely abused by aggressive white riffraff. I felt ashamed to be British.

Mrs Burdon was kind to us. She could see we were tired and had little money and suggested we go and stay with her for a week at her cottage at Ringstead Bay in Dorset. It was to be our first holiday since we got married and we both needed a rest. One Friday she took Elizabeth and Jane down there in her car and I set off from College in the early evening driving my motorcycle and sidecar out of London and across the New Forest, arriving at Ringstead very late in pitch darkness. When I eventually found the cottage and turned off the engine and removed my helmet, it was blissfully quiet, though I could just hear the sound of waves gently breaking on the seashore across the fields and the hooting of a single owl. It was wonderful to be away from pavements and the noise of urban life and it lifted my spirits no end. Then next morning something totally unexpected happened.

I slept soundly but was awake before Elizabeth and baby Jane and decided to tiptoe out before breakfast and walk in the early morning sunshine down to the sea. Stepping outside I found that the cottage was set in a lovely garden full of flowers and backed by a bank of tall trees. I saw a little wooden slatted gate that led into the field that stretched between the cottage and the shore. There wasn't a cloud in the sky. It was perfect. I felt liberated, opened the gate and walk towards the ocean with a joyous spring in my step. But I never got to the shore. Despite the bright morning sunshine when I reached the middle of the field a dreadful feeling suddenly overwhelmed me: as if I were about to die horribly. The intensity of the terror rooted me to the spot.

As soon as the ability to move returned I unsteadily made my way back to the cottage, startling Mrs Burdon when I stumbled into the kitchen where she was preparing breakfast. 'What's the matter?' she said. 'You're as white as a sheet!' Somewhat shamefacedly I told her what had just happened. She then totally confused me by saying, 'Oh, that'll be the French Pirates! It's happened before. You're not the first they've frightened since we've been here.'

Over breakfast she explained that the cottage was converted into a home for a fisherman's family in the 14th century. But before that it had been a tiny church. She pointed out clear indications in its construction that showed this to be true. Apparently the field I was crossing was the site of an old village. 'If you look at the bumps in the grass you can make out where the buildings were,' she said. 'French pirates landed here and massacred the villagers. Some of the people managed to get into the church for sanctuary but the pirates burnt it down. We still find human bones in the garden.' Over breakfast she showed me a book about the history of Dorset that described the event.

This revelation startled me. Had I really divined facts concerning an ancient event simply through being in close proximity to where it happened? How could that be? Was such divining a genuine human capacity? A similar thing had happened to me once before in an abandoned gun emplacement from the Second World War on the Welsh coast near Fishguard where Elizabeth and I once spent an uncomfortable night curled up in our sleeping bag sheltering from a storm. We were woken by the high winds and rain to distinctly hear the sound of several men talking and clattering about purposively. We both heard them. Yet there was no one there. It alarmed us and the voices continued for some while. Up until that point I had not believed in hauntings. But that experience caused me to wonder…

Once I'd recovered from the shock of the Ringstead's haunted field we went on to have a wonderful time visiting Weymouth, the swannery at Abbotsbury and ancient sites like Maiden Castle, a large Iron Age fort outside Dorchester, and the priapic Cerne Abbas Giant. I remember reading John Cowper Powys novels that year.

* * * * *

Sometime after that we decided that I should finish my College course because of the notion, common then, that a qualification would help me earn more money and that would be good for the family in the long run (in fact my qualification in Fine Art made no difference to my life whatsoever, just as gaining a university degree today in most subjects carries little weight, apart from that of the burden of debt). My married student grant was £6 a week. I supplemented it by printing fly posters for pop groups and doing various holiday jobs such as working for the local council weeding the centre of dual carriageways and helping the Post Office with Christmas deliveries.

One summer I worked for six weeks as a labourer for a small building company who were renovating lifts in Banstead Mental Hospital. Whenever lift doors were removed and the shafts exposed it was my job to stop people jumping down them. Whilst working there I saw severe cases of psychotic behaviour. There was one woman whose legs had grown unnaturally muscular by years spent pacing up and down a green corridor keeping her face to the wall all day. There was a mad professor of mathematics who kept tearing his clothes off and wandering naked around the grounds anxiously turning over stones as if looking for something. And several patients exhibited catatonia; standing or sitting immobile in unnatural poses for long periods.

Working in the mental hospital, although interesting, was also more than a little unnerving and, by contrast, I much preferred working for the Post Office helping with the pre-Christmas rush. The straightforwardness of doing a postal round, delivering letters and parcels, was satisfying and didn't take long. But there were two aspects to that job that I didn't like that stayed with me. The first was what happened when we sorted out our round in a big hall full of bags and shelves. Some of the younger full-time postmen had a game: they deliberately threw any parcel marked 'fragile' around until they could tell, by the sound of breaking glass or the smell and leaking liquid, that they had smashed whatever it contained. This meant there was a strong smell of alcoholic spirits in the hall, weirdly mixed with scent from the perfume bottles they had also broken. They seemed to rejoice in the certainty that they were spoiling the pleasure of the givers and receivers of the gifts. I was outraged that they thought damaging people's presents was funny and they mocked me as a spoilsport when I objected. They were clearly showing off to the girl students. No one was reprimanded. No supervisors intervened. No one was sacked. So I was always glad to get out in the fresh air to deliver my round.

The second unpleasantness began on the first occasion we students came back from our first delivery round. The rounds were so quick and easy that we assumed we would collect another bag to take out and deliver once we had finished with the first. But when we arrived back at the centre less than a couple of hours later we were met outside on the street by a couple of union men. They explained that we should take our empty bags home and come back after lunch for the afternoon shift. It seems that a day's 'work' for these postmen was actually only two or three hours in total. This seemed to me to be undermining what unions were supposed to be about: a fair day's pay for a fair day's work.

This wasn't my only experience of British working practices in the 1960s. In my third year at college a group of us got summer jobs at the local Charrington brewery. We were given the grottiest jobs but that was understandable. It was pretty tedious work made worse by the atmosphere of stale beer; every time a lorry came in with crates of empty bottles we had to load each crate on to a conveyer belt and the workforce was happy to let us students do it.

The problem arose because we students could all see that one person to each belt, not the two allocated, could easily do this job. This gave me the idea that each of us should work hard for two hours and have two hours off so we could take a mug of tea up to the roof and read or play chess. Which is what we did for a couple of weeks. I read *Catch-22* up there. But the union took a dislike to this. One day a small group of men led by a communist shop steward, realising I was the ringleader, bundled me among towers of crates and held a knife at my throat, ordering me to stop the students from continuing with this innovation. They didn't like that we were demonstrating how unnecessary it was for two people to load conveyor belts and thereby threatening jobs. (This same man had previously assumed I was a young communist because of my name and had been quite friendly at first.) In a way I could sympathise, but not much.

The manager of the factory got involved and apologised. He told us privately that what we were doing was reasonable but for the sake of peace on the factory floor could we please conduct ourselves as the union wanted. So we did: we all needed the money.

Most students entering the art college were 16 years old. I was nearly 20. At that time Croydon Council had ambitions for its colleges and gave them sizable budgets to employ good teachers. That was how I got a taste of the art scene of the sixties. After a year or so, being one of the older students, I often lunched with the tutors including Bridget Riley, who was becoming famous for her op art paintings; John Hoyland who was making his name as an abstract artist and Allen Jones who was becoming notorious for his erotic pop art paintings and prints. As far as I could see the talk mainly consisted of pretentious art babble - about publicity, getting famous, shocking people, making money from exhibitions in New York and selling their work. Although art colleges were the source of the creativity that fuelled pop music and fashion in the swinging sixties and created a feeling in Britain that anyone with talent could start a business or achieve success, which was great, most content – what the creativity represented – had no depth, lacked philosophical substance, was hedonistic and encouraged people to become more self-centred. We were, after all, right in the middle of what Adam Curtis was to call, 'The Century of the Self' where all the old moral certainties, traditional ideas and social structures had been battered and crushed. We didn't know how to think about ourselves, causing our identities to become fragile and leading to an age of anything goes. Art not founded on deep enquiry was whatever an artist said it was. 'Art for Art's sake' was nothing more than a money-making cult.

The shallowness of it all was so disappointing that I began reading about art history to find out why the arts had degenerated to such an extent. The otherworldly quality of Chinese painting particularly attracted me then because the artists were clearly seeking to symbolically make visible the enigmatic mysteries of the universe: the hidden. One 13th century Chinese painter, Chou Tung-ch'ing, inscribed on one of his works these words: 'We can only take an idea and make it into a painting. To probe the subtleties of the ordinary, we must describe the indescribable.' That is what I felt art should be doing. It was Chinese art that introduced me to Taoism and deepened my youthful interest in esoteric matters.

The tutor I got on best with was Barry Fantoni who was only three years older than me and very funny. We became friendly and I went up to London with him a few times, ostensibly to attend art exhibitions as part of our course – although I quickly realised that his main purpose was to go to the Soho office of *Private Eye* magazine to deliver cartoons for the next edition. This was about 1965 and by then the magazine was already a thorn in the side of the establishment: lambasting hypocrisy, sanctimony, corruption and humbug wherever its writers saw it. Various characters that later became famous wandered in and out, including Richard Ingrams, Willie Rushton and one of my favourite investigative journalists, Christopher Brooker.

The atmosphere in Private Eye's scruffy office – a blend of serious anti-cant commitment with a fun, dynamic feeling of competitive earnestness punctuated by bouts of hysterical laughter – was in tune with the mood of those few rebellious years in the 60s when everything seemed in flux and possibilities endless.

CHAPTER THREE

Meeting Idries Shah

IT WAS also in 1965 when I first heard Idries Shah speak. This was in a tall nine-sided building known as the Djamichoonatra (nicknamed 'The Jami'), whose design derived from the enneagram, a nine-sided geometrical figure said to represent the nine major and interconnecting personality types. It was set in the grounds of Coombe Springs, an estate near Kingston upon Thames a short distance from Richmond Park, my childhood playground. It was there that a community of followers of the late George Gurdjieff studied what they called 'The Work'. Gurdjieff was a Greco-Armenian mystic who taught that mankind is asleep and has no real consciousness or will. He asserted that some people, under the right circumstances and with correct training, could undergo a trans-formation and become properly conscious and find his or her true place in creation as a real human being.

The chain of events that led me to Coombe Springs began at art college when I became interested in the distinction between 'subjective' and 'objective' art and 'exoteric' and 'esoteric' knowledge. Like many youngsters in the early 60s I was lapping up books such as Colin Wilson's *The Outsider*, Aldous Huxley's *Perennial Philosophy* and *The Doors of Perception*, Jung and Jaffe's *Memories, Dreams, Reflections*, as well as the works of Dostoevsky, Hesse and Camus. Then a young man named Francis Snooks, with whom I had become friendly, introduced me to *In Search of the Miraculous* by P.D. Ouspensky and George Gurdjieff's *Meetings with Remarkable Men*. This material fascinated me and, having become disillusioned with the contemporary 'fine' art scene but greatly enjoying the part of the course where we studied the history of art, I resolved to write my dissertation on 'objective art'.

This is the passage from *In Search of the Miraculous*, where the author quoted Gurdjieff, that inspired me to do so:

'There is art and art. You have doubtless noticed that during our lectures and talks I have often been asked various questions by those present relating to art but I have always avoided talks on this subject. This was because I consider all ordinary talks about art as absolutely meaning-less. People speak of one thing while they imply something quite different and they have no idea whatever what they are implying. At the same time it is quite useless to try to explain the real relationship of things to a man who does not know the A B C about himself, that is to say, about man. We have talked together now for some time and by now you ought to know this A B C, so that I can perhaps talk to you now even about art.

'You must first of all remember that there are two kinds of art, one quite different from the other – objective art and subjective art. All that you know, all that you call art, is subjective art, that is, something that I do not call art at all because it is only objective art that I call art.

'To define what I call objective art is difficult first of all because you ascribe to subjective art the characteristics of objective art, and secondly because when you happen upon objective works of art you take them as being on the same level as subjective works of art.

'I will try to make my idea clear. You say – an artist creates. I say this only in connection with objective art. In relation to subjective art I say that with him 'it is created.' You do not differentiate between these, but this is where the whole difference lies. Further you ascribe to subjective art an invariable action, that is, you expect works of subjective art to have the same reaction on everybody. You think, for instance, that a funeral march should provoke in everyone sad and solemn thoughts and that any dance music, a komarinsky for instance, will provoke happy thoughts. But in actual fact this is not so at all. Everything depends upon association. If on a day that a great misfortune happens to me I hear some lively tune for the first time this tune will evoke in me sad and oppressive thoughts for my whole life afterwards. And if on a day when I am particularly happy I hear a sad tune, this tune will always evoke happy thoughts. And so with everything else.

'The difference between objective art and subjective art is that in objective art the artist really does 'create,' that is, he makes what he intended, he puts into his work whatever ideas and feelings he wants to put into it. And the action of this work upon men is absolutely definite; they will, of course each according to his own level, receive the same ideas and the same feelings that the artist wanted to transmit to them.

There can be nothing accidental either in the creation or in the impressions of objective art.

'In subjective art everything is accidental. The artist, as I have already said, does not create; with him 'it creates itself.' This means that he is in the power of ideas, thoughts, and moods which he himself does not understand and over which he has no control whatever. They rule him and they express themselves in one form or another. And when they have accidentally taken this or that form, this form just as accidentally produces on man this or that action according to his mood, tastes, habits, the nature of the hypnosis under which he lives, and so on. There is nothing invariable; nothing is definite here. In objective art there is nothing indefinite.'

These thoughts were at such variance to the meaningless art babble I was hearing at college that I asked our Liberal Studies philosophy tutor a simple question that was to mark a turning point in my life, although I didn't realize it at the time: 'Was there anywhere I could go to learn more about objective art?' He said he would make some enquiries – and was as good as his word. A few days later he gave me the number of an organisation called the Institute for the Comparative Study of History, Philosophy and the Sciences that was directed by John G. Bennett. I found a phone box and called Bennett's office and spoke to a lady called Joan Edwards, who invited me to a talk to be given by Bennett at Coombe Springs the following weekend.

Bennett had known Gurdjieff since 1923 and had also been a student of Ouspensky. The two, like thousands of teachers before them, attracted many lost souls – gullible and perhaps slightly autistic intellectual or creative types who were trying to understand what life was all about.

Somewhat nervously, being gauche and shy, I went along with a friend who was also interested, and I can't say we understood much of what Bennett was going on about. Despite that, over the next few months I spent spare time on weekends working on the Coombe Springs estate, meeting people, doing Gurdjieff's 'stop' exercises and listening to lectures in the hope that, eventually, I would. The stop exercise was thought to be impossible to do on one's own. The aim of it was that, when the instruction 'Stop!' was shouted out by Bennett, we should immediately stop whatever we were doing and freeze in that position, mentally, emotionally and physically, so as to observe our current inner state and what we were identifying with at that moment. The first time Bennett shouted 'Stop!' in my presence took me by surprise. I was planting shrubs on a steep bank and fell over as I tried to 'freeze'.

On another occasion I tried to learn the special Gurdjieff dance 'movements' in the Djamichoonatra where the ritual dancing and other meditations took place. Bennett was instructing us and when he noticed my deformed elbow he came over and, without speaking, took hold of my arm and examined it, moving it about as if it was a separate inanimate thing, not part of me at all. I remember feeling embarrassed and deeply discouraged, thinking that because I couldn't straighten it the harmony of the dance would be spoilt. (What with my Scottish dancing experience at school and my abject failure at Gurdjieff dances I never got to dance much, which I regret. The most I ever manage is a sort of rhythmic Neanderthal stomp when the Rolling Stones, or similar, are played at parties).

I never joined the community of people living at Coombe Springs, partly because I now had a wife and babies to support, and also because I found a lot of the behaviour there too intense for my liking; and more than a little weird. But I was young, and it was far more exciting than art college and Bennett seemed a vastly intelligent, sincere and kindly man.

One day he advised everyone to read *The Sufis*, by Idries Shah, whom at that time nobody I knew had heard of. It had an introduction by Robert Graves. Although ignorant of Sufism I devoured it. Even on the first reading it revealed a deep and subtle psychology that directly impacted on my mind. I couldn't stop thinking about it. The book offered a vision for humanity far in advance of anything I had heard about before and contained the first explanation I'd come across for why we find it difficult to see things from different points of view (it happens because our brain is a pattern-matching organ and our mind can only view experiences through the tangle of patterns and expectations we are conditioned with).

It took me years to grasp that a Sufi is someone who has the cast of mind to grapple with this conditioning problem, usually with the help of others who have done so before. Such a person has discovered how to overcome their associative thinking style and see beyond their conditioned 'Self' and attained knowledge of a higher extra-dimensional reality: often referred to as 'the divine'. This gives them capacities not otherwise available. Only such a person is a Sufi: one who is 'in the world but not of it'. Abu Said, a medieval Persian poet wrote: 'Being a Sufi is to put away what is in your head – imagined truth, preconceptions, conditioning – and face what may happen to you.' Those of us still struggling to do that are said to be 'on the Path'.

Sufism, we learned from Shah, is not an exclusively Islamic manifestation, as many scholars and pseudo-Sufi cultists believe. It's not just 'the inner mystical tradition of Islam' or 'an ascetic Islamic sect' as academics often describe it. It's not an ideology that seeks to indoctrinate people to certain beliefs and 'right' actions. Although the inner experiential dimension of all religions is Sufic, there can be no history of Sufism since it is made up of lived experience – not recorded information. It is beyond religion as understood in ordinary cultures and interpenetrates the people of differing religions.

Sufis operating in the Islamic world, like Ibn Arabi, have said that there were Sufis on Earth in ancient times, long before Muhammad was born. This 'ancient spiritual freemasonry', as Robert Graves described it, included Gnostically inclined Christians, Essenes, Pythagoreans, members of Egyptian and Zoroastrian mystery schools, Hindus, Buddhists, Taoists: every age has produced awakened individuals. As Shah explained in a subsequent work, *The Way of the Sufi*, 'The connection between the ancient practical philosophies and the present ones is based upon the higher-level unity of knowledge, not upon appearances.' So violent has much of our history been, however, that over the ages the gnostic wisdom stream has often retired underground to await favourable cultural opportunities and suitable individuals to arise before it can safely emerge once more.

Sufism only appears to be an Islamic 'oriental' phenomenon because Muslims were taught by Muhammad that seeking knowledge was obligatory and so they set about gathering together as much of the writings of earlier times and established centres of learning to translate and study the material. Once the writings were protected in the Islamic world the Gnostic wisdom connection revealed itself again, resulting in a great outpouring of creativity that reached its highest peak in the Golden Age of Islam – a time when wise men and women were often valued. From there it spread and influenced the West and Far East. As Graves explained in his introduction to *The Sufis*, 'The natural Sufi may be as common in the West as in the East, and may come dressed as a general, a peasant, a merchant, a lawyer, a schoolmaster, a housewife, anything. To be ... free from ambition, greed, intellectual pride, blind obedience to custom, or awe of persons higher in rank – that is the Sufi's ideal.'

Well-known Western figures like Meister Eckhart, Shakespeare, Goethe and his friend Alexander von Humboldt, and Ralph Waldo Emerson would be recognised by Sufis as kindred spirits.

Sufis state that the mystical goal is closer to us than is generally believed and can be attained in many ways – but it cannot be engendered through repetitive activity. It is only ignorance that makes us assume that esoteric transcendental knowledge is complex, remote from our everyday lives and difficult to achieve.

Over the years, I have read *The Sufis* more than 20 times. So rich is its prose and so vast the implications it triggers in the mind that I, like many others, have noticed, that on each reading it is like coming across an entirely new book. It's an active instrument designed to lay down the groundwork for genuine transformation of the inner life and prepare sincere seekers for connection to reality. If any one work could be said to have changed my life it is this. It undoubtedly had a similar effect on others. It was, as Doris Lessing described it: 'A book that at once announced itself as unlike any other.' For me, its publication was by far the greatest cultural event of the 1960s – bigger than Bob Dylan, The Beatles and the Rolling Stones put together. And its impact continues to resonate, as I'm sure it will for centuries to come.

In the print department at college one day I heard roars of laughter from the other end of the room. They came from another older student, Fred Carver, who to my astonishment was reading the same book and had reached the chapter on Mulla Nasrudin – the wise fool and joke figure who appears in some Sufi stories. Fred was already exhibiting 'op art' paintings with Bridget Riley and Victor Vasarely in London galleries and we soon became friends.

* * * * *

Inspired by *The Sufis* and Gurdjieff's *Meetings with Remarkable Men*, and beginning to realise how limited our schooling had been, Fred and I decided to organise a group of fellow students to get together and catch up on our education. A dozen or more of us started a sort of mini-university together, in which every member took a topic he or she wanted to know more about and studied it intensely until they felt able to deliver a talk on it to the whole group. We would then type out our talks. Our studies covered prehistory, ancient civilizations, the history of art, American Indian culture, Eskimo myths, Australian Aboriginal beliefs, Chinese history and art, the history of magic, optical illusions, music and much else. We delivered our talks over an amazing three days in my large basement flat in Peckham Rye culminating in a twelve-course feast prepared by Francis Snooks, who was training to be a chef, and his lovely French wife, Anne Marie. It was quite a party…

The art colleges of London in those days were generating a buzz in pop music and fashion. There was eye-ball kicking op art, pop art, psychedelic art and performance art to attract media attention and excite the young. And the beautiful girls wearing mini-skirts were a constant distraction to us chaps. The Kinks strode into the college canteen for lunch looking exotic and confident in flowery clothes and high-heeled boots: two of their number were students at the college before the group took off and became hot property.

One day I was browsing around an army surplus shop in Charing Cross Road and came across a large bin of small transparent plastic prisms. On an impulse I bought the lot for £1 convinced I could think of a way to make money out of them. And I did. On one surface of each one I worked out a method of printing swirly patterns in day-glow psyche-delic colours. Then I drilled tiny holes in one corner big enough to take an earring clip and sold them to boutiques. To my astonishment my plastic earrings became fashionable. The next thing I knew they were on TV! Another friend began making flowery ties by cutting up colourful Indian material and getting his mother and her friends to make them. Soon trendy young men all over London were wearing flowery ties and he made a fortune.

It was an exciting time. To bright young people in London anything seemed possible in the 60s. But the highlight of that period for me began when I heard that Bennett had asked Idries Shah to give a talk at Coombe Springs to an invited audience of his students who had read *The Sufis* and Shah had agreed, letting it be known that he was prepared to answer any questions arising. I made sure to be there.

Listening to Shah speak was a quite different experience from listening to Bennett. Whereas Bennett spoke slowly and earnestly and often, to me, impenetrably, like a deeply benevolent Victorian patrician, Shah was a breath of fresh air: modern, irreverent and serious all at once. It was not so much the person himself, though he was direct, often funny and not in the least bit obscure, it was what he said – his message if you like – that captivated many in the audience, including me. He was indicating a new kind of sensibility.

By confirming what we in the audience already thought we knew – that humanity is asleep, 'in a state of fitful sleep, generally more resembling a nightmare,' echoing what Gurdjieff, Ouspensky, Bennett, and many spiritual teachers over the millennia had stated – he gained our attention. For example, 'Peace is the fruit of activity, not of sleep,' was recorded on a temple wall by an Egyptian master in 2,000 BC. And, nearly 900 years ago, the Afghan sage, Hakim Sanai wrote, 'Humanity is asleep, concerned only with what is useless, living in a wrong world.' As a callow young man this idea seemed obviously true to me, but it was years before I really understood it.

However Shah added another observation: he emphasized that we are evolving to a certain destiny in terms of a purpose in the distant future. We are taking part in that process whether we like it or not – whether asleep or not. He cited Rumi saying that organs of perception come into being as a result of the need for them and that in this age where scientists are puzzling over the nature of time and space, these organs are concerned with the transcending of time and space.

He wrote in *The Sufis* that the function of a spiritual teacher is to open the mind of the seeker in such a way that he can come to recognise his destiny. In order to succeed in this, the seeker must first realize how much of his ordinary thinking is cramped by assumptions. Until this point is reached *true* understanding is impossible and the candidate is only fit for one or another of the more usual human organizations which train him to think along certain lines: 'Open the door of your mind to the waif of understanding,' Rumi writes. 'For you are poor and it is rich.'

Thus it was that the contention that within each human being there is the potential of another personality beneath the outer husk of our crudely conditioned ones became a real consideration for me. It seemed that, whether it was true or not, one had nothing to lose by dwelling on the possibility.

Shah described this inner potential as a latent organ of perception that was of such a nature that, if it is to develop, our mind must first conceive of it as a possibility. Only then might it become the means by which we can connect to a dimension beyond space and time and through which we can attain permanence. He said that to talk, write or theorise about it was of limited use in its development because a person needs preparation in order to attain it. And that preparation must, in part, consist of calming down those aspects of the personality that hinder, or even kill off, the possibilities of an inner life. These aspects would be such as most religions have warned about, even though the psychological reasons behind the teachings are not usually understood by conventional religious authorities. The religions with which we are mostly familiar operate on a pre-spiritual level, working to create social and mental balance. A person who is too obsessed is unable to see within himself. Likewise a person who is too emotional, whose emotions rule him, cannot make progress because his emotions blind him to finer perceptions. 'The coarse drives out the fine.'

This was a rather formal way of introducing the possibility of an advanced and subtle intuitive way of thinking more in tune with objectivity reality.

About that time, two papers by Shah were circulated: *Declaration of the People of the Tradition*, and *Twenty-two Principles* (both easily obtainable on the Internet and well worth reading). No document could have been better calculated to grab the attention of anyone who had become curious about esotericism than these. They affirmed that there was a deep meaning to life over and above what our shallow, materialistic culture had to offer, but that a particular kind of effort was required to connect to it, which seemed reasonable to me. We had to learn how to distinguish between wants and needs. It's hard to realize that making this distinction back then was a significant breakthrough, a revolutionary idea, for most people. In those days public demonstrations and protest marches usually consisted of excitable people chanting, 'What do we want?' followed by their demands. They never began with, 'What do we need?' Everyone thought that a want was the same as a need. And, sadly, many still do today.

Shah made it clear that he regarded himself as having a task: to make available in the West real knowledge about human development, psychology and evolution from the Sufi tradition he was heir to. 'Because this knowledge, in its nature and operation, is different from what people are accustomed to expect of knowledge, attempts to find out and make use of it generally fail. It will respond and operate fully only if approached in a certain manner. This is the first of the difficulties encountered in the path.'

It was the Sufi capacity to detach from objects and concerns that enabled them to go beyond familiar dimensions and transcend the ignorance produced by regarding secondary phenomena, such as time and space, as primary. He emphasised that this capacity could only be gained according to what was possible and the needs of the current situation; not what we wanted, or what our expectations of spiritual development were. Sufism, he wrote in *The Sufis*, 'is not a mystical system, not a religion, but a body of knowledge.' He was making this knowledge available by way of extensive written materials (not always under his own name), by arranging study groups, and also by directly interacting with people, often engaging with them in cultural or business projects.

In his talks and writings he stressed that what we sought – the metaphorical 'treasure' that Sufi poets allude to – was to be found in the way we responded to life and worked in the world, not by disconnecting from ordinary life. The subtle knowledge arises from experience, not through books, academic activities or indulging in random 'spiritual' exercises. He also stressed that real human development depends as much on discarding habits of thinking as it does about gaining new ones. He gently, and sometimes not so gently, mocked those supposed seekers after truth; the cultists who adopt eastern clothes, pose as 'spiritual' people and indulge in auto-hypnotic whirling, chanting, fasting and mumbling mantras in foreign tongues, all of which are merely imitating the vestigial bits and pieces of once valuable techniques that are no longer viable.

New learning is not possible without having patterns already existing in the mind for it to attach to. I see that more clearly now than I ever did back then. A baby comes into the world with knowledge that we usually call reflexes – it knows how to feed and swallow and attract attention when hungry for example – and this innate knowledge is programmed into each baby from its genes. Each programme is a pattern on which new knowledge can be built. So my reading of Gurdjieff, Ouspensky and Bennett had provided some fragments of the patterns my mind needed for the teaching to latch on to as surely as a baby latches on to a nipple. Of course Shah was looking for people who were attracted to these ideas and insights about conscious evolution.

Another idea already installed in me was that we are not the same creature from one moment to the next and that somehow we have to accommodate that fact. As Gurdjieff said, 'It is the greatest mistake to think that man is always one and the same. A man is never the same for long. He is continually changing.' And I knew that. Shah described the problem by saying that each individual mind acts like a crowd, a multiplicity of separate selves, and that this 'multimind' constitutes what we imagine to be our individuality. Because of this it is hard for us to see ourselves for what we are.

It was at a fancy weekend dress party that I next saw Shah. He was enjoying the honky-tonk piano playing of a young man called Leon Flamholc in the Djamichoonatra, to the consternation of those who regarded the building as some kind of sacred place. Bennett had given over the Coombe Springs property to Shah, who moved with his wife into the Gatehouse. Shah immediately set about dissolving the cultish elements of the community and obsessions about Gurdjieff. The party was one way of doing that. It was an astonishing event organised quickly and efficiently by groups of talented creative people who transformed the look of the house and grounds into a colourful pleasure garden. These strangers all seemed to know Shah. Pavilions were erected, acrobats, conjurors and belly dancers performed and all the time there was music ranging from eastern Afghan bands to jazz, folk and pop music. Many hundreds of guests circulated. This upset and embittered many of Bennett's more earnest followers, some of whom harried Shah over it for the rest of his life. But it was always obvious to me that it was necessary.

* * * * *

When I left art college with a wife, toddler and baby to support, I had no job and no regular income. What did sometimes bring in money was designing and printing posters for pop groups. But this was impractical to do in the Peckham Rye hostel. Understandably the resident students didn't like the awful acrid smell of drying silk-screen inks and objected – so I rented a large studio suitable for my purpose for 10 shillings a week in an 18th century mews off Portobello Road. Elizabeth and I gave up the wardenship of the hostel and we moved to a ground floor flat next to Bushy Park, not far from my birthplace at Hampton Court. Our new home was also much closer to Coombe Springs than Peckham. The new landlord was a sleazy fellow who often inspected the flat when we were out, which we knew about because of the smell and piles of fag ash he left all over the place. However, the rent was £2 a week and we could just about afford it. To save money I would cycle every day through Kingston and Richmond Park, across Hammersmith Bridge and up to Notting Hill and the studio because it was cheaper and easier than using the motorbike.

I enjoyed the Portobello Road atmosphere in the 60s, before it become a tourist destination. It was full of characters selling all sorts of knick-knacks or running antique shops and market stalls. It was also a haunt of London's growing ethnic communities. It all seemed exotic to me at the time. I had a classical guitarist friend who helped me on the big print runs and when we weren't preparing artwork or printing in the studio we would wander around savouring the relaxed cosmopolitan atmosphere. We would end up at a small Greek restaurant where the owner took pity on our poverty and gave us free baklavas whenever we bought anything from him, even a cup of tea.

In the studio I designed posters for pop groups to promote their gigs, prepared the silkscreens and printed them. I worked hard at this – the printing in particular was backbreaking – but was often swindled by wide-boy agents who had the habit of disappearing with the posters leaving behind a smile and promise: 'I'll put a cheque in the post'. Within a few months I realised a pattern was emerging: half the time the cheques never came. London was full of ex art students like me ducking and diving, trying to make a living out of printing posters, so all these budding pop impresarios had to do was move on and find another sucker.

I became disheartened, exhausted and disillusioned – so much effort for so little reward. Things took a further turn for the worse when we were woken one morning to the unearthly sound of anguished wailing. The sweet little baby of the couple in the flat above had turned a funny colour and gone limp. It was dead, although still making gurgling sounds – the death rattle. The mother was hysterical and the father in shock. I ran to the nearest phone box to call 999 for an ambulance. To my astonishment the woman who took my call calmly started asking me a series of questions such as what was the baby's full name and who was its doctor. She seemed to have no appreciation of what 'emergency' meant. In the end in my frustration I just screamed at her, 'Send an ambulance. At once! A baby is dying!' I gave our address, slammed the phone down and sprinted back to the house. A cot death is a dreadful tragedy and we were all affected by it.

* * * * *

After nine months I gave up the mews studio and got a job as a petrol pump attendant in an ESSO garage at the bottom of Coombe Lane, not far from Coombe Springs. The steady work and reliable income quickly stabilised me and I soon cheered up. There were two other attendants and we shared shifts. One of them, Colin Wilson, had a degree in Russian and a desire to train as an accountant, which he went on to do. The other, Mike, was the son of the then principal of Kingston Art College and was mad on motorcycles. He was saving up to bike to India on the hippy trail, which he duly did. Twice.

Between us we found we could more than double our wages by

earning good tips and using a bit of entrepreneurial acumen. At the end of the evening shift, for example, when we were turning off the lights and beginning to take readings from the pumps for closing down, police cars would turn up and ask us to fill up their cars but put a couple of gallons of fuel in cans for them to use in their lawn mowers, saying, 'split the difference'. (Not very honest I admit, but who were we to argue with the police?) We quickly identified other opportunities for extra earnings. Every time we put a pint or quart of oil in a customer's engine, for example, we would take the can with its leftover oil round the back and let it completely drain into a large can. When that can was full we would sell it for half price to anyone we felt sorry for or who had treated us politely (not all customers did). Most drivers liked the fact that we were capable and took an interest in them. Whenever we fitted new tyres or batteries they invariably gave good tips that we put into a jar and split equally between us at the end of each week. It became clear that good service is worth money.

One month ESSO put on a promotion to encourage us workers to sell oil more enthusiastically. The deal was that if, when we tore off the strip from the oilcan, it had stars printed on the underside we could claim a free gift. One star represented a modest gift, two stars something more substantial, like a transistor radio or hairdryer, and three stars got us into the realm of big white goods. This was a national promotion and the special cans were meant for distribution evenly among garages around the country. To our astonishment we had a box of 24 one pint cans where every one we sold from it had three stars printed on the strip. It was a mistake but the person who organised the campaign didn't want to get the sack over his cockup and said that, if we kept quiet about it, he would honour the deal and we could claim whatever we wanted from the list of gifts. We were awash with fridges, electric kettles, hi-fi equipment and the like.

Working at the garage was my first experience of dealing with the public, which I thoroughly enjoyed. It was a lovely hot summer and when business on the forecourt was slack I stripped my Triumph bike and sidecar down to paint them in psychedelic colours: purples, reds, greens, yellows and orange swirls. Every spoke was a different colour. Occasionally people I was getting to know at Coombe Springs would call in to fill up. They included Neil Hall and Leon Flamholc who were starting up an interior design and decorating firm at the time; and Count Tassilo Wolff-Metternich, who, when he saw my bike in all its newly coloured glory, told me he had bought a riverboat, which was moored on the Thames at Kingston. He was a wealthy young man who wafted about attracted to the hippy lifestyle. He wanted his boat painted in psychedelic colours and asked me if I'd do it for him. I agreed. And so, after finishing my shift at 3 pm, I would go down to the river and spend three or four hours in the afternoon sun earning extra money painting his boat. Our finances were looking up.

A strange event occurred whilst we were living in Bushy Park. At precisely 4'oclock one morning Elizabeth suddenly jerked out of sleep, sat bolt upright and cried out, 'Something's happened to Dad!' Kenneth was her father and she was clearly upset so I tried to comfort her. 'Don't worry,' I said. 'It was only a dream.' But she was strongly affected by the feeling. Just as we were both drifting back to sleep about an hour later, the phone rang with the news that her father had died unexpectedly of a heart attack - at the very moment Elizabeth had cried out.

Because of witnessing a succession of such unusual incidents, and experiencing 'psychic' phenomena in my teens and twenties, such as foreseeing several times who was about to walk round a corner in town, my curiosity about what all this might mean for the conventional view of how the world worked grew. I read various books on the topic, including some outlandish though exciting ones by the eccentric archaeologist T. C. Lethbridge, like *ESP: Beyond Time and Distance*. He believed that places where emotionally strong events had occurred in the past held a charge that could be detected by sensitive people. This idea attracted me because of my experience of the French Pirate attack at Ringstead Bay. He thought dowsing with a pendulum was an affective tool to trace such events. Maybe he was on to something. Despite scientists finding that there is no evidence that dowsing worked above chance when tested, I preferred to trust my own experience that it could.

My father had often used metal dowsing rods to locate pipes under streets and pavements before instructing his team of Irish navies to dig the trenches to take out the heavy-duty electricity cables, so I couldn't dismiss such an idea out of hand. Especially when I knew that the

London Electricity Board issued metal dowsing rods for the purpose. Dad kept his set in the boot of his car. Although he did not believe in the supernatural he demonstrated the effect for me in the garden, but couldn't explain it either.

That autumn I had a call at the garage from Fred Carver asking me if I knew anything about psychedelic art. I told him about my work on the bike and the boat. After leaving college he had moved down to the South Coast and somehow blagged a commission to produce three psyche-delic posters for Bill, an American beat poet who owned Brighton's Unicorn Bookshop, which, I was to find out, was becoming a notorious haven for hippies, mind altering drug dealers, 'free' thinkers and New Age occultists. Having taken an advance for three posters without producing anything other than his arty appearance as evidence that he could fulfil the contract, Fred felt out of his depth somewhat and needed help. But he had a deadline, which was only a week away and he was getting desperate.

Not wanting to spend the rest of my life working as a petrol pump attendant and in need of a change I made the decision to decamp to Hove immediately to help Fred design and print the posters. By then Shah had sold Coombe Springs to developers and used the money to buy a much better situated house at Langton Green near Tunbridge Wells in Kent. The house came with an estate of nearly 50 acres.

I decided there was little to keep me in Kingston. Elizabeth took the children to her mother's house in Carshalton Beeches and we decided that I would spend the weekdays in Hove with Fred, his wife Jan and their numerous cats, and return to the family for the weekend. Any spare time was to be spent flat hunting by the coast.

Fred and I worked furiously for several days and nights in his attic studio, hardly sleeping. We came up with ideas by studying examples of psychedelic graphics and posters from the USA and Britain as well as Art Nouveau drawings and paintings. We called ourselves 'Firebird Visions' and produced passable posters that caught a bit of the mood of the times, printing them in fluorescent colours and gold and silver inks. One of the designs featured a 43 word extract from *The Crystal World* by J.G. Ballard, which American Bill had permission for us to incorporate. When we finished we loaded them into my sidecar and delivered them to Unicorn Bookshop. Inside there was a haze of cannabis smoke, with which I was not familiar, and various odd characters that looked to me as if they hadn't been out in sunshine for a long while.

When we unpacked the posters these befuddled would-be hippies gathered around to view our efforts and one of them, nonchalantly flicking his long hair back over his head, drawled, 'They're great man... great. Did you do them on acid?' Thinking he was referring to the lithographic printing process where acid is used I said, 'No. They're silk-screen prints,' and was rewarded with a blank stare from a clearly puzzled young man. It was only when we got outside and Fred explained that 'acid' was slang for LSD that I understood why. The drug scene had passed me by. I had tried to smoke cannabis a couple of times at art college, hoping for some revelation, but it only made me feel nauseous, for which I am eternally grateful having now come to know what damage cannabis can do to the brain.

Bill liked the posters and immediately ordered more for dispatch to America, France and Japan. Ballard signed 50 copies himself and they were sold at a premium. So we were kept busy for a few weeks during which time I also looked for a flat so Elizabeth and the children could join me down by the sea in what I was finding to be a less claustrophobic environment than London. And it's true; sea air really is bracing.

I always parked my motorbike in the wide back alley outside Fred's flat and one morning went down to find someone had stolen the engine. I wrote off to the insurance company to make a claim for a replacement and they promptly wrote back saying that as I did not have fully comprehensive insurance, only 'third party, fire and theft', and since they claimed the engine was classed as an accessory no payment would be forthcoming. I was outraged at the duplicity. Without an engine the bike could not be moved so clearly it was not an accessory. I complained on the phone, in person at one of their offices and in writing several times until they finally relented. Three months later, on the day when the £30 cheque for a new engine finally arrived, I went outside and found that the previous night the rest of the bike had been spirited away, presumably by the same thieves. I phoned up the company to explain how the situation had changed and the person on the phone laughed at me, clearly implying that I had made the story up. Thus I developed a deep mistrust of the insurance industry.

I put the £30 towards buying a second-hand Matchless 650cc and sidecar to replace the Triumph.

* * * * *

A great atmosphere undoubtedly existed in Brighton and Hove in the 1960s, generated by creative people and the many exotic characters that lived there, but my most memorable experience was quite unexpected. That year, not long before Christmas, a foot of snow fell along the coast in a couple of hours, just as I was due to catch the train back to Carshalton. All traffic stopped. Buses, cars and lorries were left abandoned at odd angles on roads and pavements. So I decided to walk from Hove through the deep snow along Western Road and up to Brighton Station to see if trains were still running. What struck me was the soft hush. It was uncanny but delightful. Not a single vehicle engine was running, the normally noisy seagulls were struck dumb and I could hear conversations people were having 100s of yards away as strangers helped strangers. The snow muffled all sound. The contrast with our normal lives made me realize just how noisy we have become and I remember thinking that people living in smaller communities before the Industrial Revolution must have experienced such silence far more often than we do today.

I managed to get on the last train out of the station before all lines were blocked. Once north of the South Downs there was hardly any snow at all: it was very cold but sunny. But along the coast it continued snowing heavily for several hours and Brighton and Hove were cut off from the rest of the country for four days. We then heard that, because the snow had come down so quickly and heavily, some poor people became trapped in their cars on the cliff top coast road, couldn't be reached, and froze to death.

In the New Year I found a flat in Wilbury Road opposite the County Cricket Ground in Hove, but at £5 a week the rent was more than twice we had been paying in Bushy Park. I took it though because I missed Elizabeth and the children and found living on a mattress in Fred's studio uncomfortable. The flat was not ideal as there was no garden access but the rooms were clean, large and airy and not far away were parks, the promenade and the beach, plus all the attractions of the South Downs and Sussex countryside.

That spring, on a trip to the beach, that we met David Pendlebury and his wife, Barbara, with their little daughter Sarah, who was the same age as Jane. Having left Coombe Springs they had also moved to the coast and by coincidence were living in a flat only a couple of streets away from us.

By this time the psychedelic poster business had not proved as profitable as we'd hoped. American Bill was the first homosexual I'd ever knowingly met and was always being harassed by police raids on his bookshop. He was a born rebel and inevitably got embroiled in court cases about drugs and publishing and selling obscene books. The increasing pressure to pay legal fees meant his commitment to pay Fred and I moved down his list of priorities. This meant I had to quickly get a job otherwise I wouldn't be able to pay the bills. Fortunately in the 1960s, if you were willing to work, jobs were easy to come by. That was how, in 1968, I became a commuter, travelling every day up to London to a position in a small studio in Great Russell Street. My first project was to put together a one-page announcement to appear in *The Times*. It was about the formation of a new town: Milton Keynes.

* * * * *

One morning I received through the post from Octagon Press (Idries Shah's publishing company) a 16-page pamphlet, *Sufi Studies Today*. The last sentence read as follows: 'There are two kinds of community: one, the community produced and maintained by what is today called indoctrination; the other, the one accumulated and harmonised by starting with the right materials and the right knowledge.' I read it a couple of times and knew at once that it was the second type of community that interested me more than anything; so I sent off a letter of thanks expressing my interest in the material. Shortly after that I received an invitation to attend an interview with Professor Denis Fry in London concerning the possibility that I might join a group under Shah's direction, which duly came about.

A chap called Reggie Hoare, who had known Gurdjieff and Ouspensky, ran the first study meetings I attended in a studio in Holland Park. Later I was asked to join fortnightly meetings with a different group in Connaught Square, the spacious London home of Aubrey Walton, and, later still, was moved to a group that held its meetings in Richard and Mireille Burton's home in Kentish Town. (Later, after I stopped commuting, travelling to North London from Brighton was quite a commitment. However, for several years until the group stopped meeting in 1987, David Pendlebury would accompany me in the car and our discussions made the journeys more interesting. This was at the time when David was busy translating various Sufi Classics for Octagon Press.)

Back in 1969 my workplace was only two minutes walk from the British Museum in one direction and three minutes from the great bookshops in Tottenham Court Road such as Foyles and Watkins in the other. So lunchtimes were spent either exploring the museum or pouring over books. And the hour-long train journey each day, from Hove to London-Victoria and back, meant I got a lot of uninterrupted reading time. Watkins was London's specialist bookshop on all matters esoteric and every couple of weeks I went there to see if any more books by Octagon Press had been published. Shah was producing material at a phenomenal rate during those years and they always seemed to have his books in first.

Like the works of the playwright William Shakespeare, who, school-children and tourists are told, was born and died in Stratford-on-Avon, a town thirty minutes drive from where I now live, Shah's Sufi tales, jokes and observations arrived like exotic migrants in our country seeking a foothold in a culture that needed spiritually reinvigorating, each migrant's knapsack carrying a store of sustaining magical nutri-ment; in its pockets the information, poetry and wisdom needed for a special kind of journey.

(In *The Sufis* Shah had pointed out that Shakespeare's name is sometimes rendered in perfectly correct and acceptable Persian as Sheikh-Peer, 'the ancient sage'. It was this that first alerted me to the possibility that Shakespeare was not the unlettered 'Wil Shakspere' of Stratford, but someone who deliberately remained anonymous and was steeped in Sufi lore, which he clearly drew extensively from. Whoever wrote Shakespeare's plays was a widely travelled polymath, master of several languages, of classics, law, medical knowledge, hermeticism and the behaviour of people in the courts of Europe. There is no substantive evidence that the 'sage' who injected such wisdom into England was the tax-evading provincial businessman from Stratford.)

The thrill of familiarising myself with every new collection Octagon Press was releasing is hard to explain, though others who tuned into his work back then will know what I mean. He was writing not to give us a dry translation of texts or exploit them for his own advantage but to convey the spirit of them effectively to a modern Western audience, free from what David described as, 'the distressingly irrational restrictions and distortions of the academic arena and placing them fairly where they belong – within reach of ordinary people.'

After a few months working in Great Russell Street I got a better paid job in a larger studio in nearby Russell Square where I really learned a lot under the tutelage of the Hungarian studio manager, 'Rusty', a refugee from the Russian invasion of Hungary. I stayed at 'Russell Arts' for a couple of years then obtained a studio manager's job at the princely salary of £2,000 a year at an advertising agency in Dorking, twice what I had been previously earning in London. It was owned by a couple of flashy young men whom I soon discovered were corrupt: building their business by giving paybacks to individuals responsible for giving out work from corporations. Their modus operandi was that they would offer to overcharge massively for big projects and share the extra with the dishonest employee who was then tempted by the easy money to give them more and more work and let them overcharge even more outrageously. Their largest client where this was happening was British Steel. Their accountant was panicking at their blatant thieving but they ignored his warnings and eventually the business collapsed under a cloud. But long before then I had decided to leave and set up as a freelance designer working from home and thus avoid the tiresome daily motorbike trip in all weathers to and from Dorking.

I faced three problems as a would-be freelancer: lack of proper business experience, no assets and no start up capital.

Unfortunately my father couldn't help me. Due to his left-wing views he had no knowledge of how to get a business running. The only time he had gone freelance was after the war ended when he teamed up with a plumber for a while. This man, as Mum described it, was one of those who 'clocked on' and 'clocked off' and spent his earnings down the pub relying on Dad's conscientiousness and willingness to put in long hours to get jobs finished. Dad couldn't sell himself and negotiate proper fees. My own experiences in silk-screen printing had likewise foundered on the rocks of my own naiveté. He advised me to get a 'proper' job.

Realising I needed capital to start up, and since Aubrey Walton was in business, I arranged an appointment with him to ask his advice and told him of my predicament, saying that my bank had turned me down for an overdraft and I was getting desperate. (I think I secretly hoped he would lend me the amount of money that I had worked out would get me started and cover three months living expenses: £300.) Aubrey heard me out, thought a moment and then said, 'How many banks are there in Brighton and Hove?' I said I thought about 20 branches. 'Just visit each one, show them your portfolio, tell them what your plans are and how much money you need, and keep knocking on doors until you find a bank manager who likes the cut of your jib. You'll soon get your overdraft.'

And that's what happened. I began to do the rounds of banks and soon met an old style bank manager, Mr Archer, who told me that he envied me starting up on my own and had always wished he could work in a creative field. His hobby was landscape painting. He took me under his wing, gave me good advice and the overdraft I asked for. I could relax, pay off some bills and begin trying to sell my services by sending out individually typed sales letters to local companies and following them up with phone calls asking for an appointment.

I waited – nothing. Three months went by. Still nothing. The overdraft was almost used up and still no company would give me an appointment. It looked like I'd made a big miscalculation. A sick feeling parked itself in the pit of my stomach and wouldn't go away – until my luck changed.

One morning the phone rang and the managing director of Panorama Holidays was on the line saying he had my letter and could I come and see him as soon as possible. His name was Peter Hayes; a young man not much older than me. His office was only a few hundred yards away in Church Road so I smartened up and hurried down there. He told me he had been let down by his usual production team and needed a 72-page colour brochure designed and made ready for printing in three months. He asked me if I could do it. With a confidence born of desperation I said I could do all he required, provided I had a substantial cash advance. He was clearly relieved and agreed to my terms and organised his accounts department to bring me £300 there and then. It was all very unorthodox. Then he asked me if I knew anyone who could go to Spain to take photographs. Spurred on by my change in fortune I said I was a photographer too and would go and take the pictures myself, adding it would make my work more 'authentic' if it were informed by visiting the places the brochure was advertising. He thought that was reasonable and quickly organised my flight tickets and hotel accommodation. I was to fly out from Gatwick Airport in two days time!

In the meeting, being so carried away by the prospect of a trip to Spain and the sight of money, I'd forgotten I had no camera. The two days just gave me enough time to rush over to my parents' house in Inkpen and borrow Dad's Yashica Mat and buy some rolls of film.

Thus, from being trapped by circumstances and feeling a failure, I was released into the Mediterranean sunshine to spend a week driving around Catalonia taking pictures of picturesque scenes: castles, markets and the beaches where holidaymakers were enjoying themselves. In Barcelona I looked over Gaudi's wonderful buildings, visited art galleries and took photographs of Spaniards and flowers as I strolled down La Rambla. I also had my first sight of beggars thrusting filthy, scab-covered babies at people and demanding money. I was shocked by this and never thought that one day such a sight would become common again in England, but it did.

When I got back and had the films developed, Peter Hayes and the Panorama sales team were pleased with the result. Though not quite the typical cliché shots used in holiday brochures of the time, they recognised that, since the pictures in their brochure were their main shop-window, if they were a little different it would make them stand out.

Without pause I set about the task of designing the brochure around the photographs, planning the page layout, writing the copy, organising typesetting and preparing the artwork ready for printing. Nowadays this is all done on computer screens but in those times it was all 'cut and paste' using Cow Gum on sheets of card fixed to a drawing board.

Commandeering the kitchen table I worked 16 hours a day, seven days a week to complete the job on time. My new client never suspected I was working in such straightened circumstances.

I then had the responsibility of approving the proofs on a big web offset press at a print company in Crawley. It was a sobering experience, not only because of the work (the print sales manager gave me a crash course in how to judge the quality of printing, how to use a loupe and instruct the printers to adjust the colour strengths and so on) but what I saw of British working practices and the power of the unions. I happened to say to this helpful sales manager that I could see that only three or four people were needed to operate the press. Why then were there about another twelve people standing around, leaning on brooms doing nothing. Nervously he quickly ushered me away to a private room where he quietly suggested that I should never mention this on the factory floor again in case anyone heard me. Apparently the union could stop the job at the drop of a hat. After that I never believed the politicians when they claimed 'Britain has the best workforce in the world' and other such tripe about how intelligent and wonderful the British worker was. The print unions representing them were powerful bullies.

The following year we used a company in Rotterdam to print the brochures and the difference was stark. Not only had the Dutch come up with a better price than the English quotes we received (even when allowing for my travelling costs flying over there a few times to approve proofs), everything in the print works was as clean as one would expect a laboratory to be: the printers wore white coats not the dirty overalls I had seen in Crawley. And only three people were needed to work the big web offset machine.

After finishing that first job for Panorama I was mentally and physically exhausted. However I was paid promptly and we had enough money to put a £1,500 deposit on our first house, which we bought for £6,250. That was the beginning of my graphic design business. I joined up with Fred Carver who had a darkroom in his attic studio. Peter Hayes, who was delighted with my work, kept giving us brochures to produce and other smaller items requiring artwork. We called ourselves 'Carver Tyrrell' and for several years Panorama Holidays was our biggest client. But others came our way too and we soon had to move to proper premises so we could invite clients to see us in business-like surroundings. We moved into offices in Station Road, Portslade. The rent was a sobering £20 a week, four times more than I paid for the flat in Wilbury Road. As work came in we advertised for creative staff and a receptionist, who could double as a secretary and bookkeeper, and in no time we had several people working for us.

To drum up business I started a monthly magazine called *Sussex Business Times* (which still exists, although we sold it long ago). My reasoning was that companies who wanted to advertise or have articles written about themselves in it would consider our studio as a supplier of creative services. This generated quite a bit of work.

There is a big drawback to earning a living in a creative service industry however: as soon as you've finished one job you have to have another following on to keep paying the bills. By contrast, if you produce products to sell, or provide a service for which there is a constant demand, you can build a more stable business. This took me a while to digest. Also, being on the south coast limited my market. As one London street trader friend of mine said to me, 'You're crazy starting a business on the coast Ivan, half your potential clients are only fish!'

However, I persisted and gradually built up a small business. Meanwhile I was seeing more of Shah and intently reading his books and the papers given out at the group meetings for us to think about, absorb and reflect on. If anything I write in this memoir about Shah's work leads readers to go and find his books and study them it will have been worth writing.

* * * * *

About that time we went on holiday to the West Country where I gained the trust of an intense fellow who lived with his young family on a remote old farm on the border between Devon and Cornwall near were we were staying. He was mysterious and earnest about a belief he held that he kept hinting at but wouldn't explain. In the end, however, he could not contain himself and took me through a trapdoor in the ceiling by means of a steep ladder to a hidden but surprisingly large room. Once there he revealed that he was the custodian of secret knowledge. He said he had conclusive evidence that the lost tribe of Israel had finally settled in Cornwall, England. One wall in his private hideaway was devoted to a huge annotated map of Asia, Europe and Africa with multiple lines indicating the routes and journeys taken by the lost tribe together with dates. It turned out he was the leader of a small cult centred on this belief and he explained all about this theory to me with that strange pious voice cultists use when they are so certain they possess 'truth'.

* * * * *

During the many years I ran Carver Tyrrell I always felt I was not particularly good at graphics, having only a fine art training and limited experience as a lowly artworker. My way round this was to employ talented people. My own skills, such as they were, consisted of being a good copyist (I could mimic art nouveau lettering, psychedelic art and recreate the style of Moghul paintings but rarely produced anything original). I could also come up with pertinent ideas and gradually learned how to write effective sales copy.

However, there was a lot of psychology involved in trying to influence clients to buy our services and I began to study books about sales psychology. One incident taught me a lot about this – and about how suggestible people are.

We had been given the opportunity to pitch for a prestigious corporate brochure in the nuclear industry. Our designers got excited about the job and I set them the task of creating what we called in those days a 'visual': an illustrated mock-up of what our design would look like. I then went on holiday and was due to present the visual to the client the day I returned. To my horror, my studio had created an image for the brochure that was garish in the extreme and heavily influenced by the 'punk' aesthetic – not at all suitable for representing this respectable international company operating in such a politically sensitive industry. My designers were pleased with what they'd produced, but somewhat context blind and I instantly knew that we would not be considered for the job if I showed it to the potential client.

The only thing I could think of doing was to show the client examples of our work for other companies and then take them through a blank paper dummy mocked up of the 48-page production describing what each page would look like. Needless to say I was exceedingly nervous on entering their company boardroom that afternoon. The company's top brass, including the chairman, managing director, marketing director, production director and finance director were sitting around a vast shiny wooden table with a few others. They were clearly taking their new corporate brochure seriously.

After introducing our company and client list I passed around examples of our work. And then, as if it was a precious artefact, I slowly drew out from a black sleeve the blank dummy made out of high quality paper that represented their corporate brochure. Everyone in the room looked perplexed as I began my 'spiel' but they politely let me speak rather than eject me from the building, as I had feared they might. This gave me the confidence to describe what the cover was going to look like in vivid detail, making it up as I went along. It was going to be a shot of the earth taken from space, I said, with the company's name emblazoned against the stars (this would seem a cliché today but back then it wasn't). This I told them would suggest that they were a truly global corporation.

Glances were exchanged as they tried to size up one another's reaction to my pitch, but they were already intrigued. Then I turned to the first inside spread. 'And here we will have a specially taken photograph of the chairman alongside a confident statement about the future of the company,' I said. 'His signature should go here.' My long fingers waved above the blank paper decisively indicating the position of every item. I noticed a minimal nod from the chairman at this and my confidence grew. Then I said the same about the next double-page spread but this time referring to the Managing Director. He was pleased at this and I detected more minimal nods coming from around the table. Gradually everyone was staring more and more intently at the blank white pages as I turned each one over and described what was to appear on them: photos of factories, research laboratories and finished projects. They were absorbed. Like a storyteller I had put them into a trance and each one had seen what their imagination wanted them to see.

At the end of this theatrical performance there was a pause. I held my breath. Then the Chairman let out a sigh, lent back in his chair and said, 'I think this is exactly what we need.' Everyone nodded in agreement.

Then another director piped up. 'Yes I agree,' he said, and to my astonishment added, 'But can I just have another look at page ten?'

After further discussion I left and a few days later we received a letter saying that, against stiff competition, the board had decided to award us the contract.

As that and other jobs piled up, I learnt a lot running the studio: how to sell, write copy, art direct photography, manage staff and deal with money. Starting the business in the early days was fun. Many challenges were overcome, including surviving the famous three-day week when for two months, because of a miners strike, the government was forced to forbid companies from working normal hours to conserve electricity, and we were often rewarded with a sense of achievement. I also enjoyed absorbing information about different industries quickly. Over the years we had a fascinating range of clients. We built up the company so that, as well as major clients in the building business we were designing brochures, exhibition stands and advertising material for the electronic, computer and nuclear industries; all kinds of manufacturing companies, including makers of lifeboats, ionizers, sunbeds, cosmetics, garden and agricultural equipment. We worked for a private school, Kew Gardens, hospitals, Shoreham Port Authority, several national house builders, a steel company, local bus companies, and Idries Shah's own Octagon Press.

One of my clients was Michael Robinson who owned an art gallery and picture-framing workshop in Haywards Heath. To generate more business for him I suggested we create The Guild of Sussex Artists. So we did and quickly gained many dozens of members. For several years we put on an annual exhibition of their work in grand surroundings, each time successfully selling most exhibits. I got to meet a range of highly talented landscape painters, some of whom earned a good living from their efforts. Of course, we also attracted eccentrics and poseurs – each one delightfully unaware of their lack of talent but with an urgent desire for attention, which they energetically pursued.

One day Alan Tunbridge, a mercurial, highly skilled creative artist whom I knew as being responsible for beautiful book jacket designs for Shah, called saying he had a proposition to put to me. He didn't want to talk about it on the phone so I invited him over. He said he and his family had been living in Spain for a while and that he had come back to the UK to rebuild his finances and pick up the pieces of his career. He had been asked to take on the advertising campaign for a slimming machine company called Slendertone that Shah had an interest in. He said he couldn't do so unless he was part of a studio agency that could place advertisements. Alan wanted to know if I would let him join us as a creative director – a directorship being his price for introducing this bit of business. He had spent all his money in Spain and had moved his family into rented accommodation in Tunbridge Wells and needed an income. On an impulse, because we shared an interest in the Albigensian crusade and because I liked his sense of humour, I agreed to his suggestion that we became 'Carver Tyrrell & Tunbridge'.

Because of the commute he would have to do between Tunbridge Wells and Hove, as part of the package Alan needed a company car. His old banger and my reliable, comfortable Renault 16 had to go, he said, because they didn't suit the go-ahead image of an advertising company that he had in mind. So he suggested we lease a Lancia each, which we did. The Lancias looked flash but mine turned out to be the most unreliable car I've ever had. Although our turnover went up considerably, without a turnover of millions in advertising revenue, I found advertising was not a particularly profitable business to be in, so this was not a hugely successful partnership from the financial point of view.

Gradually the pressure of selling our services, being responsible for paying salaries, rent and all the other costs involved in running a business, palled. In addition I was not a particularly good graphic designer myself and, although I often had good ideas, I had to employ people to carry them out – and creative types were often difficult to manage. Nevertheless, finding out things about different products and industries and copywriting was enjoyable. And directing photography also stretched me: working with the brilliant photographer, James Beaton, was always great fun.

CHAPTER FOUR

Hidden patterns

UNLIKE Coombe Springs, Langton House had no cultish aura attached to it. Its only claim to fame was that it was once the family home of Lord Baden Powell who founded the Boy Scout movement. The grounds and various buildings took a lot of maintaining and people were invited to join weekend teams on a monthly rota basis to help with this. On Saturday evenings we all got together for dinner in a building nick-named 'The Elephant', after the famous "Elephant in the Dark" story in which blind men grope an elephant and describe it as though it con-sisted only of the part they had touched. I felt we were like the blind men in the story and, over the years, by continual demonstration, Shah represented to us the idea that it was possible to know what the 'whole-ness of an elephant' meant. It was not the sum of separate parts.

Shah usually joined us for a pre-dinner drink in the bar before the meal. The only thing not to like about this was that many people, including Shah, were heavy smokers and I would go home afterwards with a sore throat and my clothes stinking of cigarettes, which I found unpleasant – the smell didn't go down well with the family either. But I reasoned that if I was to learn anything I had to overcome my irritation and put up with it. Shah even mentioned once that he was on the lookout for people who changed their brand of cigarettes to the same ones he smoked: they were potential cult material and he didn't want them around.

These Saturday evening gatherings were unlike anything else most people have experienced. For a start they consisted of an extraordinary mix of people from all walks of life: scientists, artists, authors, labourers, actors, film-makers, farmers, housewives, teachers, academics, students, builders, architects, business people, carpenters, doctors, psychiatrists, diplomats, mechanics, engineers, civil servants, antique dealers, estate managers, journalists, judges, cooks, inventors and gardeners. Everyone treated each other with a natural respect. There was no class barrier to make people uncomfortable, perhaps because we had been working together for several hours on ordinary tasks such as gardening, lawn mowing, tree felling, painting and decorating, wine making and preparing food for the evening meal. We were all relaxed with one another at the end of the day.

However, in these moments we knew that, just as we were conscious of Shah in the room and paying him close attention, he was also studying us. One of the traits he observed and drew out from us, for instance, was our differing degrees of gullibility. One evening he was standing on one side of the room talking animatedly to a small group of people before dinner and asked for the lights to be turned down. Then, in a moment of melodrama he said he could summon up the power of electricity with his own body. Wearing a serious expression he then put a light bulb into his mouth and earnestly lifted up his arm to the heavens as if invoking some higher power – and the light bulb lit up. Some of us smiled immediately seeing that, although he *had* summoned up the power of electricity, as he truthfully said he could, his little performance was a trick. That was my immediate reaction, having entertained children with simple magic tricks in the past. But others clearly saw this as a demonstration of special powers, as seen by the look of wonder on their faces (the bulb had a battery in it so that when the tongue touched the electrical contact point at the screw end it completed the circuit causing the filament to glow brightly). He was a joker.

On another occasion in the early 1970s an Israeli magician, Uri Geller, had been bending spoons on television claiming he was doing this by means of psychic powers. A conversation started around the table in which Shah didn't take part. Someone picked up a spoon and started to stroke it like Geller, and went on doing so for a long time. Of course nothing happened to the spoon. But I noticed Shah paid close attention to the reactions from the assembly.

Meals at Langton House would be served and eaten amidst a convivial hubbub of friendly conversation with Shah just talking with his immediate neighbours. His children, Saira and the twins Tahir and Safia, would often serve. Then, as is the way with Sufi dinner meetings (as described accurately in an essay by Abdul-Wahab Tirmizi published in *Sufi Thought and Action*, Chapter 7), a little after the meal was over the atmosphere in the room changed and all general chatter ceased, only Shah's voice could be heard. And what he said throughout the rest of the evening, whatever topic he addressed, always had the effect of inviting us to see things from unusual and multiple viewpoints, thus making us conscious of how conditioned our beliefs and behaviour were. It often seemed to me as if he spoke in the way an empathetic anthropologist from an advanced culture might when trying to communicate to a lost tribe about what he confidently knew lay beyond their limited horizons. He was continually emphasising the limitations of seeing the world through the filter of the culture we lived in and emphasising that greater understanding could only arise when we had overcome such conditioning to a considerable degree.

Almost every comment, question or action by someone, however casual, would produce a response from Shah that made people think differently. For example, I overheard a middle aged woman say to him that his daughter, Saira, was exquisitely beautiful. He smiled and then said, 'Thank you. Yes she is, but I can't help pointing out that she is just seventeen.'

For those interested, the flavour of such gatherings is also caught in Rumi's *Fihi Ma Fihi* (In it what is in it).

Here is an example of how a topic arose at the dinner meetings. Shah had picked up on a conversation some people in the room had been having about how lucky we were to be living in such a great country as England. Later during his talk, which was on another topic to start with, he effortlessly segued into how he often experienced English people trying to extract his agreement to the idea that this was a great country to live in. This led to a series of descriptions of why ours was *not* such a great country. He elaborated on the points he raised for hours afterwards, and on my way home I noted some of them down;

'We live in a JOKE country,' he said, with great emphasis. 'A joke country with joke money, joke leadership and a joke parliament that pretends we have freedoms that we don't in fact have, and a ridiculous educational system.

'Your culture has contributed little that is new to the corpus of psychological and evolutionary material produced by other cultures in the past.' He backed this up with example after example and one only has to read his many book to see how true this is.

Then he talked about how we are a nation of boasters and blusterers and said this was due to... 'You English are losing confidence in yourselves. You lack 'sand', which means you are likely to become the slaves of whatever group comes to dominate the world next. Your conquerors will use you to satisfy the technological requirements of their culture ... and they will be hard taskmasters by your standards.'

He didn't stop there. 'A prime English characteristic is your lack of humility. Yet humility is essential to human development. It is something you had your chance to learn – it was, after all, a fundamental of Jesus's teachings – but no one here knows that humility is a means, a technique, not a posture. Your lightweight cultural heritage is not infused with the appropriate habits of thought conducive to human development. You have no exemplars. Humility will now probably be forced upon you by events – by war, by a conquering power, by poverty, by starvation or plague.'

He then went on to talk about the West in general: 'Western culture, art, music, architecture, and its study of Mankind are not of great importance from the long-term view. These preoccupations have only served to keep you amused and that is all. As for adding to the stock of human understanding, the West has done nothing in these areas that has not appeared before in other cultures. You ignore the wisdom in the saying, 'to continue verifying what has already been verified is stupid.'

'In evolutionary terms you are low-grade material, caring little about future generations, smug, arrogant, dishonest and not prepared to learn how to learn.'

As you can imagine, the faces of those who had expressed the notion earlier about how lucky we were to be living in Great Britain today, remained deeply solemn throughout. I'm sure they were forced to reassess their belief about being British – but so were we all.

Those who thought about what Shah was offering soon came to realize that he had delved deeply into the vast riches of human insight, culture and science that had gradually accumulated along the Silk Roads of Central Asia over millennia. He studied and absorbed them until they became part of his essence. He had found these esoteric riches in oral traditions, centres of learning and writings and was presenting them to us in forms digestible for Westerners. And, from the point of view of developing human potential and understanding, the quality of this information was far more sophisticated and useful than Europe had managed to produce in the previous 3,000 years. He explained this to me in his study once while we looked through a Russian book of evocative photographs of Khiva, which was just one of the hundreds of centres of trade and learning that thrived in Central Asia during the hundreds of years that Europe by comparison was an insignificant cultural backwater.

It was obvious to those who knew him that Shah's desire was that people should learn from the information that he made available, not put him on any kind of pedestal. No flexibility of thought is possible to an obsessional and he therefore worked hard to discourage a cult forming around himself and his activities. One way he did this was to teach us about cult behaviour and encourage us to read psychological research about it. In effect he was inoculating us with sufficient information to ensure we would not wish to create or operate a cult in any way, especially one associated with his work (when I say 'us' I mean the interested people who were invited to meet, or work, with him when he discussed such matters).

Over the years I also came to realize that a Sufi is someone who has a certain disposition: he or she is not bound by possessions or people and does not bind things or people to themselves. This means they are free from the usual behaviour of acting out of conditioned responses, compulsions and obsessions. It is a mistake to think this attitude is only found in any one culture or time; Sufis are not only associated with Islam, even though many of them lived in and were nurtured in Islamic cultures. This is simply because, for nearly a thousand years those cultures were by far the most advanced in the arts, sciences and in philosophy and spiritual matters. Individuals with this disposition arise among all peoples and always have. They can exist amidst cultures of any religious manifestation, or none, since they are not bound by belief, ritual or dogma. And because to be one involves a disposition, a particular attitude to life, genuine Sufis recognise each other even though there are no obvious identifiable markers that others can see.

* * * * *

Although I had decided in the 1960s that I wanted no part of the art scene – modern art seemed little more than a pretentious epiphenomenon of emotionality and greed for attention and money to me – it wasn't until 1973, when the Octagon Press published a book entitled *Among the Dervishes* by Omar Burke, that I was given a handle on what was wrong with art that clarified my thinking about it by giving it a bigger context. There is a passage in the book where Shah was reported talking to an artist about communicating human experience: '... almost all artists are merely the forerunners of the mass-communications media. They may transmit, convey experience in one form, but this is not active but vicarious experience. To us, you see, art is not the ability to stimulate certain emotions. It is the ability to share feelings and also *live* living. I show you a photograph of a cartoon and you smile. I show you a television programme and you laugh or cry. Is that living life? Is that contributing to life? You may feel, of course, that this has a function: it makes people happy or relaxed. It also dwarfs their intellect, robs them of volition.'

Shah could see much about our society and behaviour that at that time was invisible to most of us in the room. He made it clear to every-one that he wanted us to rise above our conditioning so that we, too, could develop the freedom to observe what goes on and think more objectively about it. He was continually pointing out that we all lived with sets of assumptions that are so deeply ingrained that we cannot see them ourselves. For decades I have weighed Shah's assessment of the state of our culture and found it to be true, although it is only in recent years that the corruption, waste and stupidity he described back then became obvious to all. For example, we now know that those countries where violence and fundamentalist contagions grow, mainly do so because the people in them are living in kleptocratic systems totally corrupted from the lowest to the highest in the land; where extreme poverty, unfairness, bribery and theft are rampant. The kleptocracies are often seen as being supported by Western countries and the NGOs who pour money into the coffers of crooked rulers and their officials. Among the ordinary population the innate need for volition and to have a degree of control over their finances is forever hampered – they cannot keep a fair portion of their earnings for a reasonable subsistence. The frustration this generates drives them to revolt by escaping into 'purist' fundamentalism, such as preached by the Taliban, Al Qaeda or Daesh, and take extremely violent measures to fight and steal back what they regard as theirs.

Of course corruption is not just a problem in Asia, the Middle East or Africa. The government and business community in the UK, for example, are no longer independent but in thrall to corrupt financial institutions, multinational companies and organisations like the EU where everyone knows that the elite power groups award themselves huge salaries and bonuses out of all proportion to the amount of work they do. The moral collapse of our banks, the National Health Service (NHS), our system of law enforcement, the Church, schools, universities and civil service have all produced a corrosive feeling of helplessness in the general population. It is a pervasive, profound disillusionment with our institutions that has encouraged the degeneration in manners and lessening of consideration for the less fortunate. Even giving charity has turned into a sentimental public performance, which itself is a form of corruption since real charity is given anonymously.

We mainly use the word 'corruption' when describing dishonesty or fraudulent conduct by someone in power: typically involving bribery or the enrichment of the corrupt person in some way. In such cases corruption is always conducted by improper manipulation of circumstances in a way that violates proper duty toward others (as when committing a crime) and involves the undermining of the integrity of individuals and groups. Examples include the 2012 Libor manipulation scandal at Barclays, one of the world's largest banks, and the more recent FIFA scandal, in which two dozen people working for the international governing body of football under the presidency of Sepp Blatter, were indicted for wire fraud, racketeering and money laundering.

The Second Law of Thermodynamics states that there is a natural tendency of any isolated system to degenerate into a more disordered state: what alchemists used to call 'The Arc of Descent.' And so the word corruption is also used with reference to decay: as with a rotting cow's carcass, or a business going rogue as Enron did, or when a wicked government collapses amidst wanton criminality as happened to Muammar Gaddafi's Libya, or when an individual slides into a life of moral depravity like the Indian Guru Sai Baba who exploited millions of followers by using conjuring tricks to produce 'miracles' and then went on to launder money, sexually abuse young children (especially boys), and was involved in six deaths in his bedroom.

When someone who is considered pure or honest is corrupted, those qualities of purity and honesty are taken from them – that is why corruption of minors is such a serious offense in our legal system.

Corruption can also refer to the process by which the meaning of a word, or an expression, is changed from its original state to one regarded as erroneous or debased. One such word is 'discrimination', which used to have a useful positive meaning: that of recognising a distinction, the ability to differentiate. That word is now corrupted so that in the minds of many it has an accusative negative connotation; that of unjust prejudice against a category of person, usually based on race, class, gender or age.

The noun *corruption* comes from the Latin *com* meaning 'with, together,' and *rumpere*, meaning 'to break'. So corruption is what breaks your trustworthiness, your good reputation with others. A civilized society cannot evolve without trust, which is why, when public trust in government declines, it is such a tragedy - as it is when one loses trust in relatives, friends or colleagues.

Unfortunately we have all become used to hearing about the extent of corruption in our financial institutions and are still being affected by the multi trillion pound scandals that recently resulted in the near total collapse of the global banking system and only prevented, for a while at least, by ordinary taxpayers being forced to bail out the rich. I saw such an event coming when I got involved with Nick Leeson, the original 'rogue trader' who, in 1995, caused the collapse of the world's second oldest merchant bank, Barings.

The executive chairman of Virgin Books, Adrian Sington asked me to help Nick write a book about stress in the modern world. Leeson's true-life story is exceptional – a modern day *Arabian Nights* adventure. In a few short years from being an unremarkable working-class lad, Leeson catapulted himself to the echelons of corporate power. He gained access to enormous riches, worked hard, played hard, fell in love, became corrupted by circumstances, cunningly lived a lie in order to maintain his position, brought down the ancient banking empire, achieved worldwide notoriety as a consequence, went on the run, was caught and imprisoned for several years in Changi prison, was abandoned by his wife, suffered cruelty and solitary confinement in a tiny concrete box, became a shadow of his former self, survived cancer, returned to the world and rebuilt his life as a changed man.

His career is a potent reminder of the remarkable swings of fortune any one of us can experience during our time on earth. On the one hand, it is an emblem for human weakness and folly and, on the other, an example of how it's possible to endure extremes of misfortune, survive and even change. For ten years, stress continually affected his physical and mental health, yet he found ways to get through it and is now healthy and flourishing, though marked for life by what he did. In the book we wrote together, *Back from the Brink: Coping with Stress*, we unpicked the psychology of corruption and predicted the financial chaos that we both saw as inevitable.

Corruption rears its ugly head in religious, political and academic life too. The appalling behaviour of Catholic and other Christian Churches with regard to covering up widespread child sex abuse by many of their priests is but one example (Christianity is not alone among religions in this regard). The bribery for access, expense frauds and 'gravy training' practised by many British MPs is also common knowledge. As are the giant scams that politicians and bureaucrats get involved in, like the UN's absurd 'tackling climate change' campaigns, the EU's sneaky 'ever-closer union' policy, and Tony Blair's concocted 'weapons of mass destruction' dossier that was so useful to the arms industry and simultaneously triggered greater chaos in the Middle East. The report of the British public inquiry into the Iraq War, called the 'Iraq Inquiry' or 'Chilcot Inquiry', was begun in 2009 and, as I write, is still not published. So little is authority trusted nowadays that people commonly regard such delays as due to corrupt influence being wielded behind the scenes. We'll probably never know.

Rarely are the people involved in corruption held to account by the law and in many areas of the world that is because they are the Law. Foreign travellers to kleptocratic countries in Africa, the Middle East, Central Asia, China and post Soviet Russia, are continually exposed to everyday corruption that is blatant and cruel in its effect. In such places the lives of ordinary people are daily made difficult and miserable by corrupt officialdom, driving many, particularly the young, into the arms of fundamentalist movements that offer simple-minded and often brutal solutions to their plight. Such corruption is the main cause of the spread of violent extremism in the Middle East, Africa and elsewhere that has begun to spill into Europe. The 'Arab Spring' was a failed uprising against such systematic thieving. It quickly collapsed. All this was not clear to most of us when we were younger. But I came to believe that if Shah thought something was important, like corruption, it was worth paying attention to. So I did.

Over the years, like everyone else, I've wondered about the lives of millions as I peered at homes, office blocks, factories and farms and tried to imagine how those inside them lived. I've seen the Kowloon beehive tower blocks of Hong Kong teaming with life; wandered in iconic cities like New York, sprawling Los Angeles, Paris, Amsterdam, Amman, Bucharest, Stockholm, Helsinki; sat on Arthur's Seat above Edinburgh; visited Dublin (home of Mollie Malone, the 'cart with the tart' as Dubliners call her) and crossed the River Danube at Budapest. In all these places one can see how corruption blights the lives of millions. Some of course have the courage to challenge it. Most don't.

Shah often commented on minor current preoccupations as well as big issues. For a while in the 1960s and 70s, for example, there was a tendency for certain media celebrities to put down and mock the middle class. Satirists, comedians and left-wing academics were prominent in the mockery. Many previously well-spoken people, from pop stars to TV pundits, even went so far as to adopt working class accents in public. Shah questioned why this should be so. 'The so-called middle class,' he said, 'is made up from those who rose out of the working class to better themselves – aspirational people – so why are intellectuals denigrating the desire of those who want to better themselves? Do they feel threatened or what!?' He said that aspiring to behave well, develop manners, seek better education and generally expand one's horizons beyond that of our parents was a healthy trait, not something to sneer at. He felt obliged to try and help anyone who was trying to better themselves. It was the decent thing to do.

For more than two decades I attended Shah's dinner meetings and heard him speak on whatever topic concerned him at the time: his travels, the strange human behaviour he encountered, characters he'd met, politics, psychological research (with which he encouraged us to familiarise ourselves), different religions, cults, the nature of evolution, baraka, academia (there were so many topics and themes it's impossible to list them all here). His main purpose seemed to me to be to stimulate in us the habit of seeing what was happening in the world from multiple viewpoints so as to appreciate the varying underlying levels of purpose in everything, and, to help us do this by giving us new information about psychology and human behaviour. All the time he emphasised that this was necessary preparatory work.

Sometimes Shah invited guests to join us at dinner. While he was talking we rarely interrupted him with questions, not because he discouraged us from doing so but because we were all in a kind of 'learning trance' and needed to digest what he was saying before genuine questioning could happen (as opposed to 'attention seeking' questioning). One evening, while he was addressing us, a youngest professor at the table, anxious to show us his academic credentials, interrupted him with a common debating tactic; 'Oh I would take issue with you on that point Mr Shah'. But before the fellow could get into his stride and take centre stage, Shah turned to him, raised his voice slightly and said, enunciating each word slowly, 'Oh … *would* … you … now?' This was said in such a way that the professor was struck dumb and a short silence followed. Then Shah asked the hapless chap, 'Are you here to learn or do you just wish to debate?' The professor mumbled something and then Shah began a tough and lengthy critique of the games academics play, illustrated with many nefarious and humorous examples that succeeded in demonstrating how divorced such games were from real teaching, learning, and pursuing the truth of things. The professor became increasingly uncomfortable and I don't believe was ever seen at Langton again.

In the mid 20th century Russell Page was one of the world's most sought after garden designers. As a long time associate of Shah, he often sat at dinner with us. He had an unusual demeanour. Princess Marella Agnelli employed him to design gardens for her and once said about him: 'His main preoccupation was not that of making a beautiful garden but of harmony.' Apparently within moments of first meeting her on a summer night at her home, Villar Perosa, Russell said, 'One must learn to serve something higher than us all, because, if not, one may easily fall prey to the basest, most material aspects of one's life.' Russell once nodded off at the table in the early hours of Sunday morning while Shah was talking at length. Shah asked the person sitting next to him to gently wake him up because he particularly wanted Russell to hear what he was about to say.

As well as picking up topical subjects in the news at the time, Shah's major themes also included what everyone can read about in his books:

- Things are not as they seem – nothing is;
- Basic motives fuel most of our behaviour including: the need for attention, control, belonging, comfort, intimacy, sex, emotional stimulation and excitement (any kind will do) and greed in all its forms;
- Most human behaviour is mechanical;
- We are easily manipulated – much more so than we like to think;
- Humankind is evolving rapidly but a positive outcome of that evolution is not inevitable;
- A guide is necessary to develop higher perceptions;
- Understanding is a skill that can develop through our actions, but does so only if they mesh well with the hidden patterns;
- There is a dimension beyond time and space that a prepared human mind can connect to;
- History, although seemingly haphazard, is not just a random succession of chance events but is the result of the human race being 'guided, encouraged or restrained into alignment with a universal plan'.

With regard to meshing with hidden patterns, Shah once said to me that a useful rule to follow whenever trying to do something, a business project for example, is to always put in a lot of effort but, if the effort produces no results and doors remain closed, stop pushing and do something different. If doors seem to open easily, however, keep going through them.

The first bit of work he asked me to help him with was to prepare a leaflet for the Institute for Cultural Research (ICR) that was to replace the Society for the Understanding of Fundamental Ideas (SUFI) that he had founded a few years previously. He had written some text and wanted to include photographs in it showing, among others, the archaeologist, Sir Mortimer Wheeler, psychiatrist William Sargant and professor Denise Fry at an ICR gathering. He then started explaining why he had founded the Institute. 'I want to attract ordinary people and help them think about psychological and cultural issues. But, as an individual, I can't easily get people to listen seriously. I discovered, however, that if I call myself an 'institute' – they will.' I heard him say many times over the years, 'We live in an appearance culture'. That is one reason why it was necessary for him to create ICR: people like to join an organisation and be part of a community. He had no trouble finding eminent speakers to give lectures or in raising audiences to attend them. He once told me that if ever I wanted to get any ideas across, to be sure first to start an institute. Years later I used this advice to great effect. But, long before that, I saw him enact the process again in a totally unexpected field and took part in it. But I'll come to that later.

* * * * *

In 1970 the BBC broadcast a documentary called *Dreamwalkers,* which featured Shah and some of his ideas. The topics covered in the film give a flavour of what we were experiencing when listening or interacting with him at that time (it can now be seen on the internet). The film began with him telling a group of children at Langton the story, now well known, of the thirsty lion, which went something like this:

'One day a lion badly needed a drink and so he went in search of a pool of water. He entered a forest and found one but, as he leant forward to drink, he saw a lion staring up at him from the water. As he was a foolish lion he roared at it to try and frighten it away. This made all the other animals laugh because they knew that he was only roaring at his own reflection. Eventually he became so thirsty that he said, 'I don't care who is in the water, I am going to have a drink anyway!' When he jumped in to slake his thirst, the lion he thought he saw suddenly disappeared.

Then Shah finished the story by saying to the children, 'That was how the lion discovered, and we should all learn from this, that you should not be afraid of something you do not understand, you should find out what it is.'

The rest of the film drew attention to a range of information discovered by Western psychology and sociology, topics typical of those that Shah spoke about at the Saturday dinner meetings, such as:

- One third of all people cannot change their mind, even when given accurate information that ought, subsequently, to correct their initial opinion;
- Adults lose the honesty and vitality of children and settle into life full of contradictions but will usually deny this when you point it out to them;
- Too often we are unaware of the way we disregard inconvenient information;
- Too often we are unconscious of the true origins of our behaviour;
- Labels are usually more effective in influencing people than reason. People will make decisions, even about things that will cost a lot of money, on the strength of a label. Research by manufacturers and advertising agencies shows that the label and the image are always more important than rational comparison when selling something; even a high price item like a car. Emotion overrides reason;
- Many other of our decisions are triggered by stimuli like labels that make us do things that we have not thought out at all because our assessments are largely made subconsciously. We are conditioned creatures mostly unaware of the ways we have been trained to react and why;
- We should realise that our desire to cooperate, and our fear of being thought inadequate in difficult circumstances, often prevents us from seeing the reality of a situation. People rarely say, 'There is insufficient evidence for me to go on', when asked their opinion about something. Nor do they say that they are personally unqualified to answer any particular question so they will happily offer an opinion on almost any topic. Shah insisted that, if we awoke to the reality of this situation we need not be disadvantaged by it.

The film also touched on ritual and he pointed out that many intellectuals nowadays think of ritual as 'religious', something bad, and are derogatory about it. Rituals, however, are increasingly coming to be understood as something that we all need in our lives and they come into play continually: in meetings, greetings, partings, buying and selling, eating, entertaining, sports and virtually all activity.

'Ritual is a form of behaviour that gives structure to our lives,' Shah said. But he stressed it is important that, just as with attention, we should take of it only as much as we need – no more.

'Attention, the need for it, to give it and receive it, is a sort of nutrition. It's as important as food and drink and many people crave it. We all know people who need it badly, and not only children. But we can get by on much less attention than we crave.

'Some might say, "Well, animals attract attention, or avoid attention, or give it, as when monkeys groom each other, after all, it is just another lower level of activity." My answer is, yes, it is a lower level activity, like your heart beating, just a pump ... but, without it, you would die. An animal is at the mercy of what attention it can or can't get. We don't have to be. That is the difference.

'You can make this a matter of your own experiment and experience. If you find an excited person who keeps on and on about something or other and give him genuine attention, you will find his views become less pronounced. He calms down and gets more interesting and may even learn to give you attention too.

'Giving attention – this is the basis of civilisation. Not culture, nor cultivated behaviour, but civilisation. It is that important.'

Some other ideas conveyed in the documentary, include:

- Information comes at us at an enormous rate from all directions, but experiments show that we retain hardly any at all. We remember only what touches us, what we recognise. All the time we look for the familiar. We are poorly equipped even to recognise new information, let alone use it. By and large, new information passes straight through us. Will our society go down in history as one that wasted almost all its knowledge?
- Some interesting research has been done with cats. We all know how difficult cats are to teach or train to do anything. It's been

discovered that, if you get a cat and train it to do something and then put it among some untrained cats, the untrained cats will learn to do that same thing very quickly, just by being with him and watching.

- This has such far-reaching consequences that all the commonly accepted educational theories about learning and how the brain works when collecting information may have to be revised. It is possible that we may discover that we learn simply by being with people and watching them do things. This casts doubt on the widely held belief that we can only learn from experience.

- The cat experiment verifies something about human education which has been known and applied in the East for thousands of years and was also applied in Europe during the Middle Ages: the Master had his apprentice. The apprentice learned from watching the Master, being in his presence and helping him.

- We always seek solutions to problems in areas with which we are already familiar; where it's easiest. We do the obvious and, often, labour at what only seems to be the right way to solve a difficulty instead of searching round for solutions from all directions.

- In real life, Shah asked, do we notice our real interests in time?

- We should rule nothing out when trying to solve a any problem.

- When we make wrong assumptions, solutions become more remote. Confined thinking can actually be dangerous because, even though it may be logical, it will almost certainly be preventing us from knowing what a problem really is, and prevent us from knowing how to solve it when it arises.

- At times in our lives we have all felt that life is rich in possibilities, but in our everyday lives we make elaborate preparation for misfortune.

- Man can further his own evolution only by breaking his psychological limitations. Although our physical capabilities have been the same for thousands of years, the four-minute mile was a psychological barrier that had to be broken. Once breached, a flood of athletes achieved it ... just by knowing that it was possible! The same is true for other capabilities.

Shah ended the film with the words, 'There's an old saying: Man is asleep, must he die before he wakes up?'

It's difficult to convey today just how refreshing this documentary programme was at that time.

* * * * *

Interesting opportunities opened up for me as a result of the time spent at Langton. One evening at dinner, for instance, I was sitting next to a jolly arty chap and we got talking. He asked me what I did and I told him I produced silkscreen prints and that I had been to art college.

'I am the principle of Chelsea Art College,' he said to my surprise, 'We need a teacher for evening classes for print making. I'd love you to come and do it.'

So it was arranged. He gave me a phone number to call and for a couple of years, when I was working in London, I augmented my meagre earnings by being an 'art teacher' for one evening a week, which basically meant showing mainly middle aged women how to make lithographic prints. On those evenings, instead of going back home to Brighton, I used to stay the night at Trish and David Schreiber's flat in Kensington and enjoy a convivial late supper with them. They were running a fine art dealership at the time but later went on to start a business called Ethos Candles.

It was also when I was working in London that I visited the Soho Square studio of the animator, Richard Williams several times, always in the evening and always he was there working. On each occasion he enthusiastically showed me what section of his major project, which was based on the stories of Mulla Nasruddin, that he was working on, and demonstrated aspects of his art.

I also met the psychiatrist Ensor Holiday at Langton and we got talking about his interest in patterns and he asked me to call in to his London home to help him prepare some artwork derived from the Islamic tile designs he had seen at the Alhambra Palace in Granada and on buildings in Damascus. He wanted to have them printed and made into pads so he could see if there might be a market selling them to schools (it was his work that formed the basis of what was to become

Altair Designs, colouring books that are still published today). Anyone staring at the lines in a poster he had created from these patterns always found that they couldn't help but try to seek out the underlining symmetry. However, as soon as they thought they'd grasped it they would suddenly realize they hadn't – their eyes were taken to another combination of patterns within the larger one.

Ensor told me that for some reason one particular complex design couldn't be reproduced by computers; and that he and, I think Roger Burrows, had tried to do so. He said that when he asked Shah why this would be the case, he was told that it was because the original geometry deliberately included an element that was not geometrical and couldn't be worked out logically but that, nevertheless, held everything together. This line couldn't be reproduced by binary means. I took this to mean that geometry that was fixed and endlessly the same, if it didn't express this 'something extra', wouldn't be representing reality, which is always moving; evolving to the next possibility.

This poster is on the hall wall in my home today and whenever I concentrate on it, the effect is as strong now as it was when I first saw it. It powerfully symbolised not only the limitations of human perception but also the limits of reductionist science.

On each occasion I visited him in his London study, Ensor was generous with his time and needed no encouragement to chat about the many interesting people he had met or known. British Prime Minister Harold MacMillan, for example, had been one of his patients. Ensor had helped him deal with his wife's continuing infidelity with the bisexual Lord, Robert Boothby. Before the war his wife's behaviour had driven MacMillan to a mental breakdown from which, according to Ensor, he had never completely recovered. Even when MacMillan became Prime Minister, he kept visiting Ensor to be calmed down and reassured before major debates in Parliament about which he was always nervous, despite his confident public persona.

My conversations with Ensor made me determined to visit the Alhambra Palace in Granada, Spain. So in the summer of 1974 Elizabeth and I booked a cheap 'Fly Drive' holiday, which included a three night stay in the Parador de Granada hotel abutting the palace gardens. The travel agent assured us that we could simply pick up the car at Alicante Airport and drive down through Spain, stopping at hotels on the way: no need to book rooms in advance, he said. This advice proved worthless. With our two children in the car we travelled from the airport into the Spanish countryside. As evening approached we stopped at hotel after hotel, all of which were full. The first night of our trip we ended up with all of us sleeping on one old bed in a stinking room full of cockroaches next to open toilets in a run down village hostelry – the only refuge we could find. Not wishing to waste any more time on our holiday searching for rooms in hotels, we went to a town the next morning and bought a small tent and sleeping bags and then drove to a nice beach where we could swim and relax. We set up the tent amid sand dunes. When eventually Jane and Mark settled down to sleep I used the remaining light to begin reading Washington Irving's *Tales of the Alhambra.*

This second night in Spain was to prove as unpleasant as the first, but in a quite unexpected way.

At about 2 o'clock we were woken up by a harsh command and found a gun barrel poking through the tent entrance directed at my head. Two rather aggressive Gardia civil policemen began shouting at us, but then calmed down when they saw the children and realised we were English. Elizabeth had studied Spanish at school and she attempted to explain that we were harmless tourists who couldn't find a hotel for the night. For a long time they didn't seem to accept this and kept gesturing for us to leave. We felt threatened and vulnerable but made no move to pack up and go. This was still the time of Franco's dictatorship and, although his government was encouraging tourism there was an uneasy period of adjustment and continuing suspicion of strangers in Spain at the time. The Civil War's psychological wounds were to take decades to heal and when we were there Franco was still alive. He died the following year. It turned out that nobody, neither tourists nor anyone else, was allowed to sleep on Spanish beaches. If you wanted to camp you had to do so in regulated campsites. It was typical top-down control freakery found throughout the world under Fascist and Socialist governments. But coming from what at that time was a relatively freer society, we didn't know about these strict rules. Fortunately however, because of tourism in the early 70s, the Franco dictatorship was losing its grip on power. So what might have been a violent episode had we been there a few years earlier just petered out. When it became evident that we had nowhere to go they eventually gave up and went for a smoke about 20 yards away, keeping us awake and nervous because we didn't know what they might do next. We could hear them mumbling to themselves for ages until they drifted away and we could finally fall asleep again.

It was quite a culture shock after camping rough for a few days to turn up in Granada at the elegant Parador in our little dust covered hire car. We must have looked tired and unkempt to the other guests, as indeed we were. However the staff were kind to us and we luxuriated in the comfortable beds, large bathroom and jolly good food in the restaurant.

The next day we went to the Alhambra and, like every visitor before us, were enchanted by this haunting expression of Moorish architectural genius: an attempt to build a paradise on earth. The profound symbolic influence on the sensibilities of architects, stonemasons, artisans, designers, artists, craftsmen, gardeners and engineers was apparent everywhere we looked. The proportions of the various halls and gardens, the pools and fountains, the exquisite tiles and arabesques and the disorientating honeycomb stalactite ceilings were created to excite a sense of otherworldly mystery and tip one into contemplating the cosmos and Mankind's place in it. We were lucky. I've been told that nowadays visiting the Alhambra can be a nightmare of timed ticketing and large crowds. It's now one of Europe's top tourist destinations.

That evening after dinner and a stroll down the bustling streets of Granada, Elizabeth and the children were tired. As Jane and Mark settled to sleep Elizabeth decided to stay with them and I went out onto the Parador's terrace to look across the valley at the floodlit Generalife Palace that we planned to visit the next day. I happened to glance over the terrace wall and notice that at the bottom of a long drop there was a large compost heap at the working end of the Alhambra gardens. There was no one else around so on impulse I jumped down onto the compost and found myself alone there.

Soft floodlighting made it easy to find my way around. The night air was African warm and suffused with Mediterranean garden fragrances. My only companions were bats flitting around and a nearby owl that hooted occasionally. The Royal Rooms, The Court of the Myrtles, The Ambassadors Room, The Court of the Lions – were all mine to enjoy alone. Enchanted and mesmerised by the sound of fountains, cicadas and nightingales I became so absorbed in the atmosphere of the place that I fell into a reverie, a sort of trance where I felt personally connected in some supernatural way to the creators of this wonderful place. After spending an hour or so exploring, looking deep into shadows, at the patterns, I sat down by one of the columns and gazed at the dark reflections in the pool in front of me that also reflected the stars. I thought about the exotic culture that did so much to cradle the wise and talented people who enriched the world all those centuries ago. It felt as though, if I tried hard enough, I could witness events that happened here.

I then returned to the wall to see if I could climb back up to the Parador terrace. I managed eventually to do it, but it wasn't easy.

Next day we visited the Generalife garden that Russell Page had told me about. He said to especially look out for the wonderful rise of steps with water rills running down either side at handrail height. These had a subtle calming effect on those sensitive to the psychological benefits of harmony found in such beautiful gardens. Perceptive people had designed it and the myriad fountains and rills generated negative ionization that had an uplifting effect. The garden worked on many levels, literally and metaphorically.

* * * * *

In August 1981 at a Langton dinner meeting the subject of the true nature of reality came up during a discussion about people who had insights derived from richer perceptions – and I think that most of us assumed meant telepathy and precognition.

'Reality, as we normally think we experience it, is not Reality at all,' Shah said. 'It is an illusory approximation of Reality, a secondary world of constructs. The ancients were right about this.'

He then referred to the well-known 'Allegory of the Cave' used by Greek philosophers, Plato and Socrates. 'Our world is illusory like the image on the cave wall in the allegory or like that thrown up on the inside wall of a camera obscura. The moving image, when you approach and try to grasp it, leaves you only experiencing the flat wall from which it's reflected. The real world lies outside.'

He then said, 'It is because we become emotionally attached to the reflections, to the constructs, that we are prevented from making contact with Reality. We are mesmerised by secondary phenomena and it is emotion that keeps us mesmerised. This mesmerisation is known by the Sufi as 'sleep.' In this sense, humanity is asleep.'

At that point I asked him how we could go about connecting to the 'Reality' beyond the constructs? He replied directly with an emphasis that made us all realise this was important; 'It is not difficult. It has to do with time. You can practice techniques that develop the ability to step out of *time* – to connect with Reality – but, take note, these techniques must not be carried out with anything to which emotion is connected. Emotion blocks the path to Reality. When such exercises are successful, try to remember the feeling you had, divorce it from the particular events and objects, and, as it were, store up this feeling so you can come to recognise it.' I wrote these words down in bed that night (the mystery of the arrow of time and why we can't repeat wonderful moments had puzzled me since childhood and his words about the nature of our relationship with time were the most pertinent I had heard on the subject up until then).

The next morning I happened to pick up Shabistari's book, *The Secret Garden*, opened it at random and read the phrase, 'In an instant, rise from time and space. Set the world aside and become a world within yourself.' I knew this was important – but how could one achieve it? Similar phrases appear in many Sufi texts. (It was long after Shah died before the question of time and space was answered for me - I'm a slow learner and it wasn't until I really discovered that experience always trumps intellect in these matters that I made progress).

During one evening dinner meeting, before the general chatter stopped, Shah was sitting just opposite me and, I forget why, but he began telling me of how as a young man he had lived for a while in a London house and discovered that it was rigged up with hidden metal rods and other devices. Apparently it was once the home of a medium, a practitioner of séances devoted to communicating with spirits, and he discovered that royalty had often visited the house to take part in them.

The rods were fitted to make objects move to impress the medium's clientele. As Shah spoke, a thought about him – a clear question – formed in my mind; 'How is it that this one man can have had so many amazing experiences and adventures and achieved so much?' At once Shah looked straight at me, lowered his voice and said, 'The reason such a variety of things happen to me Ivan is that I say, "Yes" to any opportunity, so long as it's legal. There are great advantages to having this attitude.' Since I hadn't spoken and it was such an odd intervention in the conversation about the tricks mediums got up to, I had no doubt that he had read my mind directly and told me something that I needed to know.

As many people have pointed out, incidents always seemed to happen around Shah that can help people see beyond their usual conditioning and way of carrying on. For example, as a student I had spent a lot of time reading the books of Colin Wilson who, at a young age, had written *The Outsider*, published when he was 24 years old. Like many others, I identified with the characters he wrote about and his work introduced me to many writers including Albert Camus, Dostoyevsky, William James, Herman Hesse, Friedrich Nietzsche, William Blake, Fyodor Dostoyevsky, Thomas Mann and George Bernard Shaw, to name a few. Over the years I looked out for Wilson's books and read them avidly. Consequently, in the letter I was asked to write when applying to join a study group under Shah's direction, I mentioned Colin Wilson as an influence, along with some of the writers his books had introduced me to.

Years later, in 1982, Colin Wilson was invited to chair an ICR conference in London entitled 'The Nature of Religious Man: Tradition and Experience'. As a public speaker Wilson was stilted in diction but glowed with confidence and, I felt, self-importance. During the afternoon teabreak I was in conversation with Shah when Wilson rather rudely interrupted.

'I must give you a copy of my latest work,' he said. 'I'll sign it and you can sign one of your books for me. We can do a swap.'

Shah raised his eyebrows and said, 'Look Colin, we don't have to behave like that.'

'Nonsense!' Wilson replied. 'I'm a genius. You're a genius. We geniuses must stick together.'

With that he hurried off to the bookstall to collect one of his books to sign. Shah turned to me and said, 'Try and keep that man away from me Ivan,' and he too quickly beetled off.

When Wilson returned to where we had all three been standing, Shah was nowhere in sight and I mumbled that he was attending to something or other and I didn't know where he was. Wilson, my one time hero, disconcerted by being left high and dry with me, until someone he felt was more worthy of his time attracted his attention and he could extricate himself, had been revealed, despite his undoubted intelligence, as also a bit of an idiot.

From time to time I puzzled over that incident. I knew nothing about Asperger's syndrome then and it was years later that I realised that Colin Wilson would make a good case study of a high performing and productive person on the autistic spectrum. The journalist, Lyn Barber, in a 2004 interview with him, suggested that his work 'seems to constitute an attempt to classify human feelings and behaviour as written by a Martian who has never met an Earthling.' She went on to say that this was, of course, Wilson's weakness and also, in a way, his charm – he has no understanding whatsoever of other people. When she asked him if he thought he was low in emotional intelligence, he nodded: 'That is fair, yes.' In the article Barber also suggested that he would have been diagnosed as having Asperger's today.

Shah's books often referred to 'obsessives' and their typical behaviour and how unsuitable they were for absorbing teachings. Colin Wilson was clearly a brilliant but obsessive misfit in search of an identity, which would explain why, as a newly published young man, he declared himself a 'genius', a label that from then on, it was often reported, he introduced into most conversations about himself.

* * * * *

In 1978 at Shah's request Professors Denis Fry and Rushbrook Williams with Dr Edward Cowen together with Russell Page founded 'The Sufi Trust' to promote the spiritual teaching of Sufism by means of publications, lectures and the exercise of the beliefs and practices of the Sufis. In 1984 they asked me to become Hon. Secretary, a purely functionary role that nevertheless resulted in taking part in some interesting gatherings. The trustees by that time were David Widdicombe QC, Dr Ensor Holiday, the architect Richard Burton and Dr Riad Kocache, a Syrian engineer who had made a wonderful translation of *Journey of the Soul: The story of Hai bin Yaqzan*.

A major part of Shah's mission was to present Sufi literature in a way suitable for the modern world and to disseminate it so that people around the globe might be encouraged to connect to the spirit of it. The Sufi Trust had gathered considerable funds from well-wishers and these were used to finance translations of relevant material and to donate large numbers of books to libraries around the world. This would ensure that, even if major disruptions occurred and our civilization collapsed, books would exist whereby the Sufi understanding could be reclaimed at a later time.

You can only teach a person in the way that person can learn. Shah dismissed a person's expectation about what form a teaching should take; it being only useful in so far as it tells you more about the person than it does about the teaching.

One Monday morning in his study he showed me a collection of papers he was about to publish in book form as *The Sufi Mystery*. He said that the reason he chose this title was that one ancient meaning of the word 'mystery' was 'craft.' He likened Sufism to a craft but one that was also a mystery to most people. We then went on to talk about how words evolve and change their meaning and he casually said that a great hobby of his had been reading dictionaries from cover to cover, which he told me he had found valuable on more than one level. At the time this puzzled me a lot because, although I used a dictionary from time to time to check a spelling or the meaning of a particular word, I had never considered reading one in that way.

Shah's fascination with word origins and how meanings change becomes clear when you read *Darkest England*, published in 1987. It's full of hilarious coruscating examples and anecdotes that parody the English ways of thinking and behaving that Shah felt was often more 'oriental' than that of genuine Orientals. The title is a parody of those books by English explorers and anthropologists about 'darkest Africa' and he asked me to produce to his instructions the irreverent cover for it: a drawing on parchment of an English knight sitting on a solid horse holding the sort of plastic Union Jack umbrella sold to foreign tourists. Shah had produced so much material for *Darkest England* that it had to be broken down into three books, the other two being *The Natives are Restless* and *The Englishman's Handbook*. One of the reasons he wrote them was to encourage us to look at ourselves from a viewpoint outside our normal cultural assumptions, in other words, more objectively. They offer a feast of information about words and their usages over time, how meanings change and misunderstandings arise so easily, and how our conditioning channels the use we make of words.

Years later, during my near death experience in hospital, his comment about dictionaries was put in a new light for me when I experienced for myself that the REM state is also a portal to higher realms. I found myself in a dimension with a 'guide' who, among other things, showed me a strange library that could be regarded as a kind of living dictionary of metaphor. It consisted of tiers of drawers rising up as far as I could see and which I somehow knew extended infinitely beyond what I could see. Each drawer had one word written on it but inside were all the phrases alluding to its multiple metaphorical usages. Indeed, every word I saw in any drawer I opened had infinite multiple meanings according to context. Every word and phrase was somehow interlinked with all the others. So the experience of this otherworldly library was in itself a metaphor for the interconnectedness of everything – one total consciousness.

Later, on one of my readings of *The Sufis*, I came across these lines in the chapter on Ibn El Arabi; 'Every Sufi experience is an experience in depth and qualitative infinity. It is only to the ordinary man or woman that a word has only one meaning, or an experience less than a large number of equally valid, whole significances.'

* * * * *

Beyond Shah's study in Langton House was a larger room where entertaining sometimes took place. One Monday morning we moved in there to talk about a poem by Haykali, 'Thou Art There', which he had included in the *Way of the Sufi*. Every line in the poem describes something for which there is no name and is followed by the words, 'thou art there.'

The flitting of a light in the desert dusk – thou art there.

The weary duty of the Magian's forced ritual – thou art there.

The movement in response to another movement – thou art there.

Not in the book of the scribe, but in the smile at it – thou art there.

The Grace of the graceful, not the mind of the graceful – thou art there.

The question and answer: between them, not in them – thou art there.

Between the lumbering paces of the elephant – thou art there.

In harmony, in love, in being itself, in truth, in absoluteness – thou art there.

The pearl rejected by the oyster-fancier – thou art there.

The inexplicability of non-rhythm, of seeming change – thou art there.

The interchange, pulsation, sweetness, silence, rest: In congruity and in incongruity – thou art there.

In the glow, the spark, the leaping flame, the warmth and the burning; in the relaxation and the agitation: Thou art there!

I wanted to discuss the poem and Shah answered my questions about it at some length. At the time I was acutely aware of the fact – one we easily forget – that a word is not the same as what it stands for. The word 'tree', for example, is not the tree itself; it is a convenient shorthand symbol for it. This problem of perception had interested me since my time at college. It is obvious that our ability to summarise what we see or think in the blink of an eye by using a symbol is invaluable for most day-to-day communication purposes. But I had long realised that there is a price to pay for this efficiency. Viewing everything symbolically through the lens of names means we don't really *look* at what we are seeing or *think* about what we are thinking. The reflex of using words means we mostly forget that there are other more direct and imaginative ways of perceiving reality: slower perhaps but more revealing. Our instant judgements blind us to the greater depths that could be mined from lived experiences and prevent us from developing all aspects of human life: from science to religion, from aesthetics to culture, from ethics to politics. The language that liberated us from animalism seems to impose a limit that prevents us from developing further. Unless we escape from the seductive trap of instantly translating every action and thought into words and assume that that means we have finished with a topic, we are stuck because we don't pause to reflect.

So I asked Shah if the poem was partly about the reality we can sometimes perceive before the brain 'fixes' it with words? He said that it was. Then I asked if the poem's meaning explained why in discussions he so often answered a question with another question, thus instantly expanding the frame of reference of the questioner. He agreed it was – and immediately asked me a question; 'Have you read the Tao Te Ching?' I said I had. He went on to say that, although 'Thou Art There' was a powerful poem, he thought that what it expressed and transmitted had been surpassed in succinctness by Lao-tzu in the 6th century BC and suggested it would be worth my while reading a good translation of it again (I did of course, with greater concentration than when I'd read it in my teens).

We talked for a while about this during which he said that Lao-tzu showed that real knowledge about the nature of reality went back many thousands of years but, although that was true, it was not something he wanted to go out of his way to draw attention to. This was because people's tendency to get excited by anything ancient and exotic acted as a barrier, preventing them from doing what they should be doing now in our own culture, which was absorbing preparatory information. He stressed that human gullibility and the inability to discriminate blinded most people to the more subtle requirements of a genuine search for truth, which had to be done from a basis of knowledge about the real needs of time, place and people.

Human gullibility was a frequent theme of Shah's. This after all was the age of the Moonies, spoon bending and *Chariots of the Gods: Unsolved Mysteries of the Past* – a book by Erick von Däniken claiming that alien astronauts who were revered by humans as gods introduced ancient civilizations to the technologies and religions we associate with them today. Although von Däniken was a convicted fraudster his book sold more than 63 million copies and enabled him to pay off many debts. (His second book, *Gods from Outer Space*, was written whilst serving a prison sentence for financial crimes.) Carl Sagan wrote of this phenomenon, 'That writing as careless as von Däniken's, whose principal thesis is that our ancestors were dummies, should be so popular is a sober commentary on the credulousness and despair of our times. But the idea that beings from elsewhere will save us from ourselves is a very dangerous doctrine – akin to that of the quack doctor whose ministrations prevent the patient from seeing a physician competent to help him and perhaps to cure his disease.'

Quite.

Mention of physicians reminds me of another event.

On weekdays when I visited Langton I often parked my car close to the front door rather than the car park. One morning, having finished what I was there to do, Shah and I were talking in his study when the doorbell rang. Shah jumped up to answer it and within seconds he ran back in the room and urgently whispered, 'Ivan, this fellow is a lunatic! If I can't get rid of him in a minute or two, come out and say that we have to go now or I will miss my train. And we'll jump in your car and drive off.'

He then answered the door and I could hear a man insistently whining, demanding that Shah should tell him what to do. He was getting louder and louder. So after a minute or two of this I gathered up my papers and went out with my briefcase to do as Shah had asked.

The man was middle-aged but behaving like a three-year-old having a tantrum: crying and stamping his feet. I played my part, going on about the train and the need to hurry and Shah said to the fellow, 'Look, I'm sorry old chap; I can't help you. I've got to go. You need to find a psychiatrist.' Then he quickly locked the front door and jumped in my car and we drove away in the direction of Tunbridge Wells.

A few hundred yards through Langton village Shah said, 'Quick! Turn left here. We'll hide off the main road in case he follows us to the station.' We found a quiet cul-de-sac and when I turned the engine off he explained that this unexpected visitor was a GP who had been bothering him for some time. Apparently he had read his books and tracked him down. At a previous meeting this doctor had revealed to Shah that he was homosexual but was terrified his parents and colleagues would find out and had become bizarrely obsessed with the idea that Shah could sort this out for him. Whilst we waited Shah went on to say how hard it was to find people sane enough to interact normally with him and who would give time and consideration to what he really had to offer, rather than what they thought he offered. This GP clearly thought Sufism existed to solve his personal dilemmas and that Shah in particular was offering some sort of psychotherapy.

After twenty minutes or so, Shah suddenly remembered that we had left his wife, Kashfi, alone in the house. Since the doctor was clearly unhinged he thought it best to get back home in case the man was still hanging around and frightened her. We decided to drive round the back of the estate so he could find a way in without being seen from the front. My last sight of Shah as I drove off that day was of him picking his way through brambles and climbing across a fence into the Langton Estate grounds.

* * * * *

One Monday morning Shah called me over to talk about a new book he was collating. It was to be called *World Tales*, a collection of 65 stories from many cultures, each with a short introduction tracing its history and describing the extraordinary coincidence of its appearance in different cultures. He asked me if I could locate illustrations to go with each tale. He was thinking of work by classic book illustrators like Arthur Rackham, Kay Nielsen, Edmund Dulac and Maxfield Parrish. I said I could but that, since there are so many brilliant contemporary illustrators, why not consider commissioning new work? I had good friends, Chris McEwan and Carol Lawson, who were members of the Association of Illustrators and well connected to a network of great artists and illustrators who would have loved to contribute to such a book. Chris and Carol were widely respected in the community of illustrators at the time and I had no doubt that, with their support, we could find enough artists to produce a wealth of fine work.

Shah liked the idea and asked me to cost it out so we could put it to the publisher to see if they would give us the extra money. So I prepared a budget and we went to see William Jovanovich at the London office of Harcourt Brace Jovanovich (HBJ). It was quite an experience. At that time Jovanovich was hugely influential and his publishing company was reputed to be the biggest in the world. He was wealthy beyond imagining; even his butler had a personal helicopter! When he swept into the meeting room it was with a serious entourage of a dozen or more crisply dressed American professors and writers, all no doubt hoping to further their own pet projects, plus his personal secretary. He shook hands with Shah, rudely ignored me, and we all sat round a large table with Jovanovich and his secretary at one end and myself and Shah at the other.

The meeting was devoted to *World Tales*, a project that Jovanovich himself was pushing through because he had read some of Shah's books and wanted to be associated with him. My impression was that most people at the table hadn't a clue who Shah was or why they were included in the meeting with him. After getting everyone to introduce themselves, which took some time as they were all trying to impress each other, Jovanovich asked Shah to explain 'to our distinguished colleagues here' what the book was all about.

Then an odd thing happened. Shah stood up and spoke for about 30 minutes about traditional stories and how their social and psychological importance was largely unrecognised. To illustrate what he was talking about he summarised story themes, gave examples and told a couple in a most entertaining manner. He held the attention of everyone around the table – except William Jovanovich, who assumed an air of being above it all and quietly, but nevertheless ostentatiously, dictated letters to his secretary throughout.

At the end of his presentation Shah said, 'and I think it would be a really good idea if we had *original* illustrations for this book. Ivan, please show us some examples of the quality of illustrations we could commission to complement the tales.' I stood up and passed around the table a number of exquisitely detailed illustrations from various contemporary English artists and told them that we were living in a golden age of book illustration every bit as great as that of a hundred years ago. The professors were impressed, but I quickly got the measure of them when they said such daft things as, 'Wow! Were these done by hand?' and, 'Oh! I do love picture books, they make me cry.'

Then Shah mentioned that we would need extra money to commission work of this quality from so many different artists but, if we did so, it would make *World Tales* a really special book. At the mention of 'money' and 'special' Jovanovich's attention was finally caught. He asked the assorted crew (in such a way that implied it was his notion) whether or not they liked the idea of this being an illustrated book. Everyone sycophantically assured him they did. So he concluded the meeting by saying he would think about it, went into a huddle with Shah for a few minutes, and we both left.

Out on the streets we sought out a coffee bar where we could talk and Shah asked me what I thought about the meeting. 'It was amazing,' I said. 'He's supposed to be interested in your work but he didn't take any notice of what you were saying at all! And what were all those professors doing there?'

'You don't understand Ivan. In America your importance and status is indicated by how many people you can afford to have tagging along with you. So, he just hires a plane and brings along a crowd. For example, if some professor wanted a book deal with Harcourt Brace Jovanovich, the biggest educational textbook publisher in the world by the way, he'd bring along another professor in the same field to meet and assess him. But, because Jovanovich is the big cheese and is paying the bills, all these professors have to tag along wherever he goes and sit in on the meetings he has. This ensures he always has a crowd round him, which gives him a big advantage in negotiations. As for not listening to me, he does this to emphasise how significant he is. By not appearing to take any notice of what goes on around him he is implying that whatever he does is always more important than the preoccupations of everybody else. It's a technique such people adopt to intimidate and maintain an advantage. He is declaring he is top dog, the alpha male, head honcho, the boss man.'

'So what was he talking with you about at the end?'

'He wants to see us again next week to give me his decision. He just wants more attention. He could have given his decision there and then – it's a tiny amount of money for him.'

The next time we saw Jovanovich he shook me by the hand, asked many questions and gave me lots of attention. He approved the new budget for the book and authorised an advance for the illustrators. After that meeting we went again to the coffee bar and I said, 'Well, that was different! He noticed me.'

Shah smiled and said, 'I thought he would. I spoke on the phone with him during the week and told him you were head of a large organisation employing many creative people … Never underestimate the usefulness of a ruse like that to influence a situation, we really do live in a world of appearances.'

Then began the work of selecting the illustrators, briefing and art directing them, and making sure they delivered on time. This was when Alan Tunbridge was working with me so I concentrated on the book project while he managed the business. Alan, in his spare time, also created an amazing painting to illustrate "The Tale of Mushkil Gusha" and a beautiful scraperboard illustration for "The Pilgrim from Paradise." Only one artist let us down and, as we were running out of time, I had no choice but to spend three days producing pictures to illustrate the "The Bird Maiden" story myself. Approving the colour plates involved three trips to Milan and two to New York to meet with the team who were organising the printing and marketing.

In New York HBJ had booked me in to the St. Regis Hotel, perhaps because they realised I might enjoy the iconic 'Old King Cole' painting by a favourite illustrator of mine, Maxfield Parrish, that decorated the bar – or maybe not. On my second trip to New York I went with my friends Chris and Carol who by coincidence were staying in the same hotel before setting off around America on a TV promotional trip for Carol's Franklin Mint 'collectables'– porcelain plates for which she had produced decorative nursery rhyme themed illustrations. Each evening we had our meals next to the table where a doddery Salvador Dali and his wife and mistress had theirs. They had a suite in the hotel where each year they spent the Autumn and Winter months. All of us were mesmerised by the elderly dancers on the floor below robotically waltzing with frozen stiff faces like puppets without strings. While I was staying there, psychologist Bob Ornstein contacted me to say that he was in New York too and wanted to take me to an eatery that served typical New York pastrami. When we met up, however, he brought along a girlfriend and I felt a bit of a gooseberry. She obviously wanted Bob to herself and our conversation was unexpectedly dull.

On one of my trips to Milan, I remember, having breakfast in a street café with the Italian/American production director of HJB's print company and the Milanese plate maker. At the next table a passionate blazing argument was in progress with much loud shouting, gesturing and table banging. It would surely end in fisticuffs I thought. Perhaps the Pope had died or another Italian government had fallen, as they seemed to do every few weeks in Italy then. But when I asked my companions what was going on they said, 'Oh nothing special. They're just arguing about the best way to cook breakfast!

World Tales was published in 1979 and chosen as the book of the month by the American Book of the Month Club. Although the illustrations were jewel like and evocative and it was a fun project to work on involving many talented artists, including Alan Lee, who was later responsible for visualising *The Lord of the Rings* films, I never thought for one moment that the artwork was more significant than the stories themselves. As Shah said in his introduction, 'It is the tale itself, when it emerges, which is king.'

CHAPTER FIVE

War, spies and barriers to progress

ONE of the themes Shah started talking about in the late 1970s was the possibility of nuclear war and the effects of nuclear weapons. The sustained state of political and military rivalry between the Western democratic powers led by America and the Communist Bloc of the Soviet Union and Warsaw Pact countries was a continuing background stressor for all of us back then. George Orwell coined the term 'Cold War' for it and the topic featured daily in newspapers during the 1950s. In the late 60s, the tension had subsided somewhat but in the 1970s it was reawakened as conflicts increased between the major powers with both sides becoming more militaristic.

Shah forcefully raised the point that, though hundreds of millions of pounds of public funds were being spent on nuclear shelters in Britain (the equivalent of many £billions today), none of these were intended for public use. If another major war broke out the Royal Family, Prime Minister, the Government, selected members of the civil service and military officers would occupy purpose-built bunkers, to 'preserve the continuity of government' but, if the country were attacked, the people would have no defences, despite an annual defence budget then of some £13,500,000,000. This was illogical since the word 'defence' was supposed to be about security: defending the population against attack, danger or injury. It was quite wrong to have these weapons and threaten to use them, especially when we could not to protect our own population against them, and there was no civil defence policy worth a light.

Shah gathered a group of us together in his study at Langton and it was decided to attempt to put in a corrective by forming the 'Nuclear Protection Advisory Group (NuPAG). Since I had spare office capacity at my studio I was asked to be the NuPAG Information Officer and put in a dedicated phone line to field any enquiries that might arise from our activities.

Various projects were set in motion. Richard Burton designed a nuclear shelter that could be manufactured using massive concrete tubes for maximum strength against blasts. The money was raised and we installed a fully functioning prototype in the garden at Langton fitting it out with radiation filters, toilet, kitchen and bunk beds. Volunteers stayed in it for long periods to test human endurance, the ventilation system and so on. Another team tested how quickly they could build different designs of earth covered radiation shelters in a field beyond the garden. I made a photographic record of their efforts and timed each stage of construction.

Shah gave me the manuscript of a book he had commissioned from the writer, Peter Brent. He wanted it to be a survival manual and asked me to read it with a view to having the text illustrated with drawings. I had met Peter a number of times and read his book, *Godmen of India*, which was brilliant. But reading this new manuscript showed me that studying the subject had made him by turns angry and deeply depressed. It was written in such emotional language that I was sure it would not help readers think clearly about the topic. He had overemphasised the horror with vivid metaphors – radiation plumes were carried by 'winds of death' creating 'corridors of doom' for example – and it didn't read like a survival manual at all. It contained little practical advice. It seemed to me that researching the terrible effects of nuclear weapons had stopped him thinking constructively about what might be done if such a horrible thing did happen and you weren't immediately obliterated. He hadn't addressed what people could do in advance to protect themselves against the effects of blast, fire and radiation or what they could do if they survived and had to live through the aftermath. Although the government's civil defence advice was laughably inadequate, this would be no better.

Next time the NuPAG committee met I explained that the book needed rewriting and Shah said he agreed totally. He then looked around the room and said that someone who understands the need to make it factual rather than emotional should write it. Everyone looked at me. After a long pause I said, 'Would you like me to do it then?'

'Yes,' said Shah, 'But you need to get on with it quickly.'

Within a couple of days he supplied me with boxes containing nearly 50 books and scientific papers to read, digest and fillet for facts. I have no idea how he had got hold of them. They included civil defence manuals from China, Russia, America and Switzerland. Whilst doing my full time job in the day, in the evening – right up to 2 or 3 in the morning – I was reading, researching and writing the book from scratch whilst also thinking about the illustrations and selecting an illustrator who could do the type of line drawings I envisaged.

Although Shah was encouraging me through all of this, and I had acted as copywriter for many commercial projects, I was aware that I wasn't a particularly good prose writer. My half finished book about the crimes of Christianity, for example, although it contained fascinating stories about the dark side of Christian history – the notorious cruelties and killings that I'd culled from various sources – wasn't well written. My limitations were clear to me. I talked about this to Ramsey Wood, an American friend who lived in London and whose wonderful *Kalila and Dimna, Selected fables of Bidpai* was published that year. Ramsay had a marvellous command of language and could write really well and he offered to come down and give me a crash course and we spent an intense weekend in my garden in Brighton going page by page through *The Elements of Style*, by Strunk and White, which every aspiring writer should read.

I went with Shah to the Athenaeum a couple of times to have lunch and discuss the book with his friend the literary agent, Hilary Rubenstein, who then sold it to Jonathan Cape. Tom Maschler, head of Jonathan Cape, assigned a top editor to me and we went through the manuscript together making many improvements. I learnt a lot about writing from her too.

The book came out in 1982 as *The Survival Option: A Guide to Living Through Nuclear War*. It sold well and was positively received. To promote it Maschler suggested I go on television to talk about the premise of the book and he sent me off for a screen test in Soho. Two other authors were at the same session and were keen to impress the TV company: David Starkey, the ambitious historian who became a well known author and 'go to' constitutional historian for the media (a personality guaranteed to stir up controversy in radio and television programmes), and an ex nun, Karen Armstrong, who had just produced a book about life in a convent and who went on to write a host of books about religion and mysticism. We had an enjoyable long lunch with Starkey dominating the conversation. There was an understandable polite lack of enthusiasm for discussing the grim topic of my book and I was too shy to attempt to make an impression in such eloquent company.

Shah was pleased with my work on *The Survival Option* and told me he that there were people at Oxford University that he knew would be happy to award me a PhD on the strength of it. He said I might one day find it useful to become Doctor Tyrrell. But, possessed of a crippling sense of false modesty, and assuming I was not expected to appear greedy, I said I wasn't really worthy of that and didn't see the point of a PhD since I was in design and marketing. Foolishly I didn't take him up on the offer. I realize now that, because we live in an appearance culture, it would have been invaluable to have the label 'Dr' attached to my name, years later, when promoting the Human Givens approach to psychotherapy. I have wondered if Shah had somehow intuited how my life might possibly evolve thereafter and that a label like that might be helpful.

Once the book was published it got good reviews. *The Guardian* said, 'Facts, not emotion… should be in every home in the country.' *The Listener* praised it and asked, 'Can we really duck the knowledge that careful preparations and modest expenditure might save lives?' And the *British Medical Journal* declared of it that, 'The practical information is reliable,' and pointed out that I began it with an old Chinese saying: '*To lead a people to war unprepared is to throw them away. Who dares to disagree?*'

Publication triggered a succession of strange events. One eccentric fellow with a marked humour deficit, for example, kept showing up at my office dressed all in black with a plan for an underground city that he had drawn in precise architectural detail. He wanted to enlist me in his attempt to persuade the government to start building vast underground cities that would protect the occupants from nuclear and chemical attack. His exquisite drawings were so big that to view them we had to lay them out on the floor of our large reception area. Looking back at his behaviour with what I know now, he was clearly a high functioning example of someone with Asperger's and a bee in his bonnet.

It must be difficult for young people today to appreciate the atmosphere that the Cold War engendered and how unsettling it was to have several visits from an Eastern European spy working for the USSR. But that's what happened to me. At the time, Russians were not allowed to stray far from their embassy and were always followed when they did. So they used to send out Eastern Europeans from the embassies of Warsaw Pact countries to do their dirty work for them because they were not subject to such strict travel restrictions. This charming individual turned up at the office several times, always bringing presents; chocolate and crates of lager. His English was excellent and he told me about his family, his homeland and asked me about my family and offered to take us all on a picnic. But he soon got around to his purpose for visiting my office. He said he had read *The Survival Option* and his curiosity had been aroused. He wanted to ask me a few questions about it. It quickly became clear that this was not a casual chat. He had a thorough agenda and wanted to know where I had found the information in the book about the civil defence plans of various countries like the USSR, China and so on. He also obviously thought my design business was a front for something more sinister and couldn't believe someone independent from government could write such a book and get it published.

When I told Shah about his visits he said that since we started NuPAG he was sure his phone was being tapped and mine probably was too. Our secret service would know of this chap's visit to my office. By today's digital world standards where everything you do online and electronically can be monitored, having your phone tapped seems rather quaint. Nevertheless at the time it made me a little uneasy.

Copy Laws, the co-director with Shah of Medion and designer of the Medion Ioniser, was a wonderful inventor who designed and built a prototype of a radiation detector for us that could be produced so cheaply it could be mass produced for every household at a cost of pennies each. I was told that the Home Office somehow heard of it and sent officials down to investigate. When they realised what Copy had achieved they confiscated all his work on this project and made it clear it was now subject to The Official Secrets Act and no mention of it could be made from then on. We could be prosecuted if we ignored this injunction.

Around that time NuPAG held a conference on civil defence at the London Royal Institute of British Architects. The speakers included Dr

Fritz Sager, head of Swiss Civil Defence, Cresson H. Kearney, from Oakridge National Laboratory in America, and the Architect Richard Burton, a founding member of NuPAG. The event triggered a protest demonstration and considerable media attention on national news programmes. Death threats were received at my office from people who thought that seriously discussing the topic of civil defence would make nuclear war more likely.

After that I was invited to a civil defence conference at Easingwold where I met the Home Secretary, William Whitelaw, who had a reputation for great intelligence, political cunning, old fashioned loyalty and good manners (and of whom Maggie Thatcher said, 'Every Prime Minister needs a Willie'). He was the keynote speaker and arrived in a Jaguar with two minders. His talk was bland and unmemorable. But what *was* memorable for me was that I could see, close up, that his suit was covered in egg and gravy stains. He seemed oblivious to the fact.

Back then, NATO and Warsaw Pact nations were not the only ones concerned about nuclear war. I learned, for example, that the Iraqi President, Saddam Hussein, believed that one day America would attack his country with nuclear weapons, even though at that time they were supposed to be allies. He had set in train a huge building programme of underground public nuclear shelters and was employing Western companies to build them. Ove Arup, a global firm of structural design engineers was involved in this work and they asked Richard Burton to go to Baghdad as a consultant and give a briefing on emergency crowd management to the Iraqis. But at the last moment Richard couldn't go and, on the Thursday a week before the meeting in Baghdad had been arranged, he phoned me to ask if I would go instead. The pay was £400 a day plus expenses (a good fee for me in those days) and the trip would last a week. Following Shah's hint that one should say yes to any opportunity that showed itself, so long as it was legal, I said yes.

There was no time to get a visa because the Iraqi embassy in London was closed on Friday. But I was told not to worry: I would fly to Jordan on Sunday and Ove Arup would arrange to have a visa waiting for me at the Iraqi embassy there on Monday morning. I would then fly from Amman to Baghdad that same night and arrive in good time to meet the project team and be briefed for Wednesday's meeting. The reason for the night flight was that this was only three months into the Iran-Iraq war and there were still Iranian planes active over Iraq, bombing and strafing, and domestic civilian flights were considered vulnerable targets.

On Sunday I arrived at the Amman Hilton in Jordan and first thing on Monday morning made my way, by taxi, to the Iraqi embassy. It was already hot and dusty and armed soldiers surrounded the embassy. Inside I went up to the reception desk and told them my name and said I had come to collect my visa. The man behind the desk said nothing, looked closely at my passport and then, in a tired voice said, 'No telex, no visa.'

'What do you mean, "No telex, no visa"'?

With a shrug worthy of a French waiter he wearily repeated this mantra several times, 'No telex, no visa.'

I tried to question him but the words 'no', 'telex' and 'visa' seemed to be the only English words he knew. Confronted with this dedicated, unhelpful 'jobsworth' my Middle Eastern adventure seemed to have come to a stop before it had properly started.

It was then that I realised that there were numerous other foreigners around me all looking fed up. A little man came up to me and explained everything in a strong Scottish accent.

'Look, Jimmy, some of us have been here for a couple of weeks. We can't get visas and as far as we can make out it's because their wretched telex machine isn't working.'

He pointed out that there were lots of business people and skilled workers – Dutch, Americans, Germans, Canadians, French and so on – all waiting for visas so they could get into Iraq and do business. There was even a group of Japanese dressed identically in black with white shirts standing in a tight knot packed closely together like a bunch of skittles. 'You'll just have to join the queue and wait with us.'

I went out into the hazy sunshine to think. The crowd of bored soldiers, hot in their uniforms, eyed me up and down as I paced around. Then into my mind came something Shah had once said whilst recounting his travels: 'At borders in Africa, the Middle East, and much of the rest of the world, you just have to show officials a printed document and pretend it's sufficient. They will make great play of examining it and then usually let you through.'

I had checked out of my hotel and left my bag back at the reception because my flight was not until 11 pm that night and I remembered that I had put a telex confirming my hotel booking into the waste paper basket in my room. Perhaps, if the room had not already been cleaned, I could retrieve it. I tore back to the hotel in a taxi, told reception I had left something in my vacated room and they let me in. There was the strip of telex paper with my name on it curled up in the wastebasket where I had left it. Back to the Iraqi embassy I went and strode through the disconsolate crowd up to the desk and flourished the white strip of paper at 'Mr No-telex-no-visa.'

'Look!' I said, pointing out that I was holding a telex, that it had my name on it and that it was the same name as on my British passport. 'Now can I have my visa?'

He ceremoniously took the telex away through a green door behind him. After a long pause he reappeared and ushered me into an inner sanctum where sat a man who, to my relief, spoke perfect English. He asked me a few perfunctory questions and wanted to know why I was in such a hurry. I told him about the meeting I had to attend in Baghdad, that the meeting was about Saddam's plan for civilian civil defence bunkers and that my flight was booked for that night and I had no other way of getting there. Very courteously he wrote out a visa for me and ushered me back into the waiting room. I left the building chased by the frantic and puzzled Scotsman asking me, 'How did ya do it?'

Flourishing my telex at him I said, 'I just remembered a piece of advice,' and hurried away before the Iraqis changed their minds.

After that bit of excitement I wandered into Amman's great Roman amphitheatre to calm down. It was built in the reign of Emperor Marcus Aurelius and the acoustics were amazing. It was practically empty and peaceful despite its proximity to the city streets outside. From my vantage point, on the steps near the top, I heard an English archaeologist explaining to a small group of tourists far below how studying the stones showed the way the arena had evolved. It had been quite small to start with; a theatre where poetry and plays were performed and the audience on the lower steps were close to the actors. Gradually, as Roman civilisation decayed, the entertainments became more violent until a large drop separated the first row of seating high above the floor of the arena so that the blood of wild animals and human victims could not splash the audience. This was evidence in stone of the 'blood and circuses' policy of appeasing an ignorant populace with ever more crude and violent diversions.

I am often reminded of that process whenever I see TV programmes where adults are deliberately whipped into a frenzy by 'celebrities', or encouraged to jump up and down and scream like six year olds in game shows, or laugh hysterically at whatever obscenity is displayed for them. And many films and computer games made today glorifying violence and cruelty seem to be produced and directed by depraved young psychopaths. Alas, as it was in ancient times, the subtle is still at the mercy of the crude – and restraint at the mercy of hedonism.

Whilst listening to the archaeologist an elderly Arab sat down next to me. When the group moved on he spoke to me in good English and politely asked if I would like to be shown the sights around the city. He became my guide for the rest of what turned out to be an interesting day. He was a Palestinian refugee and told me how the founders of modern Israel had taken his family home, causing him and his relatives to flee and build a new life for themselves across the border in Jordan. He said all this in a matter of fact way, without anger or looking for pity.

In the evening we said our goodbyes and I collected my bag from the hotel. I went to the airport to catch my flight across the desert to Baghdad where I was met by an English employee of Ove Arup who took me to the hotel that was to be my base for the week. To my relief he told me that the Iranian Air Force was now largely destroyed so the risk of being bombed was minimal.

The meeting I attended on Wednesday was lively. There seemed to be arguments going on around the table but I had not the slightest inkling of what they were about. Perhaps they were just excitable people. In the event none of the Iraqis had much time to listen to a quiet young Englishman talking about crowd control in an emotionally arousing emergency. At a suitable moment I said my piece. They listened politely but I was aware that they were more interested in getting back to their internal bickering. I'd finished what I was contracted to do and for the rest of the week wandered around Baghdad seeking out the older quarters, visiting sites where captured Iranian weaponry were on show and relaxing with a drink in The British Colonial Club that was founded by the British explorer and diplomat Gertrude Bell. The rest of the time I just soaked up the atmosphere of the despot's capital, viewing endless numbers of huge posters and statues of Saddam and his architectural vanity projects. It felt totally safe to do so. Sadly such idle wanderings in that region are now impossible for Westerners.

On the evening before my flight home, fed up with bland hotel food, the Ove Arup team decided we should eat out at what they had heard was the best restaurant in town. On the way we passed the modern Baghdad Opera House whose glass front stood several stories high but was sandbagged to protect it from bomb blasts. It looked ridiculous.

The restaurant was cavernous and dark, candle lit and quite crowded. We ordered and, as our eyes gradually accustomed to the gloom, sat back to enjoy the unusual dancing movements of the waiters as they served the tables. They employed a complex and amusing routine of little steps forward and back followed by occasional swivels and many ridiculous hops. When the food came we picked at it a bit. It was not good lamb, imported from Pakistan apparently, but worse was the realisation that the waiters bizarre dancing was caused by an urge to avoid stepping on one of the many hundreds of mice carpeting the floor. The vermin were everywhere, scampering up the walls, along beams and over our feet and legs.

Suddenly a public schoolboy shout went up from someone in our group, 'We're not paying for this chaps!' And we noisily stood up from the infested table and made for the door, scattering mice in all directions. The waiters followed us outside clearly believing that we should pay. I had some sympathy for them. After all, they were doing their best for us in trying circumstances. But angry exchanges followed and cooks armed to the teeth with knives and meat cleavers joined the waiters. Having committed ourselves to this course of action we ran as fast as we could down the street, furiously chased by what looked to me for all the world like a murderous band of bloodthirsty pirates.

* * * * *

One day Shah announced that we should close down the NuPAG project. He said we'd done enough and that it was important to know that stopping a project is as important as starting one. So we ceased producing newsletters and halted our experiments related to civil defence. It wasn't long after that the Berlin Wall came down and the Soviet Union was dissolved.

* * * * *

Over the years Shah talked a lot about expectation, a theme that runs through many of his books. He pointed out that expectations are almost always not fulfilled and that they stop us seeing things clearly. It is our expectations that frustrate most human endeavours, including so-called spiritual ones.

'Expectation and disappointment go hand in hand,' he said. 'We are swept along first by expectation – then by disappointment or surprise. And, once in the disappointed or surprised stage, we quickly forget our earlier expectation.

'We are not masters of ourselves when swept along like this, although, being human, expectation and disappointment will always be with us. They are major handicaps and prevent the mind and heart from perceiving the Truth.'

One Saturday evening he told what he said was a Zen story to illustrate this and I wrote it up when I got home.

> One day a young man who was interested in the spiritual life heard of a famous teacher who lived far away. He resolved to seek him out and become his pupil.
>
> He travelled far to find him suffering great hardship along the way, until he arrived at a house at the foot of a high mountain where the sage lived. It was late in the day and snow was beginning to fall. He was hungry and cold.
>
> When he knocked on the door it was opened by the great teacher himself.
>
> 'Master!' he cried. 'With great difficulty I have travelled a

thousand miles to find you. Let me in so I may serve you and learn.'

Instantly the teacher slammed the door in his face shouting, 'Get away from me you wretch!'

Shocked and getting colder by the minute the young seeker after truth huddled in the doorway. 'This must be a test,' he thought to himself and, bucking up courage, he knocked again at the door to plead his case. This time the teacher was even more forceful, sending him spinning to the ground with a mighty blow before slamming the door once more.

Even more convinced that this was a test of some kind he tried again and again. The teacher eventually relented but, before he was allowed to rest or eat, he was cuffed round the ears and ordered to clean the floors, chop wood, light fires and cook the evening meal. He was then given scraps from the table, for which he professed himself most grateful.

He was allowed to stay. For ten years he led a miserable life. He was treated like a slave, often beaten, made to work long and hard at the menial tasks around the house, all for no reward. In all that time he could detect no sign of any teaching from his master... no words of wisdom... no comforting hint of spiritual succour. All the while, however, he was convinced that one day his suffering would pay off. That was his expectation.

He was usually so tired from his labours that he went to bed early each evening to sleep off his exhaustion. But, one warm summer night, he couldn't sleep for puzzling over his circumstances and his teacher's behaviour so he rose again to walk in the garden, intent on meditating about his fate. And so it was that he made a great discovery. Unobserved he saw his master quietly leave the house and make his way by starlight up the side of the mountain. He resolved to follow him.

In less than an hour the teacher reached a mysterious cave entrance and disappeared inside. The disciple's heart missed a beat. 'This must be where my master holds his spiritual meetings,' he said to himself and sure enough, with mounting excitement, he saw other shadowy figures entering the cave. For fear of being caught he made his way back down the mountain to his room deciding that from that moment on he would work harder still for his master so that he too might one day be allowed to participate in the cave's wondrous ceremonies.

He did work harder, paying even closer attention to his master's wishes and keeping close watch every night to see how often his master took the path up the mountainside. About once or twice a week it turned out. Each time the disciple followed discreetly until, one dark night, he could contain his curiosity no longer. After he was sure that no more people were coming up the mountain, he entered the cave.

Inside he found a fabulous world of decorated chambers connected by dimly lit tunnels. From deep within he could hear the rhythm of drums and, beside himself with anticipation and keeping to the shadows he crept towards the sound anxious to see whatever ceremony was in progress.

He peeped nervously into the inner sanctum. It was more sumptuously furnished than the outer chambers and glowing with a warm light from artfully placed lanterns. The cavern was decorated with rich carpeting, colourful patterned wall hangings and huge luxurious cushions. In the centre a delightful fountain played into a deep crystal blue pool. It was a magical place. At first the disciple couldn't see his master. There were many people lounging around as if waiting for something to happen. High up in the gallery musicians played a haunting melody. Then suddenly the music changed. The rhythm grew louder and faster – more compulsive and urgent. With a shout everyone turned to look in the direction of a door that was opening and immediately began clapping in time to the music.

To his surprise the disciple saw, coming through the door, an exotic troupe of ravishingly beautiful, dark-eyed dancing girls. He watched in amazement as they brazenly circled around, erotically swinging and swaying in time to the wild music. Surely this was no spiritual assembly!

It was then that he saw his master. With a cup in one hand and a girl on his knee, surrounded by carousing companions, he was clearly the host of the party. Motionless, mesmerised, the disciple watched an orgy develop. Wine flowed, songs were sung and girls disrobed. He slunk miserably away, totally disillusioned.

At dawn the dissolute old man came staggering home to be met at the door by his erstwhile disciple.

'I'm leaving!' shouted the disciple. 'I saw you in the cave! You're a fraud! I've wasted ten years of my life with you.'

'I know, I know,' said the orgy master, 'but what amazes me is, why it took you so long to find out!'

When he finished telling the tale Shah said that the point of it was that, if you are going to bring assumptions to an activity, especially a spiritual one, you might as well stay at home for all the good it will do you. It's always the flaws within ourselves, our biases and assumptions, that prevent successful outcomes to our endeavours.

On another occasion he gave us a tip on how to overcome the handicap of being overwhelmed by expectation and disappointment. 'They are both parts of one process,' he said. 'Try to hold a memory of both expectation and disappointment together in the mind. Get used to what this feels like. When you can do this it enables something else to be seen in between the two states – the true situation. When you can do this, you will be free from the tyranny of expectation and disappointment. Also, take a more gentle, softer approach to expectation, never let it rage as a fever. Take what comes and you will never be disappointed.'

After dinner meetings, I sometimes stayed the night in the cottage situated across the courtyard from The Elephant, a sort of all-purpose hostel for visitors. In the early days Shah would often talk long into the early hours and, if there was no room for me to stay in the cottage I would leave, getting home at three or four in the morning, my mind buzzing (I had a favourite spot on the road across Ashdown forest where I sometimes stopped to write down a few notes by the interior light of my car).

One Sunday morning, after staying overnight in the cottage a group of us were invited to attend a meeting about study groups in the library. The discussion was about why study groups are needed and how they should be used. I made notes later of what Shah said:

As he so often did he began with a metaphor. 'The situation I am in is like that of a man in a group of people all seated in a room. The man stands up and goes into another room for a while and, when he returns, begins to describe to those in the first room what the other room is like.

'Some of the people don't believe there is another room.

'Some do believe it and want to see it instantly and get overexcited about it.

'Some want to hear more about the room but are not interested in going themselves to find out.

'When the man says that to understand all about this other room you first have to stand up, then walk across the floor and open a door ... people don't see the relevance.

'Sufi study is about traditional psychology and the means of 'getting to the other room'. To begin we are going to build up a body of material based on questions and answers.

'Why should we do this? Just because the possibility is there: we cannot help but evolve.

'What are we doing? We are developing new perceptions and skills associated with connecting us with a dimension beyond time and space.

'How do we proceed? By rapidly going through a vast range of questions and information in order to make ourselves ready to move to another stage.

'There is much material to be studied from the Sufi point of view. Poetry, like the quatrains of Omar Khayyam for example, are signals on the way, illustrations, not to be confused with any supposed state of Omar's. We have to learn how to understand these signals for what they are.

'We are learning a skill and we must have the aptitude and the wish to learn.

'A person too full of himself can never learn.

'There is always a disparity between the learner and the teacher. Without this disparity there is no curiosity, no reason to learn because the learner would already know. A children's teacher in an ordinary school, if he or she is any good, has to be aware that the model of the world in the child's head is different from the teacher's. The teacher has to make the relevant allowances by approaching nearer to the child's model in order to be understood. With small children connections sometimes have to be made on a trade basis to focus their attention, as when we say to them, "You can go out to play once you've learnt the twelve times table."

'To return to Omar and other Sufi suppliers of signs on the way: the signs and signals exist for us to use, to make us reflect and see things from a wider point of view. Sufi material is not intended to dominate or impress the author's mood or intellectual stance on people. This objective approach is the hallmark of Sufi poetry and prose, whatever it may seem to ordinary scholars.

'We have to practice the art of using such material. Study groups are composed in such a way that they help in this.'

* * * * *

In the 1980s when my children, Jane and Mark, were teenagers, they expressed an interest in going to Langton so I began taking them with me. Shah was always happy for family members to come along, only insisting that no one should feel pressured to be there (unlike what happens in cults). But he also emphasised that visits should not be used to satisfy emotional needs, such as for attention, friends, or the desire to belong: these should be met elsewhere. Jane and Mark both benefited enormously from this involvement. However, my wife Elizabeth, who had become wrapped up in her teaching career working in a primary school, was not remotely interested.

Shah listed politics as one of his interests and encouraged us to think more in the round about what went on, both domestically and internationally. He seemed to deliberately challenge the preconceptions we held about how we were ruled.

In1987, for example, a big scandal of the Reagan presidency was in full swing: the Iran-Contra affair or 'Irangate.' It had come to light that certain senior administration officials were secretly facilitating the sales of arms to Iran, which was subject to an arms embargo. Those officials then used that money to fund and buy arms for the Nicaraguan Contra rebels, who were waging a war against the Marxist regime in Managua (Congress made it illegal for the White House to fund the rebels directly). The people involved were being publicly cross-examined in open hearings. The topic of these hearings came up at dinner and Shah used it to point out flaws that were not obvious to us before.

'Democracy doesn't work,' he said. 'You cannot run a country with it.

Look at America for example: people from other cultures outside America look at the way they have their public hearings and don't for a moment believe that they are what they are. They cannot conceive of a country being run so openly and so they strain to try and understand what's *really* going on. It drives the Russians crazy. But doing things in the open the American way has a big drawback. It means that they cannot act decisively when needed.'

He explained how the mentality of Americans and Russians is similar in the way they both have abandoned their roots in the 'Old World.' Without proof or scientific justification, each had set up their own new worlds, totally convinced, as in the case of America, that theirs is 'Gods Own Country' and the rest of the world was just underdeveloped America, and, in the case of the Soviet Union, that their communist model represented the way all countries in the world would eventually be ruled. He said that he thought both these convictions derived from Christianity; in particular the belief that because you are 'right' you therefore have rights over other people, regardless of their thoughts and feelings on the matter.

A typical end result of such an extreme attitude could be exampled by the Catholic Church's crusade against the Cathars, the medieval gnostic Christian sect that flourished in the South of France and whose members strove to live lives of perfection, in stark contrast to the avaricious priests and powerful bishops who declared them heretics. Cathars appeared in the eleventh century, and their origins are something of a mystery though it is thought their ideas came from Persia or the Byzantine Empire, by way of the Balkans and Northern Italy. Because Cathars lived lives of simplicity compared to officers of the Catholic Church (by then the world's oldest religious institution), they were seen as a threat and the pope declared a crusade against them. He invited European knights and their armies to take part. The first major military action of the crusade led to a massacre in the town of Béziers where up to 20,000 men, women and children perished. The invading knights asked the abbot accompanying the crusaders entering the town how they would know who to slaughter because the Cathars were indistinguishable from other inhabitants. He is reputed to have replied, 'Kill them all, God will know His own'. So they did.

'People think that institutions are a mark of civilisation and are proud of them,' said Shah. 'But institutions only exist *because civilisation has failed.*' He illustrated this point with reference to the inefficiencies and hypocrisy involved in our parliament, Church, legal system and the academic and educational world.

He described our institutions as being the equivalent of corrals for restraining ungovernable wild beasts. We have institutions because we cannot behave honestly, humanely and from a body of real knowledge, he said. They are to us what barbed wire is to containing animals. Sincere people establish them in an attempt to restrain our appalling cruel and dishonest behaviour. But the trouble with that is that institutions stop civilisation from developing because they throw out any idea that men and women are perfectible.

Shah said he found our trust in institutions almost endearing, no different from the behaviour of natives in the jungle leaping about saying that one day they will invent antibiotics too but, in the meantime, doing nothing about it and carrying on using the voodoo. He often gave examples of how tyranny uses oversimplification to stop us thinking clearly in relationships, cults, organisations and governments. By contrast truly civilized people are honest, thoughtful and careful about the needs of others – not driven by greed, selfishness or vanity. When talking on this topic he also included tyranny within ourselves, in each and every one of us, as well as the tyranny on a larger scale.

Ever since Shah encouraged us to think about institutions my own experience – with the law, universities, civil servants, banks and the organisations set up to 'regulate' psychotherapy – has confirmed his observations. All institutions operate by schematization using rules, forms, questionnaires and now call-trees in an attempt to simplify and control everything. In fact in practice this generates bureaucracy and makes life more complex and frustrating. The reason for this is that the inspection regimes and procedures ignore subtleties and context because their modus operandi is to reduce activities to preconceived statistical formulae that are then mechanically enforced by applying pre-existing simple templates to complex and often ambiguous circumstances. This means that all our institutions are intrinsically tyrannical.

Bureaucracy, of course, takes away volition, undermines creative problem solving abilities and the need for individuals to take responsibility in the face of changing circumstances. Even if set up with benevolent intentions a bureaucracy creates absurdities and tries to organise them. In effect organising stupidity. Minds captured by bureaucratic procedures shrivel as they grapple with the processes and the red tape set up to ensure that people's behaviour conforms to what an institution decrees it should.

Consequently I now understand that whenever one seeks approval from an organisation one becomes its slave. Take the National Institute for Health and Care Excellence (NICE), for example. Although politicians and academics set it up with good intentions to try and address the damage being done by some practitioners of medicine, psychiatry and psychotherapy, NICE ended up stifling innovation and progress (this is certainly the case in the field of psychotherapy and counselling, an area with which I became familiar). The object was to raise standards but it confined practitioners who felt tyrannised into working to the NICE guidelines, which were drawn solely from academic peer-reviewed research and ignored practical experience and repeatable demonstrations. The peer review process is discredited partly because the research NICE relies on is often out of touch and out of date with what practitioners had found to be effective. If a technique or approach was not researched at great expense and published in a journal it was not to be used because it was not 'evidence based'. On top of that it is assumed by the general public that if a treatment is declared evidence based that there is an objective basis for it. But this is not always so. Researchers in all fields have a stake in the outcome of their research. This means they have a bias to confirm what they hope to find and ignore any information that might contradict their expectation.

The idea that there are biases, conflicts of interests and corrupt protectionism at all stages of the research process is supported by this comment by Richard Horton, the highly esteemed editor of *The Lancet*:

'The mistake, of course, is to have thought that peer review was any more than a crude means of discovering the acceptability – not the validity – of a new finding. Editors and scientists alike insist on the pivotal importance of peer review. We portray peer review to the public as a quasi-sacred process that helps to make science our most objective truth teller. But we know that the system of peer review is biased, unjust, unaccountable, incomplete, easily fixed, often insulting, usually ignorant, occasionally foolish, and frequently wrong.'

The only thing Horton leaves out of his list is that scientists desperate for funding are always seeking approval from journals to publish their papers, which means, in effect, they are slaves.

'Tyranny needs to be understood', said Shah. 'This is important. That's why examples of people tricking or overcoming tyrants are found so often in Sufi stories.'

* * * * *

Shah made a number of trips to the United States to observe that culture first hand. Americans, he said, like many people in the East, are prone to racketeering and adopting corrupt practices. The CIA, for example, is corrupt and largely unaccountable for its activities. This may stem from the 'hire and fire mentality' that runs throughout American corporate culture, which although it has advantages, also has disadvantages. It does stimulate some people to make effort and progress at work, but motivating through fear also has unfortunate and often cruel side effects on the workforce: one of which is to encourage people to cheat.

I remember him advising us after a trip he took to New York that if we were ever to go there we should remember to enthuse to its inhabitants about how wonderful the place is. He said he found Americans on the whole to be highly sentimental and that, just like the Russians, they love to be loved. On another occasion after he returned from America someone asked what advice he would give to people who had to deal with Russians. 'Swamp them with sentiment and emotion,' he said. 'The Russians are the most primitive of the Europeans – Upper Volta with rockets – a third world country with pretensions but prone to gloom. They behave in extremely stupid ways such as trying to export communism even when in their hearts they know it doesn't work, or being paranoid about minorities like the Jews. It's because they are so emotional that they cannot think things through clearly. That's why, despite their great natural wealth, their economy is in such a mess.'

But he also said he thought that there must be some people among the 240 million people or so living in the USSR at that time who could see more clearly. He suggested that perhaps there were leaders emerging at that moment who were making progress, albeit slow.

Shah's comment about Russian anti-Semitism led to a question about why the Jews in particular have been so persecuted. This was the essence of his answer: It could be because all Semitic people, with their exclusive cultures, especially Jews, tend to inbreed more than other peoples. Their strengths become concentrated and they become talented. But also, just as what happens when we breed racehorses, they become highly strung with a tendency to turn into specialists with narrow emotional views; hence more fanatical. The dangerous 'chosen people' belief that many Jewish people hold, for example, makes less talented but more tolerant people react against them. In other words, the Jews unwittingly bring the persecution on themselves. That creative talent goes hand in hand with an excess of emotional incontinence is well-documented and such people, though colourful and productive, often make life miserable for those around them.

He emphasised that we should remember that many groups are conditioned to think they are special, not just Jews. It's no different from Americans believing that they live in 'God's Own Country' and that the rest of the world is just underdeveloped America, or Catholics believing they are the only people who can enter heaven, or fundamentalist Muslims believing they have a right to kill those Muslims who don't share their views.

* * * * *

The Soviet war against Afghanistan began on Christmas Day 1979. It lasted nine years – three years longer than the Second World War. Shah was clearly distraught when the Russians invaded and over the following years he often returned to the topic of the Afghan War and made it the subject of his 1986 novel, *Kara Kush*. He mused on what might happen after the Russians left. A real civil war was unlikely, he thought, because Afghans are so fragmented: each valley and district has its own way of doing things and would not unite in countrywide civil war.

Skirmishing involving warlords and their devoted followers would always go on in Afghanistan – but that wasn't the same as civil war.

When it became apparent that the Russians were leaving I told Shah it surprised me because it meant it would be harder for them to steal Afghan mineral wealth to support their run down economy, which was a prime reason for the invasion. Shah said he thought they had no choice but to go because they couldn't stand the pace. 'The army is demoralised, run by fat cat European Russians who, when it came down to it, knew they were on a hide to nothing in an unjust war. And they weren't prepared to die for it, just as American soldiers weren't in Vietnam. They don't understand the Pathan attitude to fighting and death and the way Pathans disregard borders and government by diktat.

'Life among the egalitarian Pathans is a minute-by-minute affair. One minute they would cut your throat, the next they would lay down their life for you – literally. Their way of life probably has survival value that is unique to their environment. Pathans have little regard for material things and would easily give up their last possession in a gesture of good will, however poor they were. Life is so unstable for such people that they probably had to cultivate non-attachment to objects, including their own lives, because they are so easily taken from them.'

I found Shah's comments on Russian history and its people's character fascinating partly because when I was growing up my parents believed that communism and the Soviet Union in particular was the future hope of Mankind. Like many sincere people upset by the working conditions of the poor and the exploitation of cheap labour, they were influenced by left wing propaganda: 'one law for the rich and another for the rest' was a common refrain in our household as I grew up. *The Daily Worker*, published by the Communist Party of Great Britain was delivered regularly on weekdays; *Reynold's News* on Sundays. It was the Russian invasion of Hungary in 1956 that finally shook my father's faith in a communist utopia whereupon he switched to *The Manchester Guardian*, which soon changed its name to *The Guardian*.

The massive inequalities in the world between the rich and powerful and the poverty stricken labouring poor; the injustice and heartbreaking cruelty that continues to affect about a third of the world population today, was not solved by communism or socialism.

Here are some of the points Shah made in 1988 before the Russians finally withdrew defeated from Afghanistan, in February 1989:

Many Westerners think that Russians are an Eastern people but their history and culture has little to do with the East. Their love of classical music, ballet and European style literature all derives from Europe. Soviet President Mikhail Gorbachev and his wife are not Russians however. They are Tartars, a Eurasian Turkic people, who were traditionally looked down upon as inferior by the Russians. The opposition to Gorbachev in Russia was made up of the diehard old style communist regime supporters who use his supposed 'racial inferiority' in a smear campaigns against him.

Shah had spoken to Russian journalists who told him that Gorbachev was trained by the KGB and is the KGB's front man (he was former President Yuri Andropov's protégé – himself a former head of the KGB). In other words the KGB was Gorbachev's power base. Eduard Shevardnadze, the Georgian who Gorbachev promoted to foreign minister, was also linked to the KGB. These journalists believed that Gorbachev was placed in power because at least some people in the USSR were prepared to admit that the communist system wasn't working – and something drastic had to be done to break it up.

After the Soviet invasion of Afghanistan, Shah quickly became convinced that communism in Russia was finished. 'It just does not work!' he emphasised. 'In Russia they used to say that they had full employment but what that actually meant for large amounts of the population was that they actually only worked for half an hour a day.'

'Economically Russia is on its knees, partly because its people are so lazy. That's why when Russians go to work in the West they often return home because they cannot keep up with the hard work needed to keep a capitalist system going. What the people really got when they embraced communism was just another autocracy. Russia has never known 'democracy', which is the nearest thing to 'rule by the people' you can get, even though,' he added, 'democracy doesn't work very well either.'

Russia has always been ruled by autocrats and is bound to return to a more capitalist way of life – especially when they catch up with western technology and introduce personal computers into everyday life. That will mean it will become impossible for the rulers to stop people communicating with the 'outside' world. Once the communists lose control of the people's environment they have lost. In other words, once people are allowed to travel and get information from outside the Soviet Union, the regime cannot prevent itself from quickly crumbling.

People in the USSR once considered it an honour to belong to the Communist Party (not everyone belonged automatically as some people in the West back then believed). Of course Party membership was also a means to an end: promotions, better jobs and privileges. Shah told us that people were no longer bothering to renew their membership or even trying to join the Party. It was simply because, after 70 years, the system's failure could no longer be disguised: it was proven not to work.

Shah said he thought that Gorbachev was either stupid, not understanding the above, or, and this seemed more likely, that the KGB had decided that something sensible had to be done – and Gorbachev was their front man to try and bring about change for the better. He added that the KGB was the only power broker that was pragmatic, flexible and strong enough to overthrow the military and the Communist Party and bring about changes. The Party and Military couldn't do it because they were too set in their ways.

'Soon,' Shah predicted, 'the Soviet Union will be gone, a mere footnote in history.' And so it happened, as we now know.

When the military retreat from Afghanistan began it was largely due to the Russians being so easily demoralised. Their success against the Germans in 1944-45 was not because the Russians were brilliant soldiers but because of the ferocity of the Russian winter and the refusal of Hitler to equip his soldiers for it. Shah said, it was even harder for Russian conscript soldiers to fight in Afghanistan, a war that they saw little point in. They all knew that the Afghans were no threat to them and that they were only there for ideological reasons.

Capitalism works because it relies on human nature – greed obviously – plus it allows people who are good at fixing things to flourish, so they ensure, for example, that the electricity works and the disadvantaged are cared for. That's why capitalism was comparatively so successful, Shah said, and why Russia, with its common background with the rest of the Western world, was almost certain to head in the same direction as it tried to get its act together.

For many of us who were listening to Shah, it seemed incredible that a global power we had all been brought up to fear and that seemed such a permanent part of the world's political landscape would soon be gone. But everything he predicted about the ending of the Soviet era came true. Russians are now capitalists, more corrupt than Western ones. And autocrats still rule them.

'Russia is a terrible tyranny and could dominate the West because our leaders have no grit in them,' he said. 'America is weak – not in material weapons but in resolve and fearlessness. They run as soon as things get difficult.'

All of this we can see playing out dangerously today.

* * * * *

One evening Shah made us laugh a lot by talking about the Salman Rushdie affair. He said that an Italian author had written a scabrous book about Jesus and Christianity to make a name for himself – and lots of money – and he achieved both these goals. Rushdie, whose background was in advertising, wanted to do the same and saw that a good opportunity to do so was to write a book insulting Islam. He knew it would get a lot of publicity. So he wrote *The Satanic Verses*, which was published in 1988 and duly become notorious as Rushdie intended. But Shah thought it really foolish of him not to realise the effect his book would have and that his foolishness was rooted in the fact that he didn't really understand the East.

He told us where Rushdie comes from in India, Indian languages aren't much used. They only speak English. Although he writes about Islam and India he is not a real Easterner. But over here of course he was the delight of Hampstead's chattering classes who liked to support him as their token Easterner.

What happened in Iran when the Ayatollah got to hear of Rushdie's book was predictable. The way to manipulate people, as we all know, is to raise people's emotions. The easiest emotion to excite the masses with is hatred. Tyrants like Hitler and the Ayatollah knew this all too well. When the Germans were looking for a leader Hitler was able to take over by bonding most Germans together through hatred of Jews, telling them that Jews were filthy, disease ridden, dishonest and the cause of all Germany's misfortunes – which of course they weren't.

Ayatollah Khomeini – as became obvious to most people outside Iran – was quite mad. To keep his regime going he simply whipped up emotions using hatred: hatred of Americans, hatred of the West and hatred of Iraq. By raising the emotional temperature at huge rallies he bonded Iranians together in a common cause and that distracted them from the way the country was being mismanaged and the dramatic drop in the standard of living.

One of the reasons it was easy for the Ayatollah to whip up harsh feelings about Salman Rushdie was that, through no fault of Salman's, his very name was already a figure of derision in Iran. To Iranians, people who come from the area in Persia called 'Rushd' are characterised as stupid and laughed at, much as the English laugh at the Irish or the Americans at the Appalachian hillbillies. 'Rushdie' means 'from Rushd'.

A typical Rushdie joke goes as follows:

Each morning Rushdie said goodbye to his wife and went off to work. When he got home there was always a queue of men outside his door. And each day the queue got longer and longer.

One day Rushdie was complaining about his wife's behaviour to a neighbour who said to him, 'Why don't you divorce her then?'

'What?' said Rushdie, 'And queue up with all the other men?!'

It seems surprising that the 'Death to Salman Rushdie!' call, the Iranian clerical fatwa, had such a far-reaching effect. But what it did was to give those Moslems who responded to it in England and elsewhere, a purpose. It was a cause that gave meaning to their lives, which they had previously lacked. The innate need for meaning can be satisfied in the most perverse ways, as we see today with the cruel behaviour of those who leave the West to join the cult of the new 'Caliphate' in the Middle East with it's abuse of women and children, sexual slavery and random beheadings. Such cults always arise when war, mass unemployment or other disaster overwhelm populations.

* * * * *

Shah often spoke about how Westerners are not trained to think properly. 'In the West you don't value your freedoms,' he said. 'You have no sense of purpose. You don't want to listen, think and learn.' As someone who is a bit right-brained, and not always good at thinking things through logically, I found these talks most helpful.

'Your so-called thinking,' he said, 'has to be dressed up with entertainment and emotional arousal – although you don't realize it – and that effectively sabotages clarity of thought. You tend not to take in straight facts or information for example, unless it's from a source you respect, are amused by or like for some other reason that's irrelevant to the meaning of the actual objective information and the true situation.'

He thought that our inability to think is mainly due to religion. 'Your religion made the development of thinking difficult for you.' He went on to describe how this happened: in nearly all the years since the Christian power structure was established, it used emotion to control and exploit people. Contrary to what is taught in universities today this slowed the growth of Western civilization. The Church was not, and still is not, a spiritual organisation. People were bamboozled by the certainties it proclaimed and were conditioned to assume it could somehow do what it claimed it could: save souls. It was common for those representing the religious establishment, from Popes down to country priests, to issue dire threats of punishment if their supposed expertise was questioned. And they often backed up their threats up with force. Fear, being a strong emotion, is not compatible with human development. That behaviour stunted our ability to think and as a result held back the development of science and psychological and spiritual understanding.

Around that time I became fascinated with the history that Shah was drawing from and told him that I was attempting to write a book about the crimes of Christianity. He said that 19th century humanist historians had largely done this work already but, if I was serious about it, I should go back to original sources. He recommended I read, *The Testament of Christian Civilisation* by Joseph McCabe, which contained numerous translations of ancient documents delineating Church history, much of it culled from the Vatican library. I eventually tracked down a copy held by a lady humanist bookseller in Cuckfield village. After reading it I was left in no doubt that Catholic Institutions throughout the ages were self-serving and deeply corrupt. She also came up with a host of other books that she thought would be useful source material. And they were.

I gradually built up a collection of works illustrating how Christianity was an amalgam of much older Pagan beliefs and practices. I learnt of the role Christians played in the destruction of the great Pagan libraries of the ancient world, such as the one at Alexandria, and how their fanaticism led to bizarre abuses such as the famous episode known as Synod Horrenda when Pope Stephen ordered that the corpse of his predecessor, Formosus, who had been dead for more than a year, be removed from its tomb and brought to the papal court for judgement. Stephen had the cadaver dressed in papal robes and propped up on a throne so he could scream and harangue it for three days. Formosus was accused of violation of canon law, of perjury, and of serving as a bishop while actually a layman. Eventually, the corpse was found guilty, stripped of its papal vestments and Stephen then cut off the three fingers of the right hand that Formosus had used in life for blessings, and formally invalidated all of his acts and ordinations. The body was finally interred in a graveyard for foreigners, only to be dug up once again, tied to weights, and cast into the Tiber.

Although many authors since then have mined such material back in the 1970s it was difficult to find out about pagan teachings or the many shameful episodes associated with the Catholic Church and its suppression of information. Through most of its time of power it persecuted anyone who wanted to expand human understanding. It held up scientific and social progress for hundreds of years, suppressing the spread of literacy and learning, which it regarded as its exclusive domain. Its excesses and corruption made it a role model for hypocritical behaviour throughout Europe and, later, in South America, Africa and the Philipines.

As I read through this material I began to realise the size of the task writing about it would be and abandoned the project when on realising how many other writers had done a better job of it than I could do.

When Shah talked about religions he would often stress that they were not what they seemed to be to most people. Neither are they what believers like to tell us they are: vehicles whose rituals and moral teachings guarantee to bring people closer to the possibility of elevating themselves. 'You should look at what people actually do, not listen to what they say they are doing,' he said. For example, for thousands of years we have been brought up to think that in some way religions are 'spiritual' operations. They claim to be, but in practice they are not. This was because in order to begin a civilisation you have to get people organised, minimise selfish, brutish behaviour and establish commonly agreed levels of good behaviour that will benefit the community. So religions are attempts of wise individuals to prepare people for real development. When that is done and a general agreement as to what constitutes good behaviour has taken hold in a culture, there is some degree of civilisation. That is the situation we are in now.

A close look at Christianity as it operates today shows that it still teaches the training system for low-grade *uncivilised* people centuries ago. That, for example, was what the Ten Commandments were about: trying to establish some ground rules for civilised behaviour. Civilised Christians do not go around killing, raping, committing adultery, coveting, stealing, bearing false witness and so on. The originators of religions knew what Mankind needed in order to develop spiritually. But the means they used to do this – the rituals, teachings, conditioned responses – invariably fossilised.

The great value of religions in their early stages was that they take the 'drill sergeant' approach and knocked backward primitive populations into shape by bullying and frightening them into obedience. Once pacified they could be conditioned and entertained enough to keep them from regressing back to the primitive state. That was the role of religions: to establish cooperative and peaceful societies. Priesthoods were established to demonstrate by their actions how individuals in communities should look after each other, particularly the elderly and vulnerable, and supervise rituals to do with birth, marriage and death in order to bind people together. Religions have a clear role when used as organisations for getting Mankind to the first stage of cohesion. But once that's done and a culture is more civilised, they cease to have a useful function, other than to satisfy social needs – which is OK so long as people are honest about it and don't pretend that the social role is a spiritual activity.

Once people are organised and, for the most part, behaving in a civilised way, they can be moved on to the next stage, which involves thinking for themselves and gaining volition. Shah hoped it would be possible to do this but also said that reaching the next stage of what was possible for humanity was not guaranteed. This was because of the ease with which we can be conditioned and the selfish, predatory nature of what Sufis call the 'Commanding Self': the 'collective' of all primitive impulses and conditioned patterns that lurk inside us and somehow dupe us into thinking we are a cohesive personality with conscious volition, which we are not.

Shah had described the Commanding Self as 'a sort of parasite, which first complements the personality, then takes over certain parts of it, and masquerades as the personality itself.' Because it is concerned purely with its own survival, and is therefore selfishness in its pure primitive form, Sufis do not attempt to destroy or undermine it. Instead, would-be students are encouraged to 'divert vanity from the spiritual arena ... to channel the Commanding Self's activities to any worldly ambition while continuing to study the Sufi Way in a modest and non-self-promoting manner.' Otherwise the Commanding Self would prevent us from entering into a relationship with reality and keep us instead in a system that is not real. For example, our system of wealth creation has made us affluent beyond the wildest dreams of our ancestors but has not dissolved our greed; instead it has expanded it at every opportunity. Human nature, it seems, is largely unconcerned about changing itself, perhaps because greed continually focusses our attention on 'wants' and puts gratitude to sleep. Yet it is clear that nudging us towards changing ourselves was Shah's mission.

Once familiar with the Commanding Self concept I found it valuable in helping me understand my own and other people's behaviour. But it's not a pleasant experience. I have felt my Commanding Self coalesce as a sudden intense feeling of egotistical importance that wants to destroy anything that tries to get in its way. It is what makes attempting to combat my own deficiencies so challenging. I have also seen it emerge on the faces of others when they feel that the survival of their addictions; prejudices or belief systems are threatened. It's a look of primitive possession, like a cornered wild animal turning vicious to defend itself. (To see it just try confiscating a youngster's mobile phone.)

Sufis realised that to have a relationship with reality, a true awareness of it, requires that benign approaches be used to overcome the barriers to progress: some element inside us has to be subtly drawn out in such a way that it bypasses the Commanding Self so as not to alarm it. As Shah wrote clearly in *The Sufis*, 'Thought, not pattern-thinking, is the method. Thought must be for all life, not for small aspects of it. Man is like someone who has the choice of traversing the earth, but has fallen asleep in a prison. The complications of misplaced intellectualism hide the truth. Silence is a prelude to speech, real speech.'

Shah stressed many times, and endlessly demonstrated, that 'It is important to be analytical – even about people who are your friends or supporters. You need to learn to think.'

I also remember him saying that however dreadful a situation is, it's important not to lose your cool. 'It's a common western belief that every problem has a solution. However experience teaches that this notion is unfounded. Some problems can never be solved. Some situations you can do nothing about.'

He often highlighted common flaws in thinking such as believing that your 'tribe' is superior to another. In the past, he said, this belief may sometimes have been useful, necessary even. It could, for example, help a tribe to rally itself to survive in a hostile world, but there always comes a point where it drives a group to behave in unsuitable or cruel ways. Like when one type of religion believes it is superior to another, or superior to no religion, or when a tribe thinks it is a 'chosen people'. This same flaw also seriously damages scientific thinking because it narrows down scientist's focus so that they only look in certain places for solutions and will not admit non-scientists into their realm – even when it would be useful to do so.

Shah's clear statements about the harmful characteristics of human behaviour, our self-delusion and inability to analyse and be objective, all of which get in the way of approaching reality directly, deeply affected many of us who heard him speak about these matters.

* * * * *

Shah did not come across as anti or pro religion; rather he encouraged us to look at religion dispassionately. He devoted many evenings talking about this. The following is based on a few notes I made after one such time when Shah began by saying how the word 'religion' comes from the root *religare*, meaning 'to bind'. Yoga, the Indian word for religion, has a similar derivation. It means 'to yoke'.

I've already mentioned that he talked about how our inability to think clearly about politics, behaviour and culture is mainly due to our religious conditioning. For nearly 2,000 years as the Christian power structure spread it used fear and emotion to control populations and bind them to dogma. This had the effect of suppressing the emotion of curiosity about anything beyond the confines of church teachings in all but the most exceptional individuals – a modus operandi that made the development of thinking difficult. He emphasised that the Church was not a spiritual organisation, although its members always pretended it was, and still do. European populations were conned by this pretence and that also stunted our potential for growth and Shah developed this theme.

The moment that striving for Truth, for understanding – higher perception in any field of activity – ceases to be the main driving force in that activity, it goes bad. When that happens to an organisation it fossilizes. It can even regress to such an extent that it becomes malevolent. As well as affecting religious movements this fossilization process can occur in schools, universities, the military, political parties, businesses and banks. This form of degeneration can also be found in the arts, media, law and in personal relationships.

No serious person interested in higher perception and spiritual matters today, for example, would look to the Church for guidance. This is because perceptive people instinctively see the hypocrisy that emanates from unthinking displays of piety and the conventional reverence for dogma. It is hypocritical, for example, for preachers to tell others to behave better, stop fighting and live in peace, when they don't even know how to do this themselves, let alone know how to go about helping others do it.

Likewise no one who observes the pitiful contribution that the so-called 'fine' arts add to our culture today, or who listen to the egotistical babbling rationalisations of artists when describing their 'art', would entertain for a moment that they were striving for objective truth or higher perception. Mostly they just want to gain attention by shocking or entertaining people and make money out of doing so, which is fair enough if they were honest about it. When I heard Tracy Emin, famous for her unmade bed art installation, say that the purpose of art was to shock I thought, what a limited, unambitious, violent and low-level aspiration to have. Why have such low standards when one could have high ones? When creative types talk about things that they claim to know about – awareness, perception, spirituality and so on – we should be aware that it doesn't mean they do know anything about these topics: someone may know the word for 'gold' but that doesn't mean they possess any. Shah suggested that we should look again at why it was that some cultures abandoned the arts altogether. The arts are rarely an automatic path to greater understanding.

Institutionalised religion was the means more highly evolved people used to bring some measure of civilisation to primitives – to 'bind' them to civilised practises so that cultures could develop in a way that allowed for Humankind's horizons to expand beyond mere day-to-day survival. The wise people who founded religions did so in order to manipulate the superstitious in order to stabilise them and fit them for more complex tasks. A religion is a kind of nursery. The religious rituals and beliefs acted as Moses baskets carrying stories, myths and parables down the ages so that they could be used in later times by insightful people to help them transform themselves and experience the great truth: 'Man is the microcosm, creation the macrocosm – the unity. All comes from One.'

Shah said that occasionally individuals spontaneously access the truth but usually it requires a certain type of group effort under guidance to do so. More often than not spiritual behaviour is muddled up with religion, and attempts are made to copy what spiritual people appear to be doing – eat less, lose interest in power and material things, or serve the vulnerable, for instance. When such practises become institutionalised in monastic orders, cults or churches, the organisations and individuals cease having a civilising function and become rotten. Shah illustrated this with simple everyday examples, for instance, saying how he intensely disliked anyone claiming that an act of kindness or a show of humanity was 'a good *Christian* thing to do'. Kindness to others, helping an old lady across the road, is a normal human duty, nothing to do with being a Christian. Research with rats showed us that even they help one another. How absurd would it be to describe an act of kindness as a good, rat-like thing to do!

'Christianity needs updating,' he said, going on to discuss how, after the Korean War, captured American soldiers who were later repatriated began saying things about the US that American authorities knew weren't true. The government set out to learn what had happened to these men during their imprisonment. And this led to the modern 'discovery' (long known and described by Sufis like Al-Ghazali hundreds of years earlier) that people can be brainwashed of their beliefs and then conditioned with new ones opposite to those they previously held.

What Shah found strange is that this new psychological information wasn't being used to look more closely at our own belief systems such as Christianity, which practised a range of conditioning methods. If Scientology and the Moonies can be seen for what they are – cults – why can't Christianity? How can people in this country consider passing laws and legislation to curb cults when the State religion is obviously made up in exactly the same way? Shah said he wasn't aware of one single Christian who had decided to look for the spirituality in Christianity by the method of discarding all the mumbo-jumbo, which stands out so obviously, and then step back and examine what is left so as to see what 'truth' remains.

It seems that people loathe to apply well-known areas of information, like the ease with which we can be conditioned and how cults form, to anything close to them. This must be because of insecurity. But surely the thing to do is discard all such rubbish when new information comes to light and to continually look for anything that is real or contains something of value?

With Islam at least you have a 'laid down' religion in the Koran, so to speak, with rules for social behaviour clearly set out. Shah had no time for a religion like Christianity that takes things from other religions and asserts that what they borrowed came by divine inspiration, making it a natural part of their religion. This is something that occurred in the earliest days of Christian history as it adapted pagan symbolism into its belief system, and it continues right up to the present day.

In the 11th century the Catholic belief in 'Purgatory' or 'Limbo', for example, was taken straight from Shia Muslim beliefs. Also, the wedding bouquet, now considered to be a Christian offering, was originally an Islamic tradition. When it first appeared in Europe, it was denounced as heretical – until it was argued to be 'a symbol of purity' and became accepted.

Shah said he would have more time for Christians if they openly said, 'We've come up with this idea or symbol from somewhere and it seems to fill in a missing part of the puzzle,' rather than laying down the law and declaring 'divine inspiration' as the source.

Instead it seems the only way people adapt or change their religion is by making pronouncements that claim that the changes come from divine inspiration – thus giving authority to each element of belief, however ridiculous it is. Shah then said that, if divine inspiration really means something to Christians, why couldn't he, or anyone else, say to them, 'I've just had this terrific divine inspiration – that such and such is nonsense and should be replaced by the true situation?'

Christianity is really an authoritarian institution and as such hates changing unless it is forced to do so. There was a time when Gospel authority was claimed as justification for self-castration so temptation could be avoided. But things got out of hand and the population started to shrink and the Church had to come up with some quick 'divine inspiration' to stop men castrating themselves and encourage people to breed for the sake of the Church.

This 'borrowing' works the other way too. An early Christian symbol was a crescent moon and star – now a familiar emblem of Islam. Shah was talking to a chap once who had just built a huge mosque next to a cathedral and, wanting to overshadow it, stuck a huge gold crescent moon and star on top of the dome of the mosque. Shah said he wanted to tell him, but had to bite his tongue!

Another example from the early Christian history is that, when people wanted to get to heaven as quickly as possible, they committed suicide by leaping from church roofs, martyring themselves. This became such a problem that Christian authorities went in search of some more divine inspiration and found it – they made suicide a 'sin'.

Shah made it clear that his attitude to all this was that it was laughable – and definitely NOT spiritual. 'Whoever heard of men *deciding* what was a sin?' He said we should look more closely at our religion.

When the religious fanatics who declare themselves ready to die for their beliefs discover that people of other faiths are equally prepared to die for theirs, they simply announce that their enemies are inspired to die by the devil. Of course, because such behaviour is so extreme, it is now largely recognised as obsession, even by some Christians, something psychologically understood. But, he asked, why can't we look at the rest of Christian behaviour from a psychological viewpoint too?

Someone asked Shah, 'Why are people so loathe to change?'

This is the gist of his reply. 'There is a village near the river Nile where plans were made to run a railway through to save the villagers some six days journey to and from market to sell their vegetables. With a railway it was argued, this could be done in one day. After thinking about it and much discussion the villagers unanimously decided 'No!' And their reason? They wouldn't know what to do with the extra five days!'

Everyone around the table laughed at this. Except Shah. He got serious, 'Yes, it seems a peculiar attitude. You laugh, but ... *it is a reflection of yourselves.* In the West you are not trained to think properly. Newspapers print drivel, for example, because the writers, editors and readers can't think. This drivel swamp is getting deeper. But, by and large, you are getting what you deserve.'

He encouraged us to look for facts for their own sake and not merely to satisfy our emotional needs. He suggested we study opinions and learn how to distinguish opinion from fact by reading newspapers. This exercise would develop our ability to think clearly, which was especially important when studying books about Sufism.

He then advised those of us who wished to progress to think about what is missing from our culture: pointing out that, for some, travel is useful to help develop this ability. Not being able to see weaknesses in our own culture is a hindrance to progress. How many English people know for example, that in Pakistan large numbers of the population believe that all Western women are sexually 'loose' and easy game and that this belief rests primarily on the fact that Western women expose their teeth to all and sundry, a sure sign in that country of an immoral woman? That is one of the weaknesses of those Pakistanis, but in the West we have equally limiting beliefs.

Scratch the surface of someone, he said (using subterfuge, aggressive questioning or whatever is needed) to irritate them if you want to find out about his or her real character.

CHAPTER SIX

Leather, nails, thread, needle

One Saturday in 1978 Shah gave me a black and white photocopy of an illustration of a seated dervish wearing a big turban and resting his head on his knees in deep contemplation. He asked me if I would turn it into a cover design for his next book, *Learning How to Learn*. Whilst working on the image I thought about it. I came to realise that an important idea it illustrated was that learning does not only occur by way of conventional methods like studying from books and listening to lectures in schools, colleges and universities – but must also involve a special effort of deep contemplation of other people's experiences as well as one's own. And the method for doing this has to be absorbed. And absorbing the material Shah was publishing could help one do this in a non-obsessional way.

One Monday morning, also in 1978, I found myself again in Shah's study talking about another book he planned to publish, called *The World of the Sufi*. He gave me a design he wanted on the cover so I could produce artwork for the jacket. He then told me about the book's contents. It was to be a collection of papers he had gathered together that he felt were useful for study, although the range of subjects and their relevance and the competence and knowledge level of the writers varied enormously. It was to be a tool to help people look at their assumptions when they read it.

During the conversation he talked about one particular paper written by a psychiatrist, Arthur J. Deikman, entitled 'Sufism and Psychiatry'. He handed me a copy and suggested I begin reading it while he popped into the kitchen to make us some tea. This is how the paper began:

> 'The questions, 'What is the purpose of living?' and 'Why do I exist?' haunt modern Western civilization and the absence of an adequate answer to them has given rise to the 'illness' of meaninglessness or anomie. Psychiatrists, themselves, are afflicted with this same illness, partly because the problem of the meaning of life is solved by a special type of perception, rather than by logic – psychiatry is trapped by its commitment to rationalism.

My parents standing on the deck of the houseboat Dad converted from a ship's lifeboat. It was moored on the Thames at Eel Pie Island. They lived on it for several years before starting a family.

Playing around in Grandfather Cheshire's garden. Wheelbarrows were invented in China over 2,000 years ago.

With my father somewhere in the countryside after the war. The scenery is similar to where I now live.

With my sister, Jenny.

This was taken in our garden in Sutton when I was struggling to get back to playing the guitar again after wrecking my elbow. The injury prevented me from holding down chords properly for several years.

My daughter Eleanor recently found examples of practice pieces I produced at the age of 16 as an apprentice miniaturist. She took this photo of the galleon alongside her hand to illustrate the scale.

Enlargement of the galleon. It was painted on vellum.

An earlier attempt at painting flowers. My task was to paint the deceased favourite flowers in Books of Remembrence.

A miniature painting done for my own amusement and to impress my girlfriend Elizabeth. We spent a lot of time wandering around at night...

With Elizabeth at a reception in the 1970s for clients at our design studio.

My eldest daughter Jane, one of the first to understand the human givens ideas and help Joe and I produce the material to promote them. She continues to play a key role at Human Givens College.

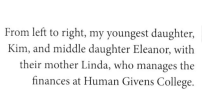

My son Mark as a teenager. This was taken in the Hameau de la Reine, the rustic retreat in the park of the Château de Versailles built for Marie Antoinette.

From left to right, my youngest daughter, Kim, and middle daughter Eleanor, with their mother Linda, who manages the finances at Human Givens College.

For my 70th birthday Jane had the inspiration to produce a dramatically large card made up of photographs of stages of my life and the family who meant so much to me. It was a moving and thoughtful gift with the bonus that it reminded me that I once had hair.

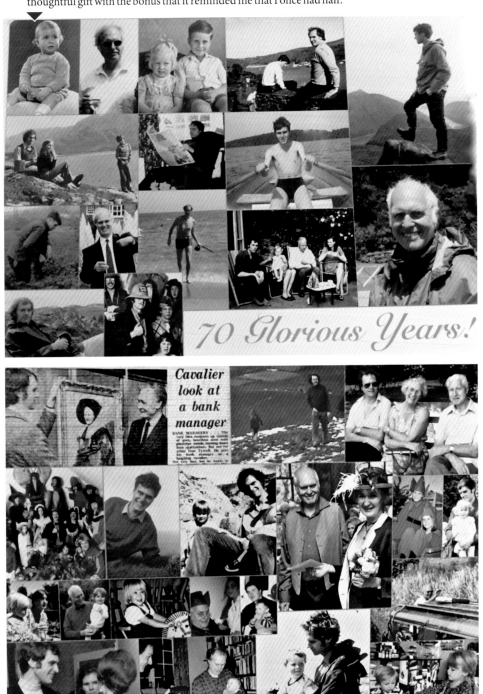

70 Glorious Years!

Cavalier look at a bank manager

Idries Shah. This was the photograph of him we most often used on book jackets and other promotional material.

Learning how to learn
by Idries Shah

My book cover painting for *Learning how to learn*.

Me inside the nuclear bunker at Langton. This was taken by Jonathan Cape's photographer for the book jacket of *The Survival Option*.

The bottom illustration was used for the cover of *The Tale of Four Dervishes* retold by Idries Shah's sister, Amina. The top one is a detail from an illustration I did for *World Tales*.

Doris Lessing who told me that there are things that we need to know about ourselves that might take generations to take root … ideas have to be planted.

▼

Symbolic book jacket. ▷ I commissioned a local airbrush artist to produce my design.

The People of the Secret

Ernest Scott
Introduction by Colin Wilson

SADI:
The Rose Garden
Introduction by Idries Shah

◁ Another painting Shah asked me to base on an Islamic original, this time for the cover of *The Rose Garden* by the immortal Sadi.

My painting for the cover of *The Dabistan of Mohsin Fani*, copied
from a detail of an Islamic original. I am forever in awe of those artists.

My illustration for the Indian story of 'The Lost Camel' in *World Tales*.

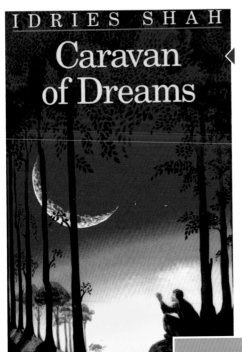

My cover for Idries Shah's *Caravan of Dreams*, which begins with a wonderful quote from Bahaudin: 'Here we are, all of us in a dream-caravan: A caravan, but a dream – but a caravan. And we know which are the dreams. Therein lies the hope.'

This is the book cover for the most up-to-date presentation of Joe Griffin's expectation fulfilment theory of dreaming, which throws new light on evolution and what it means to be human. The illustration was done by the brilliant cartoonist Michael Renouf.

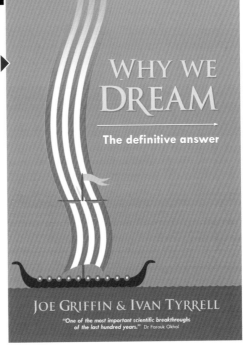

My long-term colleague and friend, psychologist Joe Griffin. We worked together for many years to make psychotherapy more sensible and effective, creating what *New Scientist* described as, 'A quiet revolution'

Joe and I preparing to speak at the first Human Givens conference in York.

Our book that has done so much to improve the practice of psychotherapy throughout the UK, Ireland and other countries. It was translated into Chinese.

GODHEAD
THE BRAIN'S BIG BANG

The explosive origin of creativity mysticism and mental illness

JOE GRIFFIN & IVAN TYRRELL

The jacket for our book about the explosive origin of creativity, mysticism and mental illness. The symbol on the cover is found throughout the world and represents the interdependence of both alpha and omega and the observer that makes the Universe manifest. A truth great mystics of all ages have intuited and quantum science has since confirmed.

I designed this mandala symbolising the oscillating universe in about 1970 and Fred Carver helped me produce a silkscreen print of it. Another example of a 'forward shadow' effect in my life?

A recent lunch with Fred Carver reminiscing about our student days.

Editing the *Human Givens* journal gave me the opportunity to meet many interesting people. This, for example, was taken in Desmond Morris's colourful Oxford studio, which is full of intriguing objects he has collected over many years, like the tribal virgin's loincloth I'm holding.

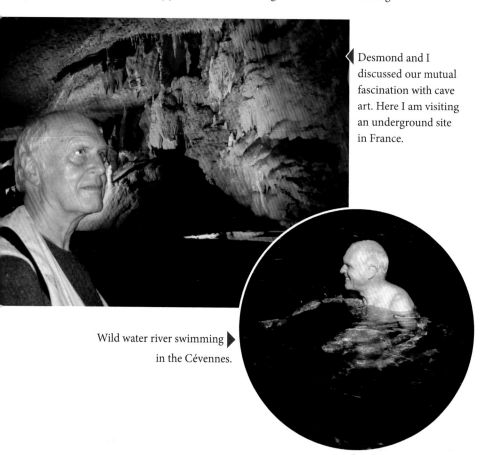

Desmond and I discussed our mutual fascination with cave art. Here I am visiting an underground site in France.

Wild water river swimming ▶ in the Cévennes.

With Véronique in Arthur's Pass, New Zealand.

My painting of a spectacular waterfall in South Island.

Enjoying the world famous Shotover boatride – I'm the bald chap in the middle at the front.

Three forest scenes in the beautiful Carpathian mountains of Romania.

Enjoying a visit to the ruins
of Volubilis in Morroco.

The pattern work and craftsmanship in Fez
blew us away!

Relaxing in a
Moroccan courtyard.

Véronique and I enjoying the sunset on the dunes at ancient Patara in Turkey.

Back home in the Cotswolds I've taken up painting again. I'll revert to childhood next no doubt.

'Sufism, on the other hand, is a tradition devoted to the development of the higher intuitive capacity needed to deal with this issue. By taking advantage of the special science of the Sufis, Western civilization may be able to extricate itself from its dilemma and contribute to the development of man's full capacities.'

In the paper Deikman described how the illness of meaninglessness and alienation from one another stems from the absence of a deeply felt purpose. Contemporary scientific culture has had little to say about meaning 'except to suggest and assume that man imposes meaning; he does not discover it.' He was saying that psychiatry lacks a theoretical framework that could provide adequate meaning for its patients, 'many of whom are badly handicapped in their struggle to overcome neurotic problems because the conceptual context within which they view themselves provides neither meaning, direction, nor hope' because it's set in the context of the modern, scientific world view of, 'an orderly, mechanical, indifferent universe in which human beings exist as an interesting biochemical phenomenon – barren of purpose. Survival is a purpose, but not enough. Working for the survival of others and to alleviate suffering is a purpose but it loses its meaning against a picture of the human race with no place to go, endlessly repeating the same patterns, or worse.'

When Shah returned with the tea I hadn't finished reading it so he told me to take the paper home as he had other copies. He wanted me to give it my full attention (Deikman's paper is easy to find online). Absorbing the contents had a big impact on me and provided one of the foundations for the attempt Joe Griffin and I were to make to try and drag psychotherapy out of the quagmire in which it was languishing and into the modern world.

On another of these Monday visits Shah said something that put me into a profound trance. I became still and could not move and was aware that I had questions in my mind I wanted to ask but couldn't. Shah sat equally still, looking at me, saying nothing. I have no idea how long it lasted, although it seemed to go on a long time. Eventually he ended it by saying, 'I think that's enough for now,' and I came out of the state feeling curious but too bewildered to talk about it. The incident was never referred to subsequently. Later he walked with me to where my car was parked to make sure I was wide-awake and fit to drive.

I have no idea if others had this type of experience with Shah.

One Saturday evening at dinner he spoke to us about an Eastern way of bringing up children. He said that in the East kids were encouraged to learn by making them perform recitations, and by praising their looks and abilities. This, he claimed, did far more for developing confidence than the English habit of not praising children. In England back then, for example it was common to hear adults say things as, 'Don't tell her she's pretty, it'll make her vain', or, 'Don't tell him how clever he is, it'll make him big-headed.'

Apparently it is easy to get children to memorise vast amounts of literature. Shah said he could recite the whole of the Koran when he was seven. And this approach to teaching children was quite common in parts of the East. He told us that there are remote regions where illiterate ploughboys can recite the entire works of Rumi and Saadi in the graceful tongue of the original. They speak, remember and understand it better than professors. And the consequence is that the richness of the material has an effect on them.

This complemented what he had said about how Western education is largely missing the experiential element whereby children and adults can gain experience through watching an experienced person, or even through being near that person. Real expertise and knowledge, Shah had said, can be passed on to someone else by just being around the knowledgeable person, especially if the learner really wants it and does not demand to be taught theory first. This is the basis of the apprenticeship system that I benefited from as a young man. At a deep level we all know this, which is why people are inclined to seek out and spend time with respected or powerful figures, even emulating them down to matters of detail. This is the reason why Sufis practice the exercise of companionship with admirable individuals. Nowadays, however, a corruption of this drive is the ubiquitous obsession with celebrities who are mostly nonentities who've succumbed to the delusion that they must be important because so many people want contact with them.

The logical, scholastic methods of learning, excellent though they are for some purposes, interrupt, or even prevent, the experiential way of study.

Because of this, wise teachers often seek out 'innocents' to teach, because those who are intensely trying to learn in conventional ways can only use those methods - the ones they were taught at school, university and in the home – and such ways interfere with real experiential learning, despite the fact that almost all of us are naturally equipped to learn experientially. That is the reason why we have to 'learn how to learn' in the spiritual field: the ways we are taught how to learn in our culture are not subtle enough to pick up advanced crafts or real wisdom.

* * * * *

One phase of my life was ending. This is how it unfolded. By now Elizabeth and I were absorbed in our work and living separate lives. We had both moved far beyond our romantic teenage selves and, with the exception of the children, who were now grown up, we had no common interests and that put a great strain on our relationship. So sadly we divorced. I gave my share of the house to Elizabeth and was free to move into the countryside, something she didn't ever want to do (never having mastered driving, which is an essential skill if you live in the countryside). Before we split I made sure Jane and Mark had obtained driving licences so they could set off on their own life journeys with cars I provided for them. Then I took a six-month lease on a cottage in Warninglid, a little village about 20 minutes out of Brighton. It was owned by a lady who was a published authority on Lord Byron and with whom I had long conversations. The cottage stood in her large garden and was a converted cow barn. I seemed to spend most of my time there bouncing my head from one low beam to another. It was the only period when I lived entirely on my own and I enjoyed it, apart from the accumulation of bruises and scabs on top of my skull.

I set about looking for an affordable country cottage of my own and settled on a semi-detached one in a village called Chalvington not far from Charleston Farmhouse, which nestled to the south at the foot of the downs and where members of the hedonistic Bloomsbury Group, champions of intellectual artistic individualism, lived back in the days. Two miles to the north of Chalvington at Chiddingly stood Farley Farm House where the photographer Lee Miller and the artist Roland Penrose lived for 35 years. Their home was a meeting place of some of the key personalities in twentieth century art. Visitors included Pablo Picasso, Man Ray, Max Ernst, Paul Éluard and Joan Miró.

During that period I became romantically involved with Linda Marchant who worked for me as a studio manager and secretary. She had split from her boyfriend and played a good game of badminton, which we both enjoyed. She moved in with me and eventually we married and raised two beautiful girls together: Eleanor and Kimberley. Eleanor obtained a degree in Psychology and was eventually to marry a fine Welsh musician, Huw, and they produced two delightful grand-sons, Mostyn and Gruff. Kimberley gained a Math's degree and, at the time of writing, is about to be married and I know she wants a baby too.

In the early part of October 1987, the world's stock markets were at record levels. By the end of the month they had crashed all around the world, not only in London but also in New York, Tokyo, Sydney and Hong Kong, where trading was suspended. The banks panicked and started calling in overdrafts. My graphic design business was wrecked almost overnight. A lot of our clients were in the construction industry, which had suffered dramatically from the financial chaos caused by companies riding high on borrowed money in the boom years, which were inevitably followed by a bust. Almost all of the projects we were working on for them were halted or indefinitely postponed. To avoid bankruptcy I had to lay off most of my staff, negotiate a personal loan with the bank to pay off the overdraft and move to smaller premises. It was a tough time.

That sixteen-year period of my life running my print and design studio was full of useful experiences but the thought of starting up again in the commercial world as the country recovered from the crash did not excite me. As well as many highs and achievements there had been also the usual downsides of working in business, and I was sick of it all. The strain of constantly having to find work to keep staff busy and pay their wages and the office rent, all for the sake of producing material designed to help companies sell things, wore me down. I became increasingly dispirited. The selling activity was supposed to be what made the world go round but I was never much good at it and no longer found it interesting.

However, new beginnings are often disguised as painful endings. In discussing with Linda how fed up I was she suggested I make a complete change of direction and develop my interest in psychology and writing. She had seen how much I had enjoyed researching and writing *The Survival Option*. Knowing I had an interest in hypnosis she also suggested I could augment that income by practicing as a hypnotherapist. I was galvanised by these two challenges and immediately felt better. I arranged for my old friend Fred Carver to convert the garage at the side of our little house into a two-roomed office/studio where I could write and continue doing graphic work for old clients. I vowed never to employ staff again.

This plan turned out well. Fred, who was one of those hands-on practical people, did a good job so I soon had somewhere to work. My remaining staff found other employment and I became a one-man band advertising my services as a ghostwriter in *The Lady* and *Country Gentleman's Magazine*. The advertisements soon lead to enquiries and the first of a series of commissions to ghost write memoirs. I charged £4,000 for the writing plus the cost of book production on which I also made a small profit. My clients were mainly wealthy enough to justify me asking for a 50% advance – a welcome alleviation of the financial pressures we were enduring at the time. I began each project by spending a couple of days with them making recordings of conversations we had about their life adventures. Linda was a brilliant touch typist and transcribed the tapes onto one of the first effective desktop publishing programmes, PageMaker, which was ideal for the purpose. I then organised the reminiscences and edited them into readable form. It was a way of working that was to serve me well later.

Involving myself in other people's lives so different from my own was wonderfully liberating and I gradually freed myself from the highly competitive world of design, marketing and printing, which, up until then had been the only way I knew how to earn a living.

The most delightful person I wrote for was Luchita, a lively 80-year-old Anglo Chilean lady. Her family commissioned me to capture the flavour of her amazing life. She was lovely, amusing and could recount a wealth of stories about her extraordinary adventures, many stranger than any fiction one could dream up. As a girl, for example, she had experienced being buried alive in an earthquake. Later, in the 1920s, she was travelling on a train that was brought to a halt by a blizzard, stranding her and the other passengers in a remote area of the Andes. The only way they could reach safety was by walking across the mountains. The outside world believed everyone on the train had perished. Their only hope was to struggle for days along the railway track from station to station through the deep snow, which they managed to do – but not without being robbed by bandits along the way. A few years later Luchita married the head of Royal Dutch Shell in South America and had an adventurous life travelling around the world with him. She was in England at the end of the Second World War when circumstances forced her to return across the Atlantic on a rust bucket of an oil tanker. During the trip she asked to be strapped into a chair on the deck so she could experience what it was like to endure the full force of a hurricane the ship was about to enter. The drama of the storm meant the captain and crew forgot all about her for several hours because the ship's outer skin had split in two and the boat lost all power. When the hurricane passed they drifted slowly towards Curaçao as the captain desperately tried to get the engine to turn the propellers so they could say it was still sailing under its own steam, otherwise salvage companies could claim it as their own.

And so it went, story after wonderful story. We produced a memoir rich in humour, romance, travel adventures and tragedy; it could have been a best seller. Unfortunately the family only wanted a couple of dozen copies printed for their private use; one of which I kept and still have.

Among other people I spent time with and wrote for was a fearless, hard working fellow who had carved out a large farm from scratch in Kenya; an unimaginative soldier who had fought the Japanese in Burma and couldn't remember anything of worth – but from whom I learned where the term 'doolally' originated (it was Indian army slang, from *Deolali*, the name of a town and site of a British military sanatorium where mentally disturbed soldiers were sent, hence 'gone doolally'); and a wealthy stamp collector who gradually revealed extreme misogynistic and anti-Semitic views to me as the work progressed. The family of that last man, knowing what he was like, became so alarmed at his intention to publish that they contacted me and offered to pay me handsomely not to finish the manuscript – an arrangement I was more than happy with.

Another book I ghost wrote was the memoir of an Indian named Ooma, who wanted his life documented, particularly his many seductions of white women who, as he put it, 'like a bit of chocolate', and his relationship with a wealthy family who kept a severely autistic 50-year-old man living in a plain, cell-like room with bars at the window in a mock castle with its own valley down to a private beach on the south coast of Cornwall. Ooma was employed there as a full time carer. His job was to feed, clean and exercise this unfortunate fellow. I visited him and his patient several times. This was my first encounter with autism and for background information and interest I read a number of books on the topic.

All these life stories made me feel my own life had been a little dull by comparison, but I was about to start a big adventure of my own.

* * * * *

While I was ghost writing memoirs Linda was pursuing the second part of her plan: to get me to earn money as a hypnotherapist. One day out of the blue she showed me a small ad for a course she had cut out of the newspaper and persuaded me to follow it up. I did so and began what was described as a 'professional hypnosis course' run over a series of weekends by the Association of Stress Management in Derby. It seemed to me to be a dismal affair run by a quack doctor who had bought his qualification in Malta. The course mainly consisted in giving us hypnotic scripts for different conditions that we were encouraged to read to patients. I managed to get out of paying for the course by doing a quid pro quo deal; offering to turn the scrappy notes he distributed into a presentable manual, which I did, considerably rewriting them in the process. A good thing about this work was that it obliged me to read widely about hypnosis and hypnotherapy.

To be fair I gained three important things from doing that course in Derby. One was that hypnotising people was easy, provided one had confidence in what one was doing. Secondly, anyone could hang up a shingle and start practicing as a psychotherapist. Before finishing the course I started advertising my services in Sussex through the local papers and in leaflets. My little office in the garage became my clinic. People came, and I found I was quite good at helping them.

The third thing I gained was that a woman there recommended another course that she said was much better and that she was going to switch to. It was on Ericksonian hypnotherapy and was run in London by an organisation called British Hypnosis Research set up by the talented Steven Brooks. She lent me a cassette tape of one of the lessons and the voice on it had a strong Irish accent. I learnt more about how to use hypnosis from that little cassette than I had the entire time spent in Derby. Since I was finding it easy to attract patients it seemed obvious that I should sign up for that course too so as to improve my understanding of the conditions people suffered from and how to treat them. Thus began a period of intense reading about Ericksonian hypnotherapy and attendance at other psychotherapy courses too.

I also considered what Shah had said about hypnosis. Once in his kitchen someone asked him about it and he said it was the easiest thing to do in the world and pointed at a spot on the wall saying, 'I could use that spot up there to hypnotise you except that hypnotising someone is not something to be done frivolously.' He had published material that showed that Sufis regarded hypnotherapy as the most elementary possible use of the hypnotic state and absolutely insignificant in comparison to its evolutionary purpose. Carelessly inducing the hypnotic state can be highly dangerous to a person's core being, which is obvious to me now that I know that all learning is posthypnotic and we are what we learn. Experiment and experience over many centuries taught Sufis this. And Shah said it was worth us investigating hypnosis.

Just how dangerous hypnosis could be was something I would soon find out for myself.

In an odd way it was Idries Shah that brought the Irish psychologist Joe Griffin and I together. Joe was teaching on the Ericksonian hypnotherapy course, which was held at St Ann's Hospital in North London and his was the strong Irish accent I had heard on the tape.

I encouraged my son Mark to do the course with me because I was worried that he had no skills with which to earn a decent living. He was drifting in and out of a succession of dead end jobs and I reasoned that, if he got interested in the subject matter and focused on it, maybe he could develop a career in this field too since one could practice in it with no formal qualifications. Anyone could set up as a therapist, as I had. So Mark did and he eventually went on to help a lot of people.

On the first day of the course Joe told a couple of Mulla Nasrudin stories that Shah had published so during the lunch break I asked him where he'd come across them. It turned out he had been reading Shah's books for a number of years. Joe was the first person I had met who devoted serious time to studying the material, wasn't in any group nor associated with Shah in any other way. Shah had often mentioned that there were people studying his writings who made more progress without meeting or being in direct contact with him and it seemed to me that Joe was one of them.

We continued our conversation over dinner that evening. He was a social psychologist with graduate and post-graduate degrees from the London School of Economics and had returned to Ireland after the 1987 crash that had affected his finances as drastically as it had affected mine. He was living with his English wife and two children in the small town of Athy, in County Kildare, and travelled to England to teach.

I told Joe that Shah had always encouraged people to study psychology and find out what scientists were discovering about human behaviour and that, to help me do that, I planned to publish a journal with a chap I met in Derby named Barry Winbolt. Barry had told me he had experience as an editor of a famous fashion magazine in New York. Like me he was in the process of changing careers and offered to help with my journal, which I planned to call *The Therapist*. The aim was to bring the best of orthodox approaches to mental health alongside the best of those complementary therapies that were excluded from the mainstream but that were clearly benefiting people, such as hypnotherapy, relaxation techniques and massage. My idea was that it would be a platform for clear thinking about emotional health, education and social issues. The aim was to try and weed out what was nonsense in both areas and extract what was useful in them. I felt that most therapeutic schools contained elements that sometimes benefited patients, though not reliably so. I also wanted to inject psychological findings that others and I thought were significant into the mix.

In this endeavour I was inspired by something Shah had said when he was interviewed in 1975 for *Psychology Today*. The interviewer, Elizabeth Hall, had asked him what, for the sake of humanity, he would like to see happen. This was his reply:

'What I really want, in case anybody is listening, is for the products of the last 50 years of psychological research to be studied by the public, by everybody, so that the findings become part of their way of thinking. At the moment, people have adopted only a few. They talk glibly about making Freudian slips and they have accepted the idea of inferiority complexes. But they have this great body of psychological information and refuse to use it.

'There is a Sufi story about a man who went into a shop and asked the shopkeeper, "Do you have leather?"

"Yes," said the shopkeeper.

"Nails?"

"Yes."

"Thread?"

"Yes."

"Needle?"

"Yes."

"Then why don't you make yourself a pair of boots?"

'That story is intended to pinpoint this failure to use available knowledge. People in this civilization are starving in the middle of plenty. This is a civilization that is going down, not because it hasn't got the knowledge that would save it, but because nobody will use the knowledge.'

Since it had become clear to me that psychological knowledge was not always being used benignly and that psychotherapy had aggrandised itself to an absurd degree – infected as it was with some really daft ideas, many of them dangerous – it occurred to me that we might do something about it. I intensely disliked the way useful information was either trivialized, fragmented and used for entertaining the simple minded. Either that or it was sucked into reductionist academia and written up in turgid ways that said more and more about less and less. I explained to Joe that I was looking for content for the first issue.

Next time we met, Joe brought along a copy of his thesis about why dreaming evolved, a topic he had spent twelve years researching. He asked me if I would read it, and perhaps publish it, because he had given up trying to interest academic publications in his ideas. He believed he had discovered something important and told me that Professor Hans Eysenck, who had read his thesis, thought he had too. At that time Eysenck was the living psychologist most frequently cited in science journals and he had found Joe's theory so convincing he wrote that it was, 'Much more acceptable than Freudian or Jungian notions' and 'his interpretation of their dreams is entirely reasonable.' Eysenck also advised Joe to present the theory in book form rather than as an academic paper so that it could be more clearly explained in terms everyone could understand.

I had read Freud's *Interpretation of Dreams* as a student and had a brief fascination with surrealism, but I hadn't asked myself *why* we evolved to dream or even thought that the answer might be important.

Dreams and dreaming are often referred to in Sufi tales and expositions. The great Arab historian, traveller, statesman and Sufi, Ibn Khaldûn, for example, in his 1377 introduction to his monumental history of the world, *The Muqaddimah*, described three types of dreams. There are 'clean' dream visions, he said, that come from God, 'allegorical' dream visions that are inspired by 'angels' (according to Sufis angels are higher human faculties of perception) and 'confused' dreams which are inspired by the material world. He wrote, 'When the spirit withdraws from the external senses during sleep, it can activate forms from memory which can then become clothed by the imagination in the form of sensory images.' He also described a technique for inducing spiritual dreams, which involved focusing a clear desire to have such dreams and the repetition of certain phrases, indicative of the 'perfection of human nature,' before falling asleep. He pointed out that this technique could only create a state of preparedness for such dream visions but provided no guarantee of receiving them.

Because Joe's thesis was written in an academic style, for me an exotic and almost impenetrable form of writing, it took a while to grasp the essence of his theory – that dreaming evolved to de-arouse unacted out expectations in the autonomic nervous system. (Academic papers always amaze me in that they are mostly concerned with preventing the communication of ideas and discoveries rather than spreading an understanding of them. But I've always been told that this was the way the system worked: always write in the third person to create the illusion of objectivity; reference every statement; qualify every thought and write formally. Boring!) I found Joe's ideas easier to absorb when listening to him explaining them.

On testing his theory with my own dream-life experiences I was soon convinced that Eysenck was right: this insight *was* a breakthrough and needed promoting as such. I also knew that the theory needed to be rewritten without academic jargon if it was to get wider recognition. So I set about editing it to make it more comprehensible. It had its first outing as a series of articles published in the first three issues of *The Therapist*. That was the beginning of our long and fruitful collaboration that resulted three years later in the publication of *The Origin of Dreams*. Joe chose the title to echo Darwin's *The Origin of Species* because he felt his discovery was equally significant in terms of the the development of mind. This was the first of many books and papers we produced together.

Following Shah's advice, before launching the journal I founded an organisation, The European Therapy Studies Institute (ETSI), and circulated a membership leaflet that also explained that members were entitled to receive the new multidisciplinary journal, aimed at all kinds of therapists – orthodox and complementary. As an added incentive I said that subscribers would be allowed to use our logo on their stationery. At the end of 1992 I persuaded several organisations to circulate the leaflet among their members and in no time enough money came in to cover production, printing and postage of the first issue. My goal was to publish the first issue in April 1993, which we achieved. And thus began the most productive period of my career. I'd never worked so hard as I did in the twenty years that followed. Much of what we published reflected my wish to use the psychological knowledge that Shah had drawn our attention to and that was widely available but largely ignored. The journal was to be a corrective to counter the general ignorance about psychology and the New Age guff that mesmerised – and still does – so many people.

As well as Joe's dream theory and numerous other articles, the first issue featured an interview with the child psychiatrist, family therapist and prolific writer, Robin Skynner. He had just published *Life and How to Survive It*, which he wrote with the comedian, John Cleese, and was supportive of my project. Twice, at his invitation, I spent several hours at his home in Hampstead Garden Suburb where he offered advice, ideas and contacts to help ensure *The Therapist's* success. Looking back it amazes me now to see how much of the way we were to develop our ideas about psychotherapy – our working methods and preoccupations – were being indicated to us in these early interviews with different people. For example, when I asked Robin what he and John Cleese had learned from writing their book, this is what he told me:

'This is something we didn't talk about in the book. I wish we had now. We started the process by brainstorming. We sat around the table or went for walks with the tape recorder and just free-associated about it all. John has this incredible capacity to turn absolutely everything upside down. He just pillaged and destroyed the knowledge I had spent decades learning. He kept coming at what I thought I knew from totally new angles – this zany lateral thinking of his. He forced me to re-jig all my thoughts and look at everything afresh from underneath rather than on top.

We also tried to boil *every* idea and word down. He was insistent that what we said should be in simple language, so that everyone could understand it. No jargon. This turned out to be important. We found that, because we were trying to express everything in simple language, we had to take everything to breaking point to sort it out. We reached down to a deeper level of simplicity, to the foundations where everything began to follow from simple principles. This meant that, although we started out trying to write an outline of existing knowledge, we actually ended up with an *integration* of existing knowledge – something that had never been achieved in this field before, and can't be achieved at an academic level because there is not enough agreement.'

This, of course, is exactly what, unbeknownst to me at the time, Joe and I were to do over the coming years. Robin went on to say:

'The other interesting thing we did was that, in order to understand more, we examined ourselves for any signs of any particular behaviour we happened to be looking at. For example, we would talk about schizophrenia and autism and I started to discover that I had elements of schizophrenic and autistic behaviour in myself. We really lived the book. I went through periods when I felt quite schizophrenic and quite autistic and came to realise that these states were part of me and, somehow, health has something to do with integrating all those elements at different levels and having access to them. John didn't have that experience exactly but he does remember getting bogged down and writing terribly slowly in the section on depression and then racing through at top speed when we were working on mania! We worked on these two books for thirteen years and both of us changed enormously as a consequence. It was a continuous process of editing and refinement. There were six or seven drafts.'

In a few words Robin had described exactly the way it turned out that Joe and I were to produce our books whilst creating our own approach to psychotherapy as we developed our understanding of hypnosis, autism and schizophrenia and puzzled over why human beings evolved to be susceptible to experiencing these states.

The second issue of *The Therapist* featured an interview with the inimitable Spike Milligan where he spoke about what it was like to live with mania and deep depression. After a few more issues, storyteller Pat Williams, whom I first got to know at Langton back in the late 60s, agreed to write a regular column for us and that became a popular highlight. She always thought carefully about every word and phrase in order to make her readers think differently about any topic she addressed.

From then on it was not difficult to find contributors and people to interview.

CHAPTER SEVEN

Doris Lessing and indoctrination

THE THIRD issue of the journal included a long discussion with Doris Lessing. I had enjoyed many long chats with her whenever we met at Langton, including about mental illness. For many years she and I were in the same group in London studying Shah's material and I got to know her quite well and was invited to some of her London soirées where Hampstead literary types gathered. At one of these, after *The Survival Option* was published, a lengthy argument about civil defence developed with me pitched against the left-wing journalist Paul Foot, who was a long time member of the Socialist Worker Party and nephew of an ex-leader of the Labour Party, the MP Michael Foot. Doris loved this passionate but, to my mind, pointless debate saying, 'Isn't it exciting! Just like the old days,' referring to her political life as a young intellectual communist. For me, though, there was little point in talking with intellectuals who are so certain in their viewpoint – even if they were famous. But they were fun to observe.

I read several of Doris's books and found them exhilarating. Here is a often quoted passage from *The Golden Notebook* that I really liked because it summed up so well my feelings about education:

'Ideally, what should be said to every child, repeatedly, throughout his or her school life is something like this: 'You are in the process of being indoctrinated. We have not yet evolved a system of education that is not a system of indoctrination. We are sorry, but it is the best we can do. What you are being taught here is an amalgam of current prejudice and the choices of this particular culture. The slightest look at history will show how impermanent these must be. You are being taught by people who have been able to accommodate themselves to a regime of thought laid down by their predecessors. It is a self-perpetuating system. Those of you who are more robust and individual than others will be encouraged to leave and find ways of educating yourself – educating your own judgments. Those that stay must remember, always, and all the time, that they are being moulded and patterned to fit into the narrow and particular needs of this particular society.'

I don't know if she wrote that before or after meeting Shah but it certainly chimed with what he was saying at the time. For example, in *Reflections* he wrote, 'Man does not have a capacity of instant comprehension. So rare is the knowledge of how to train this that most people, and almost all institutions, have compromised by playing upon man's proneness to conditioning and indoctrination instead. The end of that road is the ant-heap: or, at best, the beehive.'

Here is an extract from the discussion we had that I recorded in her kitchen as Doris cobbled together a simple lunch for us both (the full discussion is available online). It gives a flavour of how we were thinking back then, our interest and respect for what Shah was doing and why she thought our journal was a worthwhile project.

Lessing: There are other things about ourselves we don't notice because they're taken so much for granted. Politics, for a start, which seems to become more and more like theatre and less and less to do with real information. Politics has become an entertainment similar to gambling. Look at our ridiculous election days for example, where we sit up all night watching all the prediction apparatus, trying to find out who will win, a fact we will all know anyway at 8 o'clock the following morning. The nation is locked into a gambling mentality.

Tyrrell: I think it's all part of raising the emotional temperature, using anything that is happening for emotional excitement, which we then mistake for 'being more real'. But then we are being manipulated. And even the manipulators don't realise what they are doing.

Lessing: True. The common denominator is the emotional temperature. When Idries Shah, began introducing into the West new ideas from the spiritual and psychological tradition of Sufism, he said to me a long time ago that he had observed that our Western culture is soaked in two assumptions: that politics and sex are the solution to everything. We never examine this so we don't know the extent by which we're manipulated by these assumptions. The corollary is that we find it extremely hard to look at previous cultures because they didn't have these assumptions. Past cultures operated by completely different sets of expectations and demands than those that operate us today. Now I believe we have to add two other stimulants, crime and killing, to these assumptions. These are major voyeuristic features of television programmes every night. They are now doing real life reconstructions, lovingly recreating horrific crimes, two or three times a week. Even serious newspapers regularly include 'real life crime'; stories in grizzly detail because they know it sells papers.

Tyrrell: Shah also said that, when he was younger, he had expected Westerners to take on board with enthusiasm all the information that modern research was revealing about human behaviour. He said this was a necessary precursor to further human development and had hoped it would happen much as the world absorbed the necessity for hygiene in the 19th century. But, over the years, he found this information wasn't being absorbed, except in highly selective ways that unbalance us. He thought that the main reason for this was that the truth about ourselves is not emotionally exciting enough for people today.

Lessing: I know; I find this when I am interviewed. An interview is usually a map of the mind of the interviewer. I can go through the whole interview replying to questions that totally bore me. The interviewers usually say, 'What would you like to talk about?' And I say, 'Well this is what really interests me...' And I might like to talk, for example, about the discoveries of Edward T. Hall that he wrote up in books like *The Silent Language*, and *The Dance of Life*. His books are full of revolutionary observations about what we are like – he explored the unspoken ideas behind cultures and the rhythms of time and life – but he is hardly known. But the interviewers' faces fall and they quickly steer me back to my childhood, feminism or how many words a minute I write.

Tyrrell: Have you ever tried to talk to interviewers about human behaviour?

Lessing: Yes. They are not interested.

Tyrrell: And they don't publish it?

Lessing: Not only that, I can see they literally don't hear what I am saying.

Tyrrell: Have any of them asked you in any depth about your interest in what Sufis have observed and know about culture and human behaviour?

Lessing: Not really. The nearest some of them get is to say, 'Oh I hear you are a Sufi.' And by that you know immediately that they are quite ignorant of the subject. They, if they have thought about it at all, probably think Sufism is a cult – an easy mistake to make because there are many cults that call themselves Sufis. So then I stop them and what I say now is, 'I've been studying this for a long time. It's what interests me more than anything else, but I don't want to make a series of cliché remarks which will be then misunderstood by you and your readers.' And then I tell them that people who are really interested will find the necessary books that are freely available. That does the trick – they usually have amnesia about even having asked the question!

But sometimes I meet people as I travel around who are more serious and have studied the material and it has struck a chord in them. In Singapore recently I met two ordinary young men who wanted to talk about Shah's work. I can meet such people any-where and can talk seriously about it. But interviewers are gener-ally not interested in ideas and knowledge, not really.

The observations and evidence that Shah has presented about the way the world really works I continually find astonishing. Many of his ideas are now common currency. Thirty years ago they were unknown and, unless you can remember the shock of hearing these ideas when they were new to us, you cannot credit it because we think we've always thought like we do now. I see them around all over the place now. For example, he was the first to draw attention to all the different levels of importance of giving and receiving attention, and distinguishing the difference between *wants* and *needs* – which seems familiar and obvious now, but was quite startling and new in the 60s.

And the idea that most of what we do is fuelled by greed, even acts that appear altruistic, is now quite common but it wasn't at all then. When a new idea starts floating around I often think that it is something we first heard from Shah not so long ago, or it's in one of his books. I think the way he deliberately put ideas into our culture is an astonishing cultural phenomenon.

Tyrrell: It was a sort of seeding process wasn't it?

Lessing: Yes it was. There are things that we need to know about ourselves that might take generations to take root, but the ideas have to be planted. It's certainly happening. But few people notice, or are interested in, long-term changes to whole cultures, changes that take generations to occur.

Tyrrell: But certain types of people are attracted to the larger view. It's one of the reasons the best of science fiction is so stimulating.

Lessing: Yes. And the rises and falls of civilizations provide a quite distinct excitement from the 'little girl having an emergency operation' type of story that we have evolved to get excited about. An observation I think about often is to the effect that, 'Once we played with toys but now our toys play with us'. It's true! From cars to weapons! TV to computers. Everything! Our lives are determined by our inventions, which is why the Frankenstein theme is so popular.

Another thing that interests me is the fact that we have binary minds. We always have to have an 'either/or'. I see myself and others affected by this all the time. For example, if I'm giving a lecture, invariably half the questions begin, 'Mrs Lessing, do you think this or do you think that?' 'Is it A or B?' And I say, 'Well, it's both, or something else entirely.' This satisfies nobody.

But this is how we think! We take some element out of a subject or person and use that to label it or them for ever after. It's as if we can only have one idea or fact – so we have to choose. We can't have a rich pattern in our minds about the subject or person; we have to have a single label that we can refer to all the time.

Tyrrell: It is unusual to find people who can look at someone and see a pattern. We're tremendously influenced by first impressions. When we meet somebody for the first time, if they happen to be angry or sad or laughing or frivolous, that is the impression that colours our lifelong image of that person. Later, when we know them much better, we still judge their actions against that first impression.

Instead of looking at a person and saying, 'This is a person who at this moment is laughing,' and knowing, as we all must know intellectually, that this person must have a vast hinterland of other behavioural reactions in different circumstances, we still work on this ridiculous labelling assumption.

Lessing: And we can't make much progress while we simplify everything like this. But I wonder why we do it?

Tyrrell: It's left brain functioning. I suppose it had, and still has, its uses. I mean, you can get on if you remove doubt by labelling things, even if the label doesn't bear scrutiny. The trouble is, most of the time we are not aware we are doing it.

Lessing: It's easy to see it going on in another culture. In China it is so obvious. I went there recently and they have a slogan for absolutely everything. They never seem to analyse a problem, they reduce it to a label. 'Let a thousand flowers bloom...' or something similar. I spoke to a Chinese official there, one of a whole group of young directors and writers, and I said that, from the outside, China struck us as a culture that swung very easily from one extreme to another...

Tyrrell: ... like a vast shoal of fish, all moving as one...

Lessing: Yes. Immediately the Chinese in the group started laughing at me because they knew that I meant that, at the moment, they were in a liberal swing. And they told me about the story of a friend of theirs who had written a novel about the awful state of morale in China's army where the soldiers have just about as bad a time as Russian soldiers. This novel exposed the situation – he was allowed to write it because openness is supposed to reign now. But it was sent back from the censor with the following remark – 'Not every writer can be published. Not every book can be printed.' And that was the end of that. Everybody accepted it! That's what they are like. They have got labelling down to a fine art.

Tyrrell: That's worrying, the Chinese are going to have so much power over us soon.

Lessing: They don't give a damn about Europe and the things we find important. They have a saying which I find rather endearing. Every time they are criticised about ill-treating people or whatever, they will say, 'Ah yes, the Yangtze River always flows East, as they say.' And that's the end of the matter.

My father used to say that people like me have no idea at all of what the minds of people were like when he was a child. He was brought up in the country near Colchester and said that people then didn't think about the world much at all. And if they thought about something happening in Europe, it was quite rare. What they thought about was the local scene – who is going to win the race in the next school picnic etc. And going up to London was a great treat. This provincialism was what a person's mind was like. And that must have been true for the whole of Europe, unless you were very rich. Then the First World War changed everything. Suddenly the outside world exploded into everyone's consciousness and there were films, radio, and so on. He said that, between his mind and his father's mind, there was a total gulf and between his mind and my mind was a total gulf. His father would not have believed that anyone could go to the moon. He would have just laughed at the idea – and at television and so on – all facts that we now take for granted. Now we think we know everything that happens everywhere in the world. But this deceives us because we have no idea what's important. There is nothing in us that really knows how to select those bits of information that are valuable. It's all on a par. Sadly, the way we entertain new ideas seems to depend almost entirely on whether they are exciting or not.

Hardly anybody is interested in real information.

Tyrrell: People do get interested in little exciting bits, especially if they can be marketed, like NLP or 'How to Use Both Sides Of Your Brain', just little pieces of information really, but people build careers on them.

Lessing: Edward de Bono did just that with 'lateral thinking'.

Tyrrell: I know. Many people do it. Trying to exploit information instead of just absorbing it is one of my difficulties!

Lessing: For years my problem has been that I am much too emotional about everything and this over-emotional response is a great enemy. As you say, emotion stops us seeing what's really going on. But I don't know, you see, how much like other people I am. Am I worse or just the same? Is everyone so emotionally orientated? I don't know.

An interesting thing happened when I gave a lecture to the Institute of Cultural Research on 'Barriers to Perception'. I listed ten barriers to perception, one of which was guilt. Now, come question time, nobody asked a question about anything but guilt! People still stop me now and say, 'Remember that lecture you gave about guilt?' This is astonishing to me! What are we so guilty about? Why are we all so ridden with guilt? What is this about? Maybe it's the embodied accuser again.

Tyrrell: I wonder if it's because we are not doing something which some part of us, deep within, knows we should be doing?

Lessing: Well, I think that's possibly true. With these emotions I've got myself now to the point where I am able to watch them proliferating away and can detach from them. But it isn't easy. Shah once said that, if you are in a state of terrific emotion, it's possible and useful to switch to another mode by, for example, doing an arithmetic problem in your head, or something very unemotional like listening to arousing music, then switching it off and doing a crossword puzzle – you use a completely different part of your brain.

Tyrrell: To do that on command would be wonderful, wouldn't it?

Lessing: Yes. But I find it almost impossible, although I am better at it now. The interesting thing is that I wrote that tip down and forgot all about it until I re-read my diary last month. I had completely forgotten!

Tyrrell: Well, that's probably because the emotional part of your mind doesn't want you to think about it. It feels threatened and is protecting itself.

Lessing: Do you think everybody lives their lives in a tumult of emotion in one form or another? Because, if so, it's a pretty horrific thought. Even the so-called intellect is emotional. In fact, in my experience of intellectuals they are very emotional.

Tyrrell: A lot of intellectual activity seems to me to be a strategy for suppressing or dealing with emotions, and the emotions often cause intellectuals to behave in peculiar ways, which is why they so often appear, despite their 'cleverness' to be blind to the obvious. It's an unthinking strategy. Although it's intellectual, it's done automatically. We can't help doing it.

Lessing: Yes. The sad thing is, all these issues about human behaviour are so important, and so fundamental to why people get ill, anxious, sad and behave criminally, that they ought to be looked at calmly and scientifically by more people and talked about more widely. But these issues are not explored much on TV or in other media, and yet they are far more important than politics or the arts. That's why what you're doing in the journal is so valuable.

After interviewing Spike Milligan and Doris it was easy to get others to submit articles or agree to be interviewed. Fay Weldon, who had made an attack on 'Therapism' as she called it, and Ernest Rossi, who had edited the four volumes of Milton H Erickson's, *Lectures, Seminars and Workshops* were among them. As was Robert Ornstein, who wrote *The Psychology of Consciousness* – a hugely influential book that drew the attention of a mass audience to the discoveries about the different thinking styles of the right and left hemispheres of the brain. In it he used stories Shah had published to illustrate various points. Ornstein also appeared at Langton a number of times and went on to write up a number of the ideas Shah introduced, including how our brain operates as a 'multimind,' composed of different selves, each largely unaware of each other.

CHAPTER EIGHT

Cults, hypnosis, illusions and sex

MICHAEL YAPKO, an American psychologist who had written extensively about treating depression and anxiety disorders using hypnosis, gave me an interview about those topics and we got on really well. He invited me to do his one-week course on hypnosis and its uses, and, towards the end of it, we had an interesting discussion about suggestibility. I told him of my surprise at how little psychotherapists seemed to know about it. He told me he was researching how people in America were being influenced by psychotherapists to believe that they had suppressed the memories of being sexually abused as children. He was writing a book about it.

I then told Michael that I thought this was happening in the UK too, giving the example of how at our office we had recieved a disturbing pornographic document from a worried psychiatric nurse. It was a training manual for a new school of 'therapy' known as Primary Cause Analysis. This young man claimed that NHS psychotherapists were among those being trained in Primary Cause Analysis, but he was nervous about giving this obscene manual to me because before doing the course all the participants had been made to sign a document agreeing not to show it to anyone. He was worried about being sued. He only decided to do so because of what happened to him.

Hypnosis was used a lot on the course apparently, and all the participants were encouraged, while in trance, to uncover their own repressed memories of their parents sexually abusing them. The reasoning behind doing this was the old canard from psychoanalysis that therapists couldn't be expected to help others unless they had first resolved their own 'issues'. He told me that, because he had never got on particularly well with his father he came to believe it might be true that his Dad had abused him.

'But then they started asking me to remember my mother abusing me, and that did it! The idea that my mum did any of the things to me that they suggested brought me out of trance and I just knew none of it was true. Including about my Dad.' He suddenly felt frightened that he was being brainwashed and given new memories and beliefs and so he determined to let someone know what was going on.

On investigation we discovered that a completely bonkers hypnotist named James Bennett, a New Zealander who claimed that virtually everyone is sexually abused in early infancy and that the entire human race is in denial of this fact, had launched Primary Cause Analysis on the world. His mad ideas – derived from an extreme interpretation of Freudian theory – were spreading around the world and by 1987 had reached the UK. Without supplying any evidence, his bizarre training manual described 39 different abuse scenarios, which were stated to have been practised openly and performed as rituals until 2,800 BC - after which time all societies around the world banned them. Since then he declared, most children have been victims of sexual abuse but they and their parents repressed their memories of it.

The manual describes this imagined abuse in lurid, graphic 'matter of fact' detail. One of its most startling claims was the assertion that 98% of all cot deaths result from a mother holding her infant upside down by one leg inducing an act of 'double oral sex', an appalling suggestion for anyone who had suffered the tragedy of a cot death. In the manual it said that behind almost every problem for which people seek psychological help are repressed memories. Such common problems included asthma, diabetes, acne, stammering, sore throats, left handedness, headaches, cold sores, blushing, shyness, nail biting, stage-fright, yawning and hysteria. The 'analysis' involved hypnotic 'recall' and 'reliving' the abuse scenes, which, it was said would resolve the patient's problems.

Clearly the chances were high that a percentage of people generating illusory memories by the hypnotic creation of violent scenes of incest during babyhood, which they then become convinced really happened, would come to believe that they were seriously and permanently damaged by abuse. They might then make allegations against innocent people, causing families to break apart and the law to become involved. That was clearly happening and many stories were emerging about satanic abuse, alien abduction and childhood abuse – all involving psychotherapists or counsellors who themselves believed this was real. The sincerity of crazy psychotherapists – true believers – is no different from that of fundamentalist religionists of all persuasions who declare that God is on their side as they torture and kill one another.

The Primary Cause Analysis tutors were members of British Association of Counselling (now the BACP), the United Kingdom Counsel for Psychotherapy (UKCP) and The British Psychological Society (BPS). So we contacted those organisations, described the dangerous training programme to them and how it would harm the public. But none of them would condemn the cult-like training or take their members to task for teaching these malignant ideas. I was astonished at the lack of interest and so decided to show journalists the manual.

The BBC had a documentary TV series running then called Inside Story and one of its producers decided to make a programme about how some therapists were creating false memories. I helped him all I could, showing him the obscene training manual, drawing his attention to such awful books as *Courage to Heal* that had done much to foster this poison, and explained how in my experience most therapists had no idea about the dangers of hypnosis and how suggestible people are.

I also managed to get an article about Primary Cause Analysis into *The Sunday Times*.

While all this was going on I organised a conference in London to alert the media and the public to the problem. Thus it came about that our little European Therapy Studies Institute staged the first major conference in the UK on False Memory Syndrome with Michael Yapko as the main speaker. It was held at The Royal Society of Medicine in May 1994 with the title, 'Suggestions of Abuse'. Our aim was to point out how a startling proportion of psychotherapists, psychiatrists and other professionals were ignorant of how suggestible people are and did not realise how subtle cues can steer our memories away from what people really experienced, thus unwittingly leading their patients to believe they were victims of sexual abuse. The most sensitive issue arising from this debate was that those genuinely guilty of child abuse could use the 'false memory' argument to hide behind. Therefore therapists creating such situations were likely to increase the probability that victims of abuse would not be believed.

Several journalists attended, resulting in many articles in the media. For several years, whenever the topic of false memory came up, journalists and TV programme researchers would phone us for comments. But most of them were not interested in publishing quality information about hypnosis, suggestibility and behaviour: they just wanted personal horror stories.

Families suffering from the spread of this fashion for 'recovering' memories of abuse also got in touch and many of their stories were heart-breaking. We were also pestered and attacked by deluded therapists who had been taken in by these ideas. I remember one woman, Marjorie Orr, a Jungian psychiatrist and professional astrologer, who kept phoning me and was particularly irrational on the subject. She had launched a group called 'Accuracy About Abuse' and was campaigning against anyone who questioned the reality of recovered memories. She said about those who come to believe that they have recovered memories after going into therapy, 'You only have to see the emotion on their faces and hear it in their voices to know they are telling the truth.' I was so struck by her naive confidence in her absurd viewpoint that I wrote her words down.

She was quite unaware that emotional intensity, belief and sincerity are not measures of the truth of anything at all. She was also unaware of the necessity to step outside of such emotional states if we want to see what's really going on. She kept phoning me to promote her belief and as far as she was concerned we were wrong in questioning the truth of any 'memories' revealed with the help of therapists and astrologers. Orr also asserted that a personal birth chart prepared by an astrologer '...will certainly show up clearly and in some detail the psychological dysfunctions which would indicate that someone was likely to abuse or have been abused.' She would not accept that, though genuine abuse must be addressed with the full force of the law, creating false memories of abuse in ways that implicated innocent people was equally as horrible. But Orr kept insisting that, 'It just didn't happen like that with trained therapists.' I knew, however, that overwhelming evidence was accumulating that it did.

Like many people I was disillusioned by the sorry state of much of the counselling or psychotherapy training that my colleagues and I encountered. For a start I learned that tutors on many courses would solemnly begin the training by warning students to expect that their intimate relationships would suffer as a result of doing it. They explained that it was known that marriages often broke up as a result of training to be a counsellor and this was generally regarded as to be expected: in other words, it was normal.

Most counselling tutors I came across seemed uninformed about verified discoveries about human behaviour, suggestibility, conditioning or how memory works. Or, if one was to be more generous and say that they *did* know – they ignored it.

Although Primary Cause Analysis was the worst example I came across, there were other courses that exhibited cult-like elements including various forms of psychoanalysis, transactional analysis (T/A), hypno-analysis, neuro-linguistic programming (NLP), Rogerian counselling and cognitive behavioural therapy (CBT) and many variations of these. Most of them had some elements that were useful and clearly helped some people (even if only because of the placebo effect). But all carried ideological baggage that prevented any of them from developing into a really practical bio/psycho/social model that could be easily taught and applied.

On examination, just as Shah had described happens whenever groups meet regularly around an idea or practice, schools of psychotherapy and counselling reveal themselves to resemble primitive cults promoting simple minded, unscientific doctrines. In the 1990s a host of 'New Age' therapies were flourishing: Inner Child Work, Rebirthing, Alien Abduction Therapy, Janov's Primal Scream Therapy, Casriel's New Identity Process (NIP) to 'unblock what's blocked' by screaming (Casriel's scream was claimed to be a better kind of scream than Janov's), Bio Scream Psychotherapy (that claimed to be better than both Casriel's and Janov's screaming because its screaming had more 'love' in it). And so on. At the same time organisations like Landmark Forum, an offshoot of Erhard Seminars Training (EST), were, and still are drawing in large numbers of people to their 'human potential' movement courses in which speeded up cult techniques that deemphasised reason and extolled action and emotional arousal were used extensively to brainwash people into becoming more selfish and to go out and convert more people to the cult.

Since most people are unaware of the stark contrast between brainwashing and genuine learning, such organisations did enormous damage. One head teacher of a good school I knew got sucked in and did the Landmark training and then managed to persuade all the staff to do it too. In no time the school ethos was wrecked.

One way to tell if someone has been conditioned by a cult is to observe his or her eyes. If their pupils constrict to pinpricks while they are extolling the 'virtues' of the training they have subjected themselves to, it means they are referring inwards to the patterns of fixed beliefs they have been indoctrinated with rather than engaging with the outside world. In other words, pinprick pupils indicate a person is operating from strong post-hypnotic suggestions. This contraction is also observed prior to entering the REM state in order to dream.

In normal learning, the individual is given the opportunity to, at various points in the process, reset any learning they do in a larger context in order to evaluate it. By contrast, in brainwashing, information is implanted by a learning process that requires the victims to be kept in a highly emotional state with no possibility allowed for relating the new knowledge to a bigger context. This process is guaranteed to inhibit critical thought. As in all such large group awareness cults, devotees are not given time to question what they are being encouraged to absorb. Objectivity is discouraged. This type of learning is not subject to further modification because the victim's volition is taken away, even though they don't realise it. They are basically being hypnotised into believing they were finding their real selves and to then go out and sell Landmark courses to their family, friends and colleagues, which make the founders very rich indeed. This is why brainwashed people, however intelligent they are, are difficult to reason with when you try and put their beliefs under scrutiny.

When I began my psychotherapy practice I rarely found it difficult to get patients engaged in problem solving – once the problem was broken down into manageable chunks. We are compulsive problem-solving animals who need to be stretched. This trait is built into us. We are unhappy without a problem to solve and, when we have a problem, unhappy until it is solved. For most of us moments of true joy only occur at the point when something is solved, when an inner pattern engages with reality. This is a 'left brain' activity however and depressed, angry or anxious people need help to do this. It is our problem-solving ability that an effective therapist uses to good effect.

Shah pointed out, it is an understanding of the mechanism when it is at work that is important for us to know about, not the supposed problem pretending to be addressed. This is shown by the fact that an irrelevant, false problem can be created and articulated, for example, by a human potential guru, a therapist or a priest who then presents a solution and the person is 'cured' or 'converted'. There is danger here. People like Freud, for instance, would define or 'invent' a condition, diagnose people as having it, and then 'cure' them. This gave him, and people like him, power over others. It is the same mechanism that propels many religions and cults into prominence. 'Sins' are invented, denounced ... and then 'forgiven' by the cult leaders, usually at great expense, which binds his or her followers to them.

A modern version of this process is in play as I write and is wrecking the economy of many countries and undermining the reputation of science. Those promoting the manmade global warming scare are deliberately employing this same tactic. Using computer modelling they created a false problem: that an increase of a normally harmless gas that is essential to life, CO_2, from 0.03% of the atmosphere to 0.06% of the atmosphere over the course of a century will burn up the planet making life impossible. This imagined scenario was created to generate fear in the public and make people more malleable. With false data they then set about convincing politicians and the media of the need to 'fix' it at taxpayers expense with 'green' solutions involving unreliable energy sources such as wind and sunshine.

This new cult movement, endorsed by the Pope, pretends to care about the environment whilst ruining it by covering beautiful wild landscapes with windfarms, concrete service roads and pylons to convey the small amounts of electricity away to urban centres. Those propagating the dogma are being enriched beyond the wildest dreams of ordinary people. So powerful has this movement become that when it was discovered that a huge rise in worldwide CO_2 emissions, caused largely by the massive increase in the number of coal fired power stations being switched on in India and China, had not increased the earth's temperature (which has shown no signs of warming for twenty years) they simply changed the rhetoric. Instead of *global warming* they threatened us with *climate change*. And for a long while few noticed!

'Climate change', of course, is a truism: the climate has always changed, and always will, and our influence on it will always be minimal compared with the great force of the sun. You can tell it is a moneymaking cult just like Landmark and Scientology because its supporters rudely lambast anyone who questions their belief as being 'climate change deniers' thus associating them with 'holocaust deniers'. This is absurd in the extreme. (Just look for pupil pinpricks in the eyes of fanatical 'green' believers to see they have been brainwashed.) I can't imagine a human being anywhere who would deny that climate changes. And few would deny that we should look for sensible renewable energy supplies because, one day the fossil fuels will run out.

Plus ça change, plus c'est la même chose. Charles MacKay in his memoirs entitled *Extraordinary Popular Delusions and the Madness of Crowds,* published in 1841 wrote, 'Every age has its peculiar folly; some scheme, project, or phantasy into which it plunges, spurred on either by the love of gain, the necessity of excitement, or the mere force of imitation. Failing in these, it has some madness, to which it is goaded by political or religious causes, or both combined.'

* * * * *

In 1997 I had a fascinating conversation with Mark Pendergrast, author of *Victims of Memory* and board member of the American National Centre for Reason and Justice, and the English writer Frances Hill, author of *Delusions of Satan* and an internationally acknowledged expert on the Salem witch trials. It was recorded and used as the basis of a major interview about false memory syndrome with the title, *Shattered lives: Hypnosis, suggestibility, cult formation and psychotherapy malpractice.* It reveals a lot about what we were discovering about psychotherapy malpractice and the general level of ignorance about psychological discoveries, including hypnosis, at that time.

What follows is an edited selection from that conversation. As with the Doris Lessing article, the full interview can be found online.

Ivan Tyrrell: One of the many things that intrigued me in *Victims of Memory* is when you talk about the cult-like, almost religious fervour that goes along with people who got involved in recovering memories, multiple personality disorder (MPD), past lives, inner child work, satanic abuse and so on. You wrote in great detail about how cult behaviour stops people thinking clearly and yet have said that nobody who's interviewed you so far has shown any interest in this aspect of the book. Why do you think that is?

Mark Pendergrast: It's nice to hear that someone else thinks it important Ivan. Centuries ago Pascal said, 'Men never do evil so completely and cheerfully as when they do it from religious conviction.' That's just as true now as then. It's in the chapter called 'Survivorship as Religion' that I specifically compare this type of therapy with a destructive religious cult. I also say I don't much like the word 'cult' but I use it for lack of a better one. I prefer the word 'sect'. But cults and recovered memory beliefs are similar and comparable in many ways.

Tyrrell: For those still unfamiliar with how cult thinking works would you describe the similarities?

Pendergrast: Certainly. In a cult-like setting there is usually a figure of authority, a guru that you completely rely on and, in the case of recovered memory therapy, the guru is usually the individual therapist or the writer of a particular 'bible' that the therapist has bought into. I've interviewed people who say that they wouldn't do anything whatsoever without consulting their therapist. They almost ask them what they should have for dinner! They develop an over-dependent relationship with their therapist.

In cult-like settings, there is often black and white thinking where everybody is either for you or against you – good or evil – there's no grey in between. Communication with the outside world is controlled so that you are programmed only to hear or read or listen to someone who endorses the belief system and uses the proper jargon. You're supposed to block out anybody who would offer a different point of view.

Tyrrell: Do you find people doing that to your book?

Pendergrast: Yes. I keep saying to recovered memory believers, 'You know, I've read all of these books, like *The Courage to Heal* with great care and it would seem to me that, if you disagree with me, you should want to read *Victims of Memory* with great care also and then try and pick it apart and see what's the matter with it.' But they don't. They sort of say, 'Get that book away from me. It's from Satan! I can't read it.'

Another major characteristic of destructive cults is that they tend to demonise the biological family. They tend to promote the idea that your parents and your whole childhood were grim. They rewrite your past to make it terrible and emphasise any horrible thing that ever happened to you and make it worse. They also rewrite your very identity. Quite frequently, in a religious cult, they give you a new name, and that's one of the suggestions made in these incest survivor books – to rename yourself. But certainly, even if you don't rename yourself, you are defined in the movement as no longer a member of your family. You are an incest survivor, a victim with recovered memories of abuse.

One of the things I point out in that chapter is the similarity between dramatic religious conversion experiences and the experiences of people in incest survivor groups. It's a type of group dynamic. I think it's what happened in Salem where people became seized with emotion when they saw other people being seized with emotion. They literally fall to the ground, writhing and screaming. There is a vivid description of this process in *The Varieties of Religious Experience* by William James. Someone had this experience and thought they were almost dying. This sounds extraordinarily similar to experiences people have when they are 'abreacting' mythical abuse memories.

I also found a fascinating book by an anthropologist, M. Lewis – I believe he is British – called *Ecstatic Religions* and published in 1971. Incidentally, a lot of the research I did for this section of the book reinforced my belief that much of the best thinking about various subjects was done a long time ago. Anyway, Lewis talked about 'possession cults', which he called 'peripheral possession cults'. He looked at different cultures around the world, not Western ones. He noted that it was predominantly women who joined these cults and he saw that membership of the cults gave the women an enormous advantage. In the societies he looked at, women were mostly disenfranchised – the men had most of the power. By becoming 'witches', or by 'being possessed of demons', they could suddenly wield an inordinate amount of power. Everyone paid attention to them and, by being possessed, they got a great deal of sympathy.

Tyrrell: These are astonishing parallels. I remember being present when the psychiatrist William Sargant showed us films [at Langton at Shah's request] that he and his wife had made around the world to record techniques used to bring about abreaction and conversions. He filmed snake cults in America, African shamanistic cults, witch-doctor ceremonies and so on. He noted the methods common to them all. How they raised the emotional temperature so high that people hyperventilated until they entered into a particular state when catharsis takes place and a collapse follows – at which point new beliefs were introduced and absorbed by the participant. He also noted how this technique was successfully used by witchdoctors to treat psychosomatic problems.

Pendergrast: Fascinating, and you're right about the hyperventilation.

Tyrrell: Well, raising the emotional temperature is what all fundamental religions, political parties and cults do to convert people and get them to acquiesce to the belief system. The new followers lose volition and usually soon find themselves parted from a lot of money. I'm curious at the parallels because, as a culture, we need to have a clearer understanding about how easily we can be led to believe things. It doesn't just stop at recovered memories. You point out yourself that this same process was how John Wesley converted people to Methodism believing that this cathartic moment was 'the finger of God'. Just as the strong cries and tears of his congregation convinced him and them of the truth of their belief, so the strong cries and tears of recovered memory victims convince them and their therapists that the recovered memories they are experiencing are true horrors from the past.

What do you think, Frances? Does your research into the Salem witch trials throw light on this?

Frances Hill: People who witnessed the agonies of the girls in Salem who were claiming the witches afflicted them, were completely convinced they must be telling the truth. The girls' agonies were so convincing. But one of the girls, Mary Warren, later described the experience of going into an hysterical trance state when making the accusations. She said that none of the accusations were true. She felt guilty and went to the magistrate and said 'We're making all this up.' She described the state they got into, saying, to paraphrase, 'I thought I saw a hundred apparitions, but afterwards, when I was of sound mind, I knew I had seen no such things.' So, when she was in the trance state she was taken over by it and she thought she was seeing these things, but afterwards she knew she hadn't.

Pendergrast: That's one good thing about the movie about Salem, *The Crucible*, because in it they showed Mary trying to say that it wasn't happening to her and that they were all pretending. And then they challenged her and said. 'Well, go ahead, have a fainting fit now, if you were pretending so much.' And she couldn't do it. It was quite clear that she had got so involved emotionally that, while she was in that trance state, she felt as if this was real and it was only in that state that she could scream and faint and so on. And I think this is a very important point. Many of the therapists who deeply believe in this form of therapy – and who believe in it so deeply that they also believe these memories are true – have told me repeatedly, 'You, too, would not doubt these memories if you had seen the overwhelming emotion. No one could fake this emotion.' They don't understand. It's not a matter of faking. *They are actually experiencing it.* But experiencing strong emotions is not a guarantee of accurate historical recall, or anything remotely like it. I mean; there weren't witches afflicting these young women in Salem.

Hill: Witnesses at the time said the same then about those poor girls as they do about recovered memory victims. 'If you've seen these girls, you can't help believing that they were afflicted by witches.' People felt terribly sorry for them. They seemed to go through such a process, contorted and screaming in pain, that the onlookers were convinced that this possession was happening to them. It sounds to me as if exactly the same thing happens with recovered memories and the generation of multiple personalities. Strong emotions generate enormous, spurious authority.

Pendergrast: I want to read you this quote you referred to from John

Wesley. This is from 1739, shortly after the Salem witch trials: 'We understand that many were offended at the cries of those on whom the power of God came, among whom was a physician who was much afraid that there might be fraud or imposture in the case. Today, one whom he has known many years, was the first who broke out into strong cries and tears. He could hardly believe his own eyes and ears, He went and stood close to her and observed every symptom until great drops of sweat ran down her face and all her bones shook. He then knew not what to think... But when both her soul and body were healed in a moment, he acknowledged the finger of God.'

Tyrrell: It's an extraordinary parallel. The interesting thing about Wesley is that he was using a conditioning mechanism without realising it, as many therapists do today. There *are* simple, basic behavioural mechanisms that can change our beliefs and people are using and tapping into them today, getting all these strange things happening without any understanding. The fact is anyone can be made to believe almost anything!

Pendergrast: Yes. This is one of the things that I continually point out to people. They say: 'Well, there must be something dreadfully the matter in this person's family for them to make such accusations. Maybe these 'memories' of massive repression or satanic abuse are not real, but there must be something terribly wrong with the families – where there's smoke there's fire – and there must be something dreadfully wrong with these young women (it's mostly women) who have these terrible memories come back.'

But it seems to me that jumping to this conclusion is how most normal people would distance themselves from it. It's almost like saying, 'This couldn't happen to me. I couldn't ever be accused of this; my children wouldn't ever do this because they are normal.' Well, the fact of the matter is, virtually anyone under the right circumstances can be 'had'.

Tyrrell: The only inoculation against being sucked into a belief system or overcome by strong emotions that I know of is internalising accurate psychological insights: information. In the same way, we can override the limbic system's justifiable fear of jumping from a great height and leap out of an aeroplane with a parachute. The first time we do it the limbic system is screaming at us, don't jump! We're terrified. But the higher cortex has information – that parachutes work and that other people have jumped safely, that you have practised landing correctly, and so on – and, with that information, almost any fit person can learn to jump out of an aeroplane with a parachute. They may feel that they won't like it – the limbic system will be agitated – but the higher cortex will override that strong emotion of fear.

Just because the emotional centres of the brain can be turned on, and we can lose our volition and be manipulated, doesn't mean we're helpless. Many people, probably the majority, don't fall for recovering memories; they walk away from it when it's suggested.

Also, the problems with recovering memories, MPD and so on, only exist in countries where people exist who have a mind to find them, or to promote them. Developing countries don't experience these phenomena.

Pendergrast: Precisely. As a matter of fact that's what happened at Salem. You had priests who could identify that someone was being possessed or abused by witches. They were the 'experts' and had undergone a conversion to the belief in Witches.

I had many therapists tell me, over and over again, 'Well, I didn't start to hear all these memories until I was ready to hear them. I didn't start seeing multiple personalities until I started looking for them.' Over and over again I would hear this and it did not occur to any of them that *they were actually creating these memories or multiple personalities.*

I think inadvertent cueing – when people don't realise that they are leading somebody – is a terribly important point. Of course, we are all in a way constantly leading one another as we go about trying to influence people to like us, agree with us or do what we want them to do, but, in an intense relationship such as that between a psychotherapist and patient, this natural process can be extremely dangerous.

As is natural, the patient is continually looking to the therapist for clues as to how they are supposed to behave or react. It's a given in that situation. So if a therapist says, 'Well, how do you feel about that?' the patient understands from the question that the therapist is looking for hidden motives, usually negative, usually of dysfunctional families. I think it's a shame that so often, although family life is rarely easy - families are also wonderful resources - too many therapists are trained to look only for the dysfunctional in them rather than what functions well.

Hill: There is a piece of research that I'm sure you know about, but it startled me. It shows how the simple use of one word rather than another can cue people to remember something differently. People were asked in different ways about an accident they had witnessed. When they were asked, 'What did you see when you witnessed that accident?' they say something different from when they were asked 'What did you see when you saw that smash?' They would remember lots of broken glass if the word 'smash' were used – even though no broken glass was involved.

Pendergrast: Yes. That's from Elizabeth Loftus's work. I mentioned it in the book, and, of course, it is true. I find it amazing how much semantics enters into all of this. There are many cases where therapists asked people to rewrite their memories using different language and meanings so that the way they look at their past changes. For example, when Daddy was previously described as making jokes, these jokes are reinterpreted as lewd, sexist comments. And, if once Daddy accidentally came into the bathroom while you were there, says, 'excuse me' and walks out, it's reinterpreted as a grotesque boundary violation.

Tyrrell: This is what's known as 'semantic inflation'. There is another aspect of this that interests me: when people are in that type of intimate situation – a counselling or psychotherapy relationship – they are in trance most of the time. Trance is a form of focusing inwards. And in such states our brains are less in touch with the external world and *we are highly suggestible.*

Pendergrast: That's what an absent-minded Professor is, isn't it?

Tyrrell: Of course. He's in a trance, totally engrossed in solving a problem in his imagination – focused inwards. But trance states vary. In groups, for example, we often share similar trances, such as when we are watching football, a film, dancing or listening to a speaker. The more we concentrate on something important, exciting or distressing, the more we ratchet up the trance. So, when we go along to the doctor because we're worried about some symptom or other, our anxiety levels are raised because it may affect our survival or, at least, the status quo. We are focused in an anxiety trance while listening to him. We can't think straight. Then, unless the doctor quickly reassures us, the trance deepens. The limbic system is primarily concerned with survival and generates emotional trance responses accordingly fears, passions, depression, anger and so on. And in this trance state of psychic worry, depression or concentration on pain, we are open to the subtlest suggestions given by the doctor. The same goes for psychotherapy: the more focused we are, the more suggestible we are. The amazing thing is that many doctors, therapists and counsellors seem unaware of this; they sometimes say and do the most crass and psychologically destructive things.

Pendergrast: This is interesting. I'm constantly warning people against the hazards of hypnosis. I tell them never to use hypnosis to try to enhance memory because there is solid scientific evidence, replicated over and over again, that you are very likely to come up with confabulation.

But you're saying that you don't need inducing into a formal hypnotic trance to become highly suggestible? People come into therapy and they're looking for a reason for why they are the way they are. If they hear a suggestion, however subtly implied, that, say, their problem comes from repressed memories, then they are quite likely to follow up on it?

Tyrrell: Yes.

Pendergrast: A lot of therapists have suggested to their clients that they 'will probably dream about abuse'. Now we know that, if you worry about something upsetting, you are likely to dream about it. And so people do. When the patient goes back to the therapist and says they had a dream that seemed to be about being abused the therapist says, quite wrongly, that this is evidence that they were actually abused. They are generating self-fulfilling prophecies. Some of the most horrifying cases are where therapists tell their clients that they are likely to want to commit suicide – and then their clients go ahead and try to do just that! And some of them succeed.

Hill: But the hypnotic trance essentially is a state of heightened suggestibility, isn't it?

Tyrrell: Well, it's a state of focussed attention. We all go into mini-trances all the time. If you present somebody with some new information that changes their model of the universe, you see them go off into a mini-trance. It's like a moment of distraction when they stop focussing on the external world while they absorb it.

Hill: We have to form a mental picture.

Tyrrell: Exactly, and you have to go inward to do that – you have to focus and concentrate in a particular way to reconfigure your model of the world in your mind. Curiously the hypnotic state is linked to dreaming. Joe Griffin pointed this out in *The Origin of Dreams*. Hypnosis is simply an artificial way of accessing the dream state. He describes dreaming as the process whereby our introspective thoughts are clothed in metaphorical garments: during the REM state in sleep, our brain's 'reality simulator' translates unresolved introspections from the previous day in to the rich sensory reality of our dreams.

This same process seems to happen in hypnosis. In dreaming, unresolved daytime introspections are the 'dream script' and the experience is totally real. In hypnosis, the hypnotist's words replace the dream script in the mind of the subject. The subject's brain processes the words into a sensory reality, just as happens in dreaming – which is why a stage hypnotist can give someone a broom, tell them it's a beautiful woman who wants to dance with them, and they will dance with it in a convincing way. The brain evolved to look for analogies. That's how it can deal with all the ambiguous stimuli in our lives and in the environment; otherwise we would only react in pre-set, mechanical ways to everything, as a primitive, reptilian brain does. I think this same process is connected with why people can believe absolute nonsense with total sincerity. Their brain looks for analogies to deactivate patterns of emotional arousal, but sometimes finds the wrong ones.

Pendergrast: That's fascinating. You can imagine the impact when a 'script' that could totally change their world-view is presented to a patient by a therapist. This connects to the idea of cognitive dissonance that Festinger came up with in the 1950s. He realised that we can't tolerate the disharmony of two contradictory ideas or beliefs in our heads so we search for cognitive consistency. This means that, if contradictory ideas are in our minds, we have to go with one or the other. Once we choose one belief it's difficult to go back on it. So, when people are presented with the idea, and try to contain in their mind, that 'Daddy loves me and was a pretty good guy' and 'Daddy was raping me throughout my childhood', it's intolerable. You have to come down one way or the other and be firm about it.

Hill: Yes. That's what happens.

Pendergrast: Ivan. I'd like to know whether you think that what I say about hypnosis is correct. That is, that there are different ways of defining hypnosis. One way is to say it's a state of enhanced suggestibility and, given that, if you are a therapist about to hypnotise someone for a particular purpose, you should give them informed consent. I accept that it can be useful in that instance – if you want to suggest to someone to stop smoking, say – because that's what he or she want. However, I think it's malpractice, even if not intentional, for someone to hypnotise a patient and say, 'Now we're going to age regress you back to when you were three years old and remember it all,' because that's not what's going to happen.

Tyrrell: That's right. It is malpractice. The patient will fantasise about their past and you won't get accurate memories because, by and large, we can't remember things accurately much before six years-old. After all, we all find it hard enough to remember in detail what we did last year.

Pendergrast: But, with suggestion, if they expect it, they will 'remember'. They'll even remember their birth or details about pre-birth 'past lives.

Tyrrell: Yes. And they sincerely believe the confabulation. Hypnosis is, I think, a resource, a tool that all good therapists know about and use. Of course, if a therapist, counsellor or doctor doesn't know about it, they need to inform themselves pretty damn quick because people go in and out of trance states in which they are highly suggestible all the time.

Depression, for example, is a trance state. It's one of the reasons it responds so well to any therapy that snaps them out of the trance. I had someone come to see me who was deeply depressed and had been so for about twelve years. During that time she had been hospitalised three times after serious suicide attempts. She sat in front of me, sluggish, not looking at me. She was so into her depression trance it influenced everyone around her. She'd been seen by several psychiatrists and been on antidepressant drugs, which made matters worse. She kept saying life wasn't worth living and was talking about suicide again. In other words, she was doing what all depressed people do, pulling a global blanket over her life to cut out all the positive memories and resources. In that state of negative hallucination she was totally focused on ruminating about bad things in the past and worrying about the impact of this on her future. Focusing attention is a hypnotic phenomena and endless worrying is also done in a hypnotic state. And it's negative worrying that leads to depression.

After listening to her for half an hour I asked her, 'When was the last time you had a really good laugh? When did you have tears of laughter running down your face?' She just looked blank at me and said, 'I never laugh.' I said, 'Oh come on, everyone has a sense of humour.' She disagreed: 'No, I've got no sense of humour.' Then I focussed her attention into a deeper trance by saying, 'Just go back to the last time when you had tears of laughter rolling down your face.' Very soon she began to smile and then she started to laugh. She laughed until the tears flowed down her cheeks. It was wonderful to see. She had remembered an incident several years earlier when her son had accidentally sprayed himself with oil whilst trying to fix his car and she had fallen about laughing.

Now that was a resource for her. It broke the depression trance. It gave her evidence that the depression was lying to her – she *did* have a sense of humour. The negative global view was punctured. She had hope and was now on the way to a recovery. So knowledge of hypnosis is valuable. It's too easy to dismiss it just because, like any other tool, it can be misused.

Pendergrast: I would say that, so long as your client understood she was being suggested into something to help her be more cheerful, that would be okay. I just think we should realise that when we're hypnotised, we're becoming suggestible.

Tyrrell: My point is that people are *already* in a trance to some degree when they go along to a therapist, or a counsellor or a doctor. They are already more focused, introspective, looking inwards and in that focused state the conscious mind doesn't work well and we are highly suggestible.

Pendergrast: Surely there is a difference between that and the formal trance induction?

Tyrrell: Yes, a formal trance is deliberate and both parties are usually aware of what might happen and the person being put into trance will have expectations about the result. But what I'm saying is that everyone should be trained about what's going on. You know, a lot of doctors have no idea how a casual comment made to a patient can absolutely plunge them into despair or depression. But doctors are not well trained in language skills and suggestibility.

Hill: This is important. I've heard psychotherapists say, 'Oh, but I never use hypnosis.' Or, 'The only dangerous therapists recovering memories are hypnotists ...'

Pendergrast: It is important because, over and over again, the therapists I interviewed who were getting repressed memories from people would tell me how they were careful not to lead the client. Some of them were doing formal hypnosis, some of them weren't. But it is quite clear when you read the interviews that they were leading their clients in one direction or another simply by the beliefs that they brought to therapy.

Tyrrell: Exactly! It's the therapists' beliefs that are the key, that's absolutely true. With depression, for example, if your belief is that you can help a depressed person lift the depression, break the depressive trance and quickly get them back to leading a more normal life, it's going to happen. My clients never find repressed memories because I don't look for them. The few people who have come to me and mentioned childhood sexual abuse just said something like, 'Oh, I had a really rotten childhood one way or another, but I don' t want to talk about that.' They want to do something about their problem now – which is usually being depressed, anxious, obsessive or phobic. The only time I come across problems with recovered memories is when people see me after seeing a psychiatrist or counsellor who suggested that they are suppressing something terrible, and that that is the cause of their problem. A neighbour of mine went to an aromatherapist to try and get help with asthma, and the aromatherapist said, 'Well, you know what causes asthma, don't you? It's abuse when you were little, sexual, to do with your mouth and all that, which you've just forgotten.'

I had another case where a woman was having panic attacks. She went to see a psychiatrist who tried to lead her into having disturbing memories of when she was little; blatantly suggesting the panic was as a result of abuse when she was two or three years old. She thought this was awful; she couldn't remember any sexual abuse and didn't know what he was going on about. So someone recommended she come and see me because she was still having panic attacks. When I asked her what was going on in her life now it turned out she was married to a compulsive gambler, a fundamental bit of information that the psychiatrist had completely missed because he was looking for repressed memories. Her first panic attack had happened when her new husband had come home on payday with no housekeeping and no money to pay the mortgage because he'd gambled it all away. She had a new baby, she was depending on this man and her life was falling apart because her innate need for security was seriously compromised. She was having panic attacks because of her current situation. Was it surprising? No! Did the psychiatrist need to go looking in the past?

Pendergrast: Of course not! This is a tremendously important point. I try to mention it in every interview that I do because so many people do have panic attacks. I think about 35 percent of the population at one time or another have them. They are terrifying because you get dizzy, you think you're having a heart attack and dying – you don't know what's going on.

It infuriates me that by misinterpreting panic attacks, recovered memory therapists encourage them. They say something like, 'This is a flashback and you're going to keep having them until you get all the memories out.' Of course, one of the ways in which panic attacks work is that they feed on one another. As Roosevelt said, 'We have nothing to fear except fear itself.' You become afraid of having another panic attack and that fear triggers another one.

Tyrrell: Panic attacks respond well to good therapy in a relatively short time. It's been shown that you can even stop people having panic attacks just by explaining to them what they are – explaining about the limbic system and that a panic attack is just an inappropriate firing of the fight or flight response.

Pendergrast: A combination of cognitive and behavioural therapy works well. I wrote to David Barlow, the author of the definitive book about anxiety disorders, when I was researching my book. He replied, 'People have panic attacks because of current life stress. There is absolutely no evidence that it's because of a traumatic childhood.'

Hill: There is, I think, another interesting parallel with the Salem witch trials with this matter of expectations causing people to believe one thing is happening rather than another. In Salem, a group of girls started having fits. Witchcraft! And soon adults around them began to believe witches were afflicting them too. About 50 years later in Northampton, Massachusetts, a group of young people started having fits in just the same way as the girls at Salem. But this time the adults around them thought that the fits showed they were 'receiving Christ' and that was the beginning of a 'little awakening'. In Salem they were looking for Satan: in the second case they were looking for God.

Tyrrell: That's a fascinating parallel and shows why it's so important to be aware of the beliefs of therapists. *Victims of Memory* also made me think about the stresses our culture is creating, with the 'I want it NOW!' world of instant fixes, the expectation that solutions and explanations to problems should be quick, easy to understand and definitive. But why is our culture so obsessed with abuse?

Pendergrast: In some ways it's understandable, I've only been here in London for a week and there have been at least three or four reports of horrible things happening: a young girl murdered in the back of her house in Hastings, a gang rape of schoolgirls and so on. So these terrible crimes, real sexual abuse, do happen all the time. I think this has been so from time immemorial, but the difference is we weren't hearing about it constantly. Modern media has changed all that. As we said, people have panic attacks during times of stress in their lives, but I think now, overall, our whole society is going through a period of stress and uncertainty. Our economy is unstable, job security is gone, marriages are unstable, the family is falling apart – you only have a 50 percent chance of staying married if you get married. We have polluted our environment to the point where we don't know what causes what, although everything seems to cause cancer. We've lost our traditional religious and spiritual moorings, so people frantically search for miracles, guardian angels, New Age cures and astrologers. We live in disturbing and remarkable times, not that others have not done so in the past, but now it's so all-pervasive.

Tyrrell: On top of this we constantly have the means to raise the emotional temperature with music and TV. To keep sane we need to step outside, look at what we are doing and to see ourselves in the larger context.

Pendergrast: I agree. I think it is one of the more amorphous things. You can't lay your hands on it. One of the points of my book is that you can't just put your finger on something and say, 'Ah-ha! This is why I'm the way I am.' And it's the same with society. We can't just point a finger and say, 'Ah-ha! This is why we are having a witch hunt right now.' It's difficult to pin it down to any one thing.

Hill: I was on a television show the other day, where somebody said, 'These false allegations are a price we must pay because of the real sexual abuse that's coming out.' I said, 'That's a false dichotomy. We are talking about apples and oranges. You can recognise the reality of sexual abuse and be concerned about it because it is an injustice and a dreadful thing, and, at the same time, still be concerned about people who go into therapy, who were not sexually abused, but who come out with this horrible belief that they were … and ruin their family relationships. It is an equally horrible injustice.' It is very odd to me that people can't draw that elementary and logical conclusion.

Did you hear what happened with the 'Day of Repentance Conference'?

Tyrrell: What was that about?

Hill: A group of people called the Committee of Justice, who had members all over the United States, set themselves up to try to overturn false convictions for sexual abuse brought about by recovered memory therapists. They wanted to get people out of jail and try and prevent these things happening again. They decided to have a conference on the subject in Salem, Massachusetts, on January 14th, which was the 300th anniversary of the Day of Repentances. The Day of Repentances, in 1697, was five years after the Salem witch trials when a day of fasting was declared to repent the injustices that had taken place as a result of the witch trials, particularly in the light of people being hanged or pressed to death. And this was a good idea. It was going to be held at the Peabody Essex Museum but they had to change the venue to a Hotel because the Peabody Essex was swamped with e-mails from people saying, 'You mustn't let this dreadful conference take place on your premises...' Fortunately these bigots didn't stop it. But the venue had to be changed.

Pendergrast: Many luminaries contributed: Arthur Miller, William Styron, John Putnam Demos, Debbie Nathan and Mike Snedeker who wrote an incredible book called *Satan's Silence*. It was remarkable that, five years after the witch trials, the twelve jurors apologised and came out with a public statement. They said, 'We do therefore hereby signify our deep sense of, and sorrow for, our errors in acting on such evidence to the condemning of any person and do hereby declare that we justly fear we were sadly deluded and mistaken.' That took a lot of courage, just five years after the terrible events. In America we have been going through the modern equivalent witch-hunt for 15 years!

Tyrrell: But you do have a story in your book, thank goodness, of a therapist who has said she's sorry for what she did.

Pendergrast: Yes. But I have only run into two such therapists, I know it takes a lot of courage for them to look at what they have done and admit it was wrong.

Hill: It's a difficult thing for people to say sorry...

Pendergrast: I think it's going to be very difficult for them to do but I am convinced it will happen over time, just as I am quite convinced that most of the people who were separated from their families for no reason other than these illusory 'recovered' memories are going to come out of it in time.

Tyrrell: Another aspect of this is that, as more people are trained with the necessary skills to help people out of depressions, anxiety states, and other forms of distress, the public will find them. One of the reasons this false memory tragedy has happened is because psychiatry has let the public down. It's largely ineffective and relies mainly on dubious drug treatments, and that opened the door to all kinds of quackery with weird New Age beliefs flourishing like weeds and others derived from ideas of Freud and Jung.

Pendergrast: Yes. We need to address psychotherapy in a rational and scientific way, and look at what works and what doesn't. Otherwise people will continue to create nutty fads. We went from psychoanalysis, rebirthing, primal screaming, now we are doing EMDR, eye movement desensitisation response, which is essentially waving a finger in front of people's faces – going back to Mesmer. We are going to continue to do this until we make sure that anybody who calls themselves a psychotherapist is made to take decent courses in how memory works, how suggestible we are and the hazards of hypnosis.

Tyrrell: The thing that appals me is the lack of interest in useful information that some people who say they want to help others have. They call themselves therapists but are getting a huge emotional payment for what they do: for them prurient excitement and self-importance is more important than getting people better. They would rather manufacture victims than see what is really going on.

Hill: There is a story in *Victims of Memory* about a hotel receptionist who got into hypnotherapy. Suddenly, instead of checking people into the hotel every day, she was exploring people's past lives.

Pendergrast: Yes, the past-life hypnotherapist! I talked about her particularly in terms of the people who are discovering multiple personality disorder. It's exciting to feel that you are on the cutting edge of a new thing, delving into the subconscious of people, getting dramatic results. Much of the time people change slowly, people have problems but have to learn to live with them. Unfortunately, people have an expectation that they deserve to be happy. Life's just not like that. It's a little more complicated.

Tyrrell: The Declaration of Independence did so much damage by saying we have a right to pursue happiness!

Hill: If people could just be a little better educated, if they could learn in biology at school about all of this: how biology isn't just the physical but the mind as well and how the mind and body are inseparable, perhaps we could escape such madness in the future.

Pendergrast: This is a fascinating thing. Because you can cure warts with hypnosis.

Tyrrell: That's right. The mind affects the body and the body affects the mind. I had a woman hairdresser come to see me whose feet were deformed with verrucas. One of them was bigger than a 50 pence piece. She had had surgery, had been to chiropodists up and down the country and had had treatment for years. None of it had worked. She was in agony all the time because verrucas are in-growing warts and her job involved standing all day. I put her into a deep trance and just told her a story that contained a metaphor for the problem and its solution.

Hill: What was the story?

Tyrrell: It came to me in the moment. I told her that, once upon a time, there was a beautiful princess who had inherited a country when her father died. All went well for a while but then alien savages invaded the south of her country. They built formidable castles and ravaged and terrorised the people all around, draining the resources of the surrounding countryside and making everyone miserable and suffer dreadfully. She had no experience in warfare and didn't know what to do. Then one day a wise old warrior came along who understood what was necessary and instructed her on how to reclaim the land. 'Surround their castles, lay siege to them and make absolutely sure that they can't get any food or water, no sustenance at all, from the surrounding countryside.' Now that sounds daft, doesn't it? But, you know, her verrucas died and fell off within three weeks. Six weeks later, her feet were completely smooth with fresh skin. It was wonderful! The story worked because of pattern-matching: the brains operating system. Her immune system pattern-matched to the metaphor in the story and set to work to isolate the verrucas from any form of nutrition.

Pendergrast: That shows the power of suggestion.

Tyrrell: It's done all the time. And the knowledge of how to do this goes back for centuries.

Pendergrast: Some therapists talk about so-called 'body memories'. They convince people that one of the ways memories come back to you is that, if you were sodomised your anus will start to hurt, or, if someone was pinning you down in a particular place, your shoulder may hurt, or a tumour is the site of unresolved traumatic memories, things like that. It's quite remarkable that people can produce pains by thinking or worrying about them. They can even produce actual marks – stigmata, or marks around their necks if they 'discover' they had a past life in which they were hanged; they will suddenly develop this redness around their necks.

Tyrrell: That is hypnotic phenomena.

Pendergrast: In the book published in 1980, *Michelle Remembers*, which was one of the first books about recovered memories and ritual abuse, Michelle gave herself the mark of the devil's tail on her neck. There is a picture of it in the book shown as evidence of what supposedly had happened to her. But, precisely as you said, the mind can have an unbelievably powerful effect on the body and vice versa. So you have to be careful about drawing conclusions from something when suggestion is involved. Therapists have even convinced people that their cancer was caused because they had repressed memories! It's absolutely astonishing. And the range of people who suggest such nonsense goes from psychiatrists with all kinds of degrees down to your dance instructor who tells you that 'You move like someone who was sexually abused.'

As a result of this effort to expose some of the dreadful psychotherapy on offer I met three Richards: one was the world's leading expert in cult behaviour, coercion in small groups, confessions, and interrogations, Dr Richard Ofshe (*Therapy's Delusions: The Myth of the Unconscious and the Exploitation of Today's Walking Worried*, and

Making Monsters: False Memories, Psychotherapy, and Sexual Hysteria);
another was Richard Noll, who had made a deep study of Carl Jung that
indicated that Jungian ideas still do enormous harm throughout the
world (*The Jung Cult*), and the third was Richard Webster (*Why Freud
Was Wrong: Sin, Science and Psychoanalysis*). I also had dinner with
another great critic and exposer of Freudian ideology, Frederick Crews,
who wrote *The Memory Wars*. All of them contributed articles or
interviews to the journal.

* * * * *

Once the continual demands of publishing a journal had settled on me,
the required research, reading, writing and interviewing made the
following two decades the busiest of my life. The journal always lost
money however, so I also had to work for long hours pro bono and
generate earnings from other sources to produce it (once when I was
strapped for cash, Doris Lessing and other kind people injected money
to keep it going). During that time I attended many short courses in
psychotherapy and counselling and got to know the field well.
Interviewing, writing and editing articles turned out to be a necessary
preparation for developing, with Joe, a more effective approach to
psychotherapy than was currently on offer in the UK.

I did the majority of interviews in the early days, and Pat Williams,
Barry Winbolt, and Joe Griffin shared the load on some issues. Later,
when, at Pat's suggestion, Denise Winn joined us as Editor, she became
a major interviewer too. For over 25 years she was a regular contributor
to *The Sunday Times*, *The Observer*, *The Guardian*, *The Independent*, the
Daily Mirror and *Daily Mail*; and for 12 years was Cosmopolitan's
medical writer as well as a contributor to a variety of other national
magazines. Denise had also edited the UK edition of *Psychology Today*
and was the author of a dozen books on medical and psychological
topics including *The Manipulated Mind: Brainwashing, Conditioning
and Indoctrination* published by Shah's Octagon Press. It was wonderful
to have her on board. Her knowledge, plus her research, editing and
writing skills, transformed the journal and made producing it much less
of a struggle for me. With Denise in place, I took on the role of Editorial
Director.

We spoke to many of the leading figures in psychology and psycho-therapy and some also supplied articles for free that they wanted published. Looking back over them more than 20 years later it surprises me to see how many of the themes that now dominate Human Givens Psychology and practice were already in play in our minds in those early days. In my interview with the brilliant Anne Glyn-Jones in the 4th issue, for example, we discussed her book, *Holding up a mirror – how civilisations decline*, and she ended the interview by saying: '...our vision of where Reality ultimately resides, whether wholly in, or beyond, the material world, determines whether a civilization prospers or declines.' Trying to answer this question for ourselves was to eventually result in our magnum opus, *Godhead: The brain's big bang – the explosive origin of creativity, mysticism and mental illness.*

I also interviewed Ernest Rossi who kindly let me attend his hypnotherapy course in the Lake District. From watching Rossi work I realised that it was possible to use almost any slightly odd movement to hypnotise someone – waving arms around in a certain way for example – and then, if that had taken place in front of others, anybody who had seen that induction done would be much more likely to go into a trance when it was used on them. This was because of the expectation that had been set up. The implications of this as an explanation for much human behaviour astonished me. I could see how the ease with which people could be entranced and conditioned to behave like a herd was operating in such diverse fields as fashion, entertainment and politics and the rise of demagogues. Structurally there was no difference from this induction and the rapid spread of the Nazi salute. Rossi, however, seemed unaware of this implication.

Rossi also introduced me to ultradian rhythms, which he picked up from something Milton H Erickson had observed: that about every hour and a half we switch-off our outward focus of attention for about twenty minutes as the brain swaps hemispherical dominance from left to right in order to process information, lay down long-term memories and make internal mental and physical repairs. Indeed, we are designed to do this and, whenever we override our natural need for a twenty-minute break every ninety minutes or so, it always involves the production of stress hormones to keep us alert. Erickson had noticed that in those times people are more open to helpful and healing suggestions. If we continually and inappropriately override this need to switch-off and relax, as many do in our target-focused workplaces, we first become stressed, then mentally unstable and, eventually, physically ill. A lot of subsequent research confirmed these observations and it is another one of those elements that everyone can check for themselves by studying their own behaviour.

When we were wandering around London together Michael Yapko told me that he and Rossi used to share the same platform at events but Rossi would not discourage miracle seekers from lining up in wheelchairs at the front, as happens in evangelical meetings. So Yapko, who disliked cultism as much as I did, fell out with him. Rossi's great achievement was to work with Erickson, who seemed to use Rossi as a channel for his ideas, educational stories and case histories. Thereafter Rossi's contribution was minimal, apart from his book on ultradian rhythms, *The 20 Minute Break*, which was written with the help of a better writer, David Nimmons.

CHAPTER NINE

The givens of human nature

IN 1995 Joe Griffin, Pat Williams, Barry Winbolt and I began teaching weekend courses in Hammersmith Hospital. We wanted to introduce psychological interventions that could make psychotherapy and counselling more effective and improve outcomes. It was when Joe started demonstrating therapy with real patients that I realised what a brilliant psychotherapist he was. He has a razor sharp mind that gets to the nub of a person's difficulties quickly. Over the years I learnt a lot from watching him work.

Initially we called the training 'Core Skills' – but few came. We soon realised that this was because most people working in psychotherapy or mental health did not realise that they lacked information or skills. Their training had conditioned them to believe they had been given enough skills to do their work already and they did not like the implication that they needed to 'go back to school' as it were. It was frustrating because we knew we could help them do better. But we had a lot to learn ourselves. For a start we had to sell our concept: we needed to call it something that people could latch on to.

Then came the occasion when Joe and I met with a small group of Ericksonian hypnotherapists and Neuro-Linguistic Progamming (NLP) enthusiasts in a Chelsea hotel in London. They wanted to work with us and teach Core Skills basing it on what they already knew. Joe was trying to explain to them our ideas about how psychotherapy should draw on the knowledge that psychology had established and start from the basics, rather than just teach from limited models. We wanted to present a more holistic approach to wellbeing and draw on scientific findings and well-established ancient knowledge.

'It can't be right that there are so many different models of psychotherapy,' he said. 'You never find hundreds of different models in other fields.' It seemed that this thought was too complex for the others around the table and Joe got more emphatic. 'Look! We know that people need to feel secure, it's a *given*, they need attention, that's a given, they need to be connected to the community, another *given*, people need intimate relationships, they need meaning in their lives, these are all givens!' But the others round the table didn't seem to understand what he was getting at and why he was banging on the table to emphasise each point. They wanted to stick to promoting Ericksonian hypnotherapy and NLP and just link ourselves to that market.

We left the meeting feeling despondent and disappointed by how unadventurous their thinking was, fixed as it was in the belief that they already had the answers.

As we walked down the street outside it was grey and drizzling, as if to reflect our disappointment, but Joe's presentation had fired me up. I suddenly stopped on the pavement turned to him and said, 'Why don't we call what we are teaching 'Human Givens'? No one will have heard of it and curious people would ask us, 'What does it mean?' and that would give us an opportunity to explain it.' I felt sure that deep inside most people knew they had innate emotional needs – these 'givens' Joe had spoken of – and would quickly get what we were talking about if given the chance. He liked the idea and so 'the Human Givens approach' was born. We started to mention the Human Givens in our lectures and soon others started using the term.

Although we realised these innate emotional needs are not the same as the innate higher faculties awaiting development that Sufis talk about, they are nevertheless important. This is because we still have to rise above our preoccupation with, and dependence on, such emotional nutrition before higher faculties can develop. As Saadi said; 'If you do not heed first the needs of humankind, you know naught of the Sufis – nor do you deserve the name of man!'

But the emotional needs are not a simple issue. A person obsessed with security, status, community, being in control of everything, or having to be 'perfectly competent' all the time and so on, is severely hindered as regards self-development. As Shah said in *Reflections*, 'You can keep going on much less attention than you crave.' It is egotistical craving for these innate needs to be met that blocks the way forward for humankind and generates much anxiety, depression and anger. That is why we have stressed that emotional needs have only to be met in a sufficiently balanced way.

From the business point of view it was shortly after we decided to teach the Human Givens approach to psychotherapy that we hit gold.

We heard of an American company called MindMatters that was holding daylong seminars in cities all over the country. Most seminar titles included nominalisations, such as 'emotion', 'depression' and 'anger', and the people giving them were unloading the results of (mainly American) research in entertaining ways. They were attracting large crowds and the money they generated was all going back to America, which seemed wrong to us. I had heard Shah say several times that the best way to start a business was to copy a successful one – so we simply copied the business model of MindMatters. We called ourselves 'MindFields College' – a play on words because we knew we were about to step into a controversial area (a mine field, metaphorically speaking). Just as MindMatters did, we inserted thousands of leaflets into journals advertising a range of venues around the country and created a day full of fascinating facts and figures culled from our reading. And bookings came in at an overwhelming rate. Our first seminar was, *Emotional disasters in the medical and caring professions – and how to avoid them.* Barry and I presented it together over a run of nine days. Every one was a sell out.

We used a slide show of bullet points and cartoons to keep us on track throughout the day but unfortunately our presentation largely consisted of us reading material to the audience, which we soon realised was not good practice. Fortunately the material we were presenting was interesting and most in our audiences were so used to the academic style of lecturing that few commented on our performance. For my part I realised that I had to overcome my nervousness about public speaking and develop enough self-confidence to speak sincerely about what I knew, rather than just read to the audience. As we progressed through the first series of nine seminars we improved enormously and made a profit, which motivated us to keep upping our game. The fact that we had discovered a way to earn money from teaching also ensured that we could continue publishing the journal.

With MindFields up and running I soon realised that, if we could replicate the success of the first seminar at over 100 venues a year we could keep the ball rolling and earn a reasonable living. To do this we needed more seminar titles so I phoned Joe in Ireland and asked him if he would like to give seminars in this way, travelling round the country from venue to venue. He agreed at once. (Later he told me that the evening prior to my calling him he had dined with a famous Irish psychic who had told him that his life was about to change dramatically: he would soon be travelling in another country with a group of men!) We met up again in England and devised three titles on generic topics – depression, anger and anxiety – that we could turn into day-long seminars.

I then asked my son Mark if he'd like to join us. I knew his therapy practice had not taken off and he was fed up with working on the phones in a soul destroying Brighton call centre to make ends meet. He could help take phone bookings and act as a roadie when we travelled round to the different venues. He seized the opportunity and became one of the 'group of men' travelling around England with Joe.

We had about 300,000 leaflets inserted in various journals and were quickly inundated with people wanting to book on. I had to put in new telephone lines and employ people from the village to take the bookings (sometimes more than 100 a day), process them, book venues and plan ahead. We installed a computer system to cope.

One day I realised that my idea of not ever employing people again or running an office had collapsed and I went down the lane for a walk to clear my head. There were five people crammed into a space half the size of a small domestic garage. We were processing hundreds of orders and booking venues all over the country and the workload was overwhelming us. Some of the time I had to sit people in the house to work. To make matters worse I was still seeing patients in the tiny room next to the office and working long hours writing and producing the journal – this being before Denise Winn joined us.

I had to employ more staff. But where to put them?

As I walked down the lane puzzling over this I met a neighbour, the farmer Roger Fripp, who lived in a pretty old farmhouse opposite Chalvington Church and we got talking. I told him of my problems with the new business and he said he had just got planning permission to convert some old cow barns into offices and took me to see them. I asked him how long it would take to do the conversion and he thought for a moment and then said, 'Three months!' So I took a deep breath and we shook hands. I had committed myself to the premises. We just had to get through three months in my cramped garage office.

The work in the little office was relentless and frequently involved finishing at eleven at night. We had a rule that every order that came in must be dealt with in the same day; otherwise a backlog would build up and swamp our little team. We also had to plan for a new computer system, furnishings and phone lines to be installed when the new premises were ready.

Roger was as good as his word and we moved into proper offices three months later. About a year after we had settled in Mark, who could see we needed more help, introduced a friend of his from the call centre, Roger Elliott, who would help with the computer side of things and was interested in marketing. We were spending a third of a million pounds a year on leafleting and committing ourselves to venue charges, staff and travel costs. And Roger began to introduce more discipline to the process.

At that time Barry began trying to sell seminars to businesses but everything he did lost money. He also couldn't see what Joe and I valued about the human givens ideas and what we were attempting to do with them. Nor did he want us to change the name of the journal to *Human Givens* in order to consolidate the brand, so our relationship became tense.

Barry and I had both bought bigger houses on the strength of our turnover, him on the south coast in Seaford and me opposite the offices next to the pretty church graveyard, 'the dead centre of the village' as Joe quipped when he saw it. Soon after that we were in financial trouble: overtrading. It was the classic case of a business expanding too quickly without the resources to carry it. We owed over a £110,000 and were being run ragged. At least some of us were. Although Barry is very personable he refused to put in extra time in the office leaving Linda and me to carry the load. When I complained about this imbalance, he said, 'Ivan, you've got to learn to delegate like a businessman.' The problem is we had no one to delegate to and were running out of money, even though we were turning over more than £1,000,000.

Shortly after that Barry introduced Kathy Hardy to the business to look at what we were doing wrong. She came in as a consultant and he was sure she could rescue the situation because of her experience rescuing businesses in the fashion industry. But after studying what was happening for a couple of weeks she made it clear to Barry that she understood what everyone's role in the business was but didn't see what he and his wife were contributing to the day-to-day running of it, apart from him being one of the speakers. His wife was taking out the same salary as Linda but not doing any work. Although I liked Barry a lot, being tied to him in the business became a huge worry and that was one of the few times in my life I became somewhat depressed.

With Kathy's verdict in, Barry began to panic at the thought he could lose his house (our houses were securing an overdraft) and so he sold his shares to me for a nominal sum and I inherited all the debts and responsibilities. Although he couldn't afford it Joe took out an extra mortgage and lent the business £20,000 pounds so we could carry on. Both he and I thought we were doing valuable work and that the business had a future. Almost as soon as Barry left everything started to come right and within a few months we were back in profit and the company could pay Joe back.

Jane did the diploma course in 2002. Soon after that she resigned from her job running an advertising agency to join us full time and help with marketing, copyrighting and editing our books, which was a boon.

Joe and I decided that our seminar topics should contain general information but also original findings not available elsewhere, derived from our own thinking and practical experience. This meant that anyone who paid close attention would leave with a more profound understanding of the subject than they would get from conventional 'experts' and would be better equipped to help people more effectively, not least because we gave their work a sound basis to build on: the 'human givens'.

Being on the road lecturing, travelling from town to town, was gruelling for all of us. For several years as New Labour poured millions of pounds into public sector training we had large crowds at our lectures, and Joe and I would travel the country initially with my son and then with other roadies that Kathy Hardy found for us; notably Peter Lloyd, Tim Hardy and Mark Thomas. This exposure to thousands of people gave us a wonderful opportunity to spread our ideas and study human behaviour – including our own.

Some individuals, we soon realised, were attending our events simply to skive off work; they weren't paying for themselves, were clearly unmotivated, not very bright and drifted away at lunchtime to go shopping. These wastrels often demanded attendance certificates be given them before lunch so that they could fraudulently claim to their managers that they had attended the whole day. They clearly had no shame. Being in the private sector we resented this and refused to give out attendance certificates unless people left at the proper time. This made many of them indignant and they tried to bully us into giving in. They regarded their demand to leave early with a certificate of attendance as a right, whereas we saw it as a form of theft from the taxpayers who were paying them to be there.

We also sometimes watched helplessly – too busy to intervene when we had large crowds around our information table – as apparently nice people, all innocent smiles, slid journals and books into their bags. Sometimes we were able to accost these thieves and a common response they came up with was, 'Oh! I'm sorry, I thought these were free.'

We met a wide variety of characters: sincere people wanting to learn of course, but also many attention seekers; individuals determined always to be seen as a 'victim', self-declared intellectuals, emotionalists, politically correct tyrants, extreme feminists, naive socialists and over-confident right-wingers. The questions we had thrown at us and observing how people behaved meant that after a while we could often predict, just from meeting someone briefly, what they were like beneath the surface; what type of questions they would ask and how they would react to the ideas and information we were putting forward. However, it doesn't matter how easy it became to recognise the faults in the behaviour of others, it's to understanding ourselves and seeing the nature of our own heedlessness that we both needed to give attention.

On one memorable occasion in Glasgow we were teaching a workshop for about twenty psychotherapists and counsellors about the importance of being empathetic but remaining as objective as possible with patients and not getting emotionally involved in their story. 'People will come to you to borrow your brain for a while because they have become so emotional they can't think straight,' we said. 'And, if you get emotional too when you hear of their circumstances, you won't be able to think straight either and therefore will not be effective. 'In effect', we told them, 'You end up with two stupid people in the room: *because emotional arousal makes us stupid.*'

As we described this problem one man in the room, who we somehow knew from the moment he arrived would be trouble, was getting progressively more agitated until his discomfort reached such a pitch that he suddenly burst out with a wild announcement of his own, which contrasted somewhat spectacularly from ours.

'I disagree with everything you're saying!' he declared. 'I run Strathclyde University's counselling course, and I teach our students that they will make no progress with their clients until they are down on the floor with them, crying with them, sharing their pain.'

They were his exact words. Then he noisily left the room, slamming the door behind him. After this outburst it was obvious to us that Strathclyde University was employing a barking mad person to train counsellors who would consequently, if they listened to their tutor, be of little use to those suffering from the usual range of mental health problems. This man didn't even know that if a counsellor is moved to tears by a client's sad story they are in effect sending the message to their client that their situation is so bad that even their counsellor can't help them. It was a perfect illustration of the appalling psychological ignorance pervading the field; one instance that stood for a thousand.

Over the years we heard countless horror stories about counselling and psychotherapy courses. One was that students on some courses were encouraged to 'contract' clients to a large number of therapy . sessions and pay in advance for them. Many courses also stipulated that students should be 'in therapy' themselves, which of course involved extra costs and hardship for the students. This was little different than pyramid selling and we said so when we lectured. Our rigorous exposé of the sorry state of mental health training appealed to large numbers of those possessed of common sense but also made enemies of some of psychotherapy's queen bees who didn't want to hear about the research that showed brief therapy to be more helpful than long-term therapy.

Fortunately on our travels the majority of people we met were wonderfully curious, caring, intelligent individuals with a sense of humour. These were the ones who were trying to do good work in spite of the politically directed management conditions that constantly strove to attenuate their ability to do so – they could think more independently. These bright people were intrigued by hearing about what worked and why, and what didn't work or was even dangerous. And many were in agreement with us that better help for distressed individuals and families was needed more than ever and that our contention that psychological understanding in our culture is still primitive was correct. They were the ones we could talk to and who asked us to put on workshops to learn the skills we were telling them about.

One of the reasons we developed the Human Givens approach was to counter the harm that we could see many GPs, psychotherapists and counsellors were unintentionally doing to vulnerable people, largely because of the widespread ignorance of how suggestible and gullable we all are. It was amazing to us how basic psychological knowledge accumulated over thousands of years is still not generally understood today. For centuries, for instance, Sufis had circulated stories about this. And the ease with which we can get upset, become selfish, deluded, spiteful and obsessional has always been the stuff of great poetry and literature. Yet this reality and the stress it causes is not factored into the training of health professionals. Stress overload is the major trigger for mental illness and often a factor contributing to physical illnesses. The burnout rate among caring professionals is high.

Language skills were not taught in depth; neither was the need to calm people down and stimulate patient's imagination positively. And few understood the usefulness of employing guided imagery to help people mentally rehearse changes in their behaviour so as to stand a better chance of getting their innate emotional needs met. So, since our approach has always emphasised the principle of non-maleficence, 'do no harm', which is as important in psychotherapy as it is in medical ethics, we set about a programme of reforming psychotherapy and the way it is viewed.

This was the time when we began to organise our ideas and develop a consistent framework for presenting them. There are currently hundreds of different therapeutic models in the world, each claiming to know how to relieve mental distress, thus illustrating that there is a high level of confusion in the field about how best to help people. Looking for evidence of efficacy we examined as many therapy approaches as we reasonably could, and discarded any approach that was dogmatic, hypothetical, or that our own research showed was not helpful, whatever its practitioners believed. We also incorporated therapeutic wisdom from other cultures and times. Then we took what was left, stepped back and set about understanding it so we could find out why a particular approach worked (or not) and see how it matched up to the emerging findings of neuroscience.

The result was a new synthesis of everything that can reliably be said to help human beings function well. And when we coupled this with key insights derived from Joe's work on dreaming and discoveries about some long-unexplained brain mechanisms (like why humans are so vulnerable to addictive behaviour), we had created a powerful, straightforward approach to psychotherapy. People who studied diligently with us were getting outcomes far above those who were using other approaches, including the much-touted cognitive behavioural therapy.

And it was for these people that we began producing a series of monographs to encapsulate what we were saying.

The first, published in 1998, offered a new psychobiological explanation for hypnosis and trance states that had its origin when Joe and I were staying in a Manchester hotel in readiness for a seminar the next day. Over dinner we had a long discussion about hypnosis and why it is that there are thousands of ways people can be induced into trance. We wondered why this should be so? When I came down for breakfast in the morning Joe was excited. He told me he had been up several hours thinking about our discussion and had had an insight about hypnosis that not only answered our question but also explained every hitherto mysterious phenomenon associated with it. Joe always talks quickly and began to tell me what he had discovered. But I had the good sense to tell him to wait a moment while I ran up to my room to fetch down my little tape recorder. Twenty minutes later I had captured the essence of Joe's insight on tape so we could sit back and enjoy a full English breakfast. In essence he had realised that hypnosis should be defined as 'any artificial means of accessing the REM state.' (It was much later that we realised that, since trance is a focussed state of attention in the imaginative mind and that focus also occurs whenever we learn something new, in a sense all learning is post-hypnotic.)

I was immediately impatient to get home and write it up. It seemed to me that Joe had come up with what Henri Bortoft called in his book *The Wholeness of Nature*, an 'organising idea': one that pulls information together so the mind can make sense of it – in this case, making sense of hypnosis. I had met Henri a number of times and participated in a wonderful workshop he gave in Pat Williams's flat about Goethe's colour theory where he demonstrated why Newton's theory that colour comes from white light couldn't be correct. His wife, Jackie, was a psychotherapist and she brought him along to one of my seminars in London. Henri had worked with the theoretical physicist David Bohm on the problem of wholeness in quantum theory and taught physics and the philosophy of science.

As our monograph was being prepared for the printer Joe and I realized it would be easy for us to produce several more since we had so many new and useful ideas to impart. So we agreed that 'Organising Ideas' would be a good name for a series. Over the next three years we produced four more titles, each one containing original material of great help to psychotherapists and those wishing to understand human functioning: *Psychotherapy and the Human Givens; Breaking the Cycle of Depression; The APET model – Patterns in the Brain; The Shackled Brain – How to Release Locked-in Patterns of Trauma*. We sold many thousands of copies of each of these titles.

This material, much expanded upon, became part of *Human Givens: A new approach to emotional health and clear thinking,* the hardback book we published in 2003. To our astonishment in a few weeks, despite the cover price of £25, it rose to 15 on Amazon in competition with best selling novels and numerous celebrity, cookery and cat books. We had to immediately order a reprint to keep up with the demand whilst quickly preparing a paperback edition. *Human Givens* has continued to sell very well ever since and in 2013 we produced a new edition, updated with fresh material and more references to scientific research supporting our theories and practical methodology. Anyone wishing to understand the usefulness of our ideas and why they are so popular should read it.

Looking back I can see influences from Idries Shah's teachings foreshadowing some of the work Joe and I did together. The words,

'Worry is a cloud that rains destruction,' for example, appear in his *Seeker After Truth*; poetically summing up the essence of our new understanding of why so many people easily get depressed. In essence worrying always begins when someone feels an emotional need is not being met. Every little worry arouses their autonomic nervous system. If they don't act to deal with what's worrying them, a self-generated storm of emotion overtakes them and puts enormous pressure on their brain's dreaming mechanism as it attempts to de-arouse each worry scenario. From Joe's work on dreams we knew that depressed people dream far more than non-depressed people and had correspondingly less of the recuperative slow-wave sleep that we all need if we are to wake up refreshed and ready for the new day. It was, we realized, the excessive intense dreaming and sleep imbalance that caused the familiar and powerful feelings found in depression: exhaustion, loss of motivation and loss of interest in pleasurable activities. The observation that there was a connection between dreaming and depression now had an explanation.

So it was that when Joe explained his thoughts and discoveries about evolution, dreaming and consciousness that I found myself comparing his ideas to those impacts I had absorbed from Shah over the years – both the materials which he gave us to study and the content of his talks at dinner meetings and in private. This material was designed to prepare the mind for experiences over and above our conditioned automatic reactions. It was as though Shah was giving us mental blueprints ready to be drawn upon when needed.

That's why, when Joe started talking of his insight that the brain was a pattern-matching organ, I instantly knew he was right because my brain was drawing on sound mental blueprints – inner templates it had absorbed – to help me see what was true or not, which was an odd feeling.

Back at Art College in 1965, in notes for a project about ornamentation, I had underlined the words, 'Patterns Impart Knowledge' and written that our brains are cluttered up with symbols and patterns and when we become aware of something outside of us the appropriate symbol clicks into place – what we now call the brain's pattern-matching process. I also noted that I thought that, although this process must be necessary for our day-to-day survival, it also restricts our ability to see things afresh.

One thing Shah always drove home in his teaching was that the brain operates through what he called 'pattern-thinking' and the quality of the patterns the brain contains determines our thinking and behaviour. He said this idea had to be given close attention if we are to develop our potential for connecting to the reality beyond the material world. And it is why the way we live and what we experience and absorb from life is so important: our 'conditioned pattern-thinking' has to be understood and overcome wherever it impedes progress.

The problem for us all is that our Commanding Self does not like to change. When a person cannot make sense of something because it doesn't correspond with any pattern in their head, they tend either to dismiss it or adapt it so it fits in with their existing beliefs, distorting what was new in the process. In either case the larger context remains invisible to them.

Shah had explained that the way Sufis overcome this problem is to create and tell teaching stories, jokes and anecdotes that bypass conditioned thinking and behaviour. On top of that, whenever possible, they would provide experiences that do the same. He likened the process of introducing new patterns into an individual as the equivalent of providing a special type of nutrition that opens up new and richer contexts that the mind needs if it is to develop. As he explained in *Caravan of Dreams*, teaching stories are 'a means of communicating with non-verbalised truth beyond the customary limitations of our familiar dimensions.' A 'teaching-story cannot be unravelled by ordinary intellectual methods alone. Its action is direct and certain, upon the innermost part of the human being, an action incapable of manifestation by means of the emotional or intellectual apparatus.'

If we avoid or resist absorbing this nutrition, he said, we remain lost to the greater reality, trapped in a system of conditioned, selfish responses. It is real thought, not pattern-thinking, that is the method by which we can absorb the nutrition we need. And our thought should be directed at all life, not just small fragments of it, if we are to wake up to the real nature of reality and overcome the confusions that intellectualizing and emotionalising creates and that hide the truth from us.

* * * * *

Over the years as Joe and I travelled around the UK and Ireland teaching, numerous incidents taught us too: the most important of which was to expect the unexpected. The oddest example of this occurred just before lunch one day when Joe was addressing an audience of over 300 at a venue in Reading. In ringing tones he said, 'We all have to expect the unexpected' – and right on cue the stage he was standing on collapsed! The audience burst into laughter, thinking it was part of the day. Only those close to the stage realised it wasn't planned: the stage had been badly set up by the venue. To make it worse a heavy oak lectern on the stage fell on Joe's head causing a temporary concussion. Fortunately he recovered enough to continue after lunch, albeit a bit shakily. The manager of the venue, afraid we might sue, waived the fee for the day.

On another occasion we were expecting about 300 people who had booked onto our day on anger management at a big hall in London. To our surprise an extra 200 people turned up to pay at the door due to a mention of the course on TV that we were unaware of. It was bedlam in the foyer and I was desperately helping to process all the extra people and arrange for more seating. Needless to say I got a little flustered.

In those days our procedure was that at the start of each seminar I would get up to welcome everybody and speak for a few minutes to introduce the topic and the speaker, Joe. However, on this occasion, just as I was trying to calm myself and bring to mind what I intended to say, someone grabbed my arm from behind. It was an indignant man who started berating me because at the coffee stand all the biscuits had been taken and there were none left for him. I started apologising politely, explained that more people had turned up than expected and said I would arrange for someone to top up the biscuit plates as soon as I could. But this wasn't good enough for him. He held on to my arm and carried on complaining, telling me that he had got up early to attend and travelled all across London and had missed his breakfast. He seemed to think I should immediately conjure up food for him out of thin air. It seemed an age until I could break free from him and step up on the stage and by this time I was highly agitated.

Then it happened. My mind went blank as I looked out at the sea of 500 expectant faces. I'd forgotten why I was there.

After a panic stricken pause I heard myself saying, 'Welcome everybody. I'm so, so sorry about the biscuit situation.' With insane relief my brain seized upon the topic. After that all I could talk about was biscuits! Of course the only person in the audience who knew what I was babbling on about was the man who had arrived late to find all the biscuits had gone. But that didn't stop me apologising. I explained at length that we'd run out due to the unexpectedly full house and assuring anyone who felt deprived by the biscuit shortage that I intended to remedy the situation as quickly as possible … somehow. I became more forceful and emphatically assured the crowd that I liked biscuits too. I sympathised. I bemoaned their loss. In full cry I declared that I would send out for more biscuits immediately. Several kinds. 'Chocolate biscuits! Digestive biscuits! Shortcake biscuits! Don't worry about biscuits!'

The audience met this passionate declaration with bemused silence.

It was a perfect example of emotional arousal making me stupid! Realising I had suddenly become possessed of a temporary madness, Joe had to jump up, shuffle me off the stage and introduce himself to the audience.

* * * * *

Late one night, after driving a few hundred miles to a town we didn't know, Joe and I found ourselves tired and lost. The place seemed deserted. There was no one in sight to ask for directions to our hotel (this was before the days of satnav). Then with relief we saw a lone figure slowly walking along in the drizzling rain. I stopped the car alongside him and Joe wound down the window and asked the fellow if he knew the street we were looking for. 'Yesh sir,' he said and we realised at once he was pickled. He peered through the window breathing alcoholic fumes into the car and told us with great confidence and much pointing and arm waving how to get there. Like idiots we then tried to follow his instructions. After many frustrating right and left turns, we eventually found ourselves back in the street of our director, the drunken man – except he was no longer there and we were now more tired and frustrated than ever.

It's curious how, when reflected upon, everyday incidents like that reveal deeper insights into the human condition. That occasion, for example, paralleled what happens to seekers after truth who follow instructions given to them by confident 'spiritual' teachers who, drunk on their own ego, are unaware of the necessities involved in higher development: preparation, right time, right place and right people. In our case, we hadn't prepared ourselves with the information needed to find the hotel. Our timing for finding a good source of information was off: most people in town were at home in bed. We asked for directions from the wrong person and then, stupidly, tried to follow his instructions. It was a perfect metaphor for what people so often do when they get interested in 'self-development' and tag along with random gurus.

Given the somewhat self-rightous climate created by New Labour it was inevitable that we would come up against political correctness. There were often attempts to police the new ideas and insights we were introducing as if we should follow a party line. I remember once Joe was outlining to a large audience the research that had revealed why fewer men get depressed than women and why, when men do get depressed, they tend to recover more quickly. Suddenly a young woman dressed all in black with cropped black hair that made her face look as white as alabaster, stood up and angrily shouted at him: 'Are you saying that women have *anything* at all to learn from men?' The hall went silent, stunned at this unexpected, strident display of aggression. Then Joe slowly paced across the stage with everyone wondering how he would respond. He leaned towards her, stared at her for a moment, and then sharply released one word for everyone to hear: '*Yes!*'

She stormed out.

On another occasion Joe had been talking about how emotional arousal forces the brain to think in black and white terms and an earnest white man stood up and piously objected to him using the term 'black and white', describing it as an offensive racist phrase. The audience roared with laughter, especially the black people, clearly thinking he was joking. When it quickly became apparent that he was serious the laughter turned to mockery at his nonsensical attitude. Apparently he was the only person in the audience who was offended and this self-appointed adjudicator of our use of language also left, clearly upset that no one had appreciated his position on the moral high ground.

Not all of the people we taught internalised the HG ideas and skills properly and their behaviour was illustrative of much that is frustrating of the human condition. Some, recognising it had value, became greedy and wanted to monetize the HG approach by selling it online, pretending that the ideas were theirs and dumbing down the approach in the process. Others would obsess about one aspect of HG, such as our version of the rewind technique or the use of hypnosis. Yet others would immediately try to make the approach more complicated again, either by adding elements back in that we had so carefully stripped out, or by introducing unnecessary new ones. Some were unable to divest themselves of earlier training they had been saturated in, especially if they had been conditioned by psychodynamic ideas or spent time wandering the wilder shores of NLP flimflam.

In 2004 we held the first Human Givens Conference in one of my favourite cities, York. This was the occasion where Joe first described his discovery of the mechanism by which an addiction is created. At the end of his presentation the audience knew this was an important breakthrough that could revolutionise treatment for addictions and he got a standing ovation for it. At that conference we also gave away hard copies of *The Human Givens Charter*, that set the human givens in a historical and political context it has since been downloaded thousands of times in its online version.

At that event it also became apparent that those studying with us wanted a professional body to maintain standards. So, in 2005, we created 'The Human Givens Institute' (HGI), to act as a professional membership organisation containing the register of qualified HG practitioners. It would also act as a source of general information for any member of the public wishing to understand more about common psychological and emotional difficulties. The aim was for HGI to become the premier UK body concerned with effective counselling and psychotherapy since no other organisation sets out to do this. Other bodies prefer instead to value accreditation and process above therapeutic effectiveness and common sense. (There is a massive shortfall of common sense in psychotherapy and counselling as it is generally taught.)

The problem with common sense of course is that it cannot be defined – you know it when you see it. That's why, because we can all recognise it, we can say that most people have a degree of it, at least in certain circumstances: we exhibit common sense in some areas of our life but not in others. The difficulty arises when people try to define it and turn what they think it is into *process:* systems, rules and regulations. Paradoxically it's usually seen at work only when someone has the courage to fly in the face of the mechanical application of rules and regulations. Unfortunately, as we are being overwhelmed with more and more process, backed up by an army of bureaucrats employed to make sure we all stick to the rules, people have become more reluctant than ever to employ common sense when they see so many around them saluting processes that are simply not sensible. It takes courage to become an adult equivalent of the boy in the crowd who pointed out that the Emperor wore no clothes. To protect themselves from blame for things going wrong, the priority for most people has now become, 'follow process, even if it falls off a cliff' so they can always fall back on the notorious 'I was only following orders' manoeuvre.

Of course we cannot live together in a complex society without rules, but they should be minimally set to allow for a flexibility of response to changing circumstances because 'circumstances alter cases'.

Unfortunately high functioning people on the autistic spectrum thrive in any kind of bureaucratic role. They find it hard to tolerate the ambiguity and messiness of life, and tend to obsessively force everyone into their structured view of the world. Because other ways of seeing things are invisible to them they need rules of how to behave, with other people particularly, spelt out to keep their anxiety levels down. So they see nothing wrong in endlessly trying to legislate for all possible eventualities because they can only exist in an ordered world, one where they 'know' where they are and how others should behave.

A curious thing happened once we had set up the Institute: it attracted people who wanted to take it over. For instance, one person invited Joe and I to a Thai restaurant in Bristol for dinner where he set out a plan he had concocted in some detail that, he assured us, could turn our Institute into the Royal College of Psychotherapy within ten years. He could do this, he said, because he knew how, plus he had the advantage of knowing the prime minister at the time, Tony Blair. All it would require was for us to pay him a salary of £70,000 a year, and provide him with a staff of about 12 people and an office in London. He produced detailed plans and spreadsheets with a cash flow forecast setting out how he would do this. When I pointed out we had no money and were a 'shoestring' operation he said that wouldn't be a problem, he would just raise the HGI membership fee to £500 a year to cover it! And when in general conversation I further expressed a profound mistrust of Tony Blair, he forcefully told me not to traduce his hero saying, 'Tony Blair is my leader; right or wrong!'

Despite our reservations about this man's proposition, which we were clear about, over the coming months he continued to make a strong bid to take over the operation and run it himself. His concept was so out of touch with reality that Joe would often say, when we were faced with such stupidity, 'Ivan, we must remember, there is no substitute for intelligence.' Nevertheless others supported him at meetings, giving no thought to the possibility that we had our own ideas as to how to progress. As we left after one such meeting Ian Thompson quietly said, in sadness about the way some people were behaving, 'None of this would be happening if they had studied the material Shah had made available.'

It is curious how every day people act against their own best interests, exhibiting behaviour that results in destructive and even cruel effects on those around them. It takes a lot of effort to counterbalance this.

Fortunately, although some disappointed us, we also attracted many intelligent individuals who had picked up on what we were trying to do, had internalised the Human Givens approach and sincerely wanted to help with our efforts. They were the ones who got great results from employing the knowledge and skills we taught, whether they were counsellors, psychotherapists, social workers, GPs, occupational therapists, midwives, teachers, chaplains, business coaches, managers or anything else.

* * * * *

Our seminars on depression spread a lot of good information around the country and helped many people see through the myths that had grown up about the condition, especially the notion that depression was caused by a chemical imbalance in the brain. This harmful idea was deliberately developed and promoted by the corrupt partnership between the pharmaceutical industry and the American Psychiatric Association (APA). Drug companies wanted to sell more drugs and psychiatrists needed to preserve the guild status of psychiatry, which was in massive decline at the time until it began to encourage the public to regard mental disorders as 'diseases' for which medications could be prescribed by psychiatrists. Thereafter the sale of drugs soared: as did the opportunity for corruption.

Our courses on depression were both satisfying and fun to teach. On one occasion we had about 250 attendees at Weston Hall in Manchester where there were two big lecture halls side by side. One had our sign up, 'How to lift depression'. Outside the other hall there was a sign reading, 'Annual General Meeting of the British Comedy Writers Association'.

Our day was going well.

Before lunch I popped out of the lecture theatre to phone the office leaving Joe in full flow. As I emerged into the foyer as soon as the Weston Hall staff saw me they smiled broadly, obviously amused by something, so I asked them what was so funny. They said they couldn't help noticing that all morning there were gales of laughter coming from the hall where Joe was speaking about depression, whereas not even a chuckle had been heard from the comedy writer's event. To them the comedians seemed by comparison to be a miserable lot. Even though they couldn't hear what was making our audience laugh they were smiling because laughter itself is infectious and the contrast was intrinsically funny.

Many of our training days were not without drama. On one occasion, for example, when we put on the depression seminar in London, about 250 people came including a block booking from a group of psychoanalytic therapists from the Tavistock and Portman Hospital. They sat together near the front and after Joe had been speaking for a while began to give one another grim faced knowing looks. Then something happened that perfectly illustrated why the psychoanalytic tribal belief in its superiority over other forms of psychological interventions had held back the development of psychotherapy for so long.

At about midday they started challenging Joe, haranguing him about his Expectation Fulfilment Theory of Dreaming, the link between dreaming and depression and the practical methodology for treatment he had been talking about. It was obvious that our claim that the field of psychotherapy had moved on a lot since Freud and Jung was heresy to them: proper psychotherapy could only be long-term, they believed. They flatly denied all the evidence that Joe had presented that showed this wasn't the case. In long interruptions two or three of them explained how they viewed depression and how it should be treated, becoming in the process quite insulting; at one point even going so far as to say Joe's talk was dangerous as it could encourage depressed individuals to not seek out 'proper' therapy. They were clearly trying to disrupt the day.

As the row developed I noticed a woman at the back had got up and left the room in tears so I followed her outside and asked her what was wrong. She said she was upset by the attack on Joe because she had personal experience that the ideas he was putting forward were helpful. It turned out she had suffered from depression and spent two years in therapy at the Tavistock, which had only succeeded in making her worse; suicidal in fact. It was only when a friend had recommended she see a Human Givens therapist that she recovered. Her HG therapist had applied the principles Joe had been outlining in his talk and got her out of depression in a couple of sessions. She was at the seminar to find out more about how it was done and deeply resented the disruption the Tavistock people were causing.

I said, 'Why don't you wipe away your tears and go back in, put your hand up and tell the audience what you have just told me. It will do you the world of good.' And she did just that. Back inside the hall she attracted Joe's attention away from the challengers and gave an impassioned account of what had happened to her at the Tavistock and how wrong she felt the criticisms were. Her obvious sincerity captivated the audience and she sat down to loud applause. When the group from the Tavistock realised they had alienated most of the audience, who were there to learn from Joe, not hear their outdated views, the only recourse they had was to stage a fussy walkout. Which to everyone's relief they did.

Someone once asked Shah whether he thought Freudian ideas were worth studying. 'Oh yes,' he said, 'Freud's worth ten minutes of anyone's time!' That single response put the psychoanalytical movement in perspective for me, and for others I'm sure. It still puzzles me how anyone can revere Freud, a man who dismissed the suffragettes by diagnosing them as suffering from penis envy.

* * * * *

Every week or so television programmes would phone our office to ask if we could appear on their show. The researchers from Robert Kilroy-Silk's show, *Kilroy*, were the most persistent. We always turned down requests to appear in contrived shouting matches. Our experience of programme makers was not good. They lie to get you on board then, if it's a filmed programme, will keep you talking on camera all day until you say what fits their script. They're not interested in original thought, they only pretend they are.

Once two young female programme makers got in touch after a full-page article about Joe's seminar on anger management appeared in *The Telegraph*. They assured us they wanted to make a film of our ideas about anger to be shown on Channel 4. On the way to a restaurant where the plan was to discuss this, it became apparent that they had not read any of our books or attended any of our seminars, not even the one on anger. However, thinking it would impress us out-of-towners, they said they were taking us to a place where history had been made. It was to be a surprise. But this turned out to be Granita, the restaurant in Islington where Gordon Brown was supposed to have agreed to stand aside and allow Tony Blair to become leader of the Labour Party, and possible future Prime Minister.

The acoustic properties of the restaurant were awful. We couldn't hear a word these girls were saying and all four of us ended up hoarse from shouting at one another as we were forced to endlessly repeat ourselves. No wonder politicians used to meet there: there was no danger that anyone would overhear anything they said. Blair and Brown must have been good lip readers. And we had no idea why they thought it would impress us to sit in the same place where two of the biggest autistic scoundrels in modern British politics had shared a meal before they were elected and went on to bankrupt the country, wreck the UKs health and education systems and take us into an illegal war that has devastated the Middle East.

Nevertheless we agreed to help with their programme, and thus was another day of our lives wasted. Filming was done in a quiet, posh hotel room and Joe gave them brilliant material from which a fascinating programme could have been made. But they politely kept asking to reshoot it, suggesting he could say things a bit differently. It turned out that they only wanted snippets from an 'expert psychologist' so that they could insert into the programme to complete their predetermined 'story' by fitting his words into the silly scenarios they had already contrived and filmed. All the good material Joe had given them was scrapped. It was an exhausting and demoralising experience.

Not all our TV experiences were bad however. On another occasion a TV company called Chrysalis got in touch. These people were also making a film about anger, this time for the BBC, and had actually attended Joe's seminar and read our material and recognised we had some original things to say. Our relationship with them began well. But then an arrogant BBC producer, whose wife was a psychoanalyst, was seconded in to oversee the project and immediately began to under-mine it and dumb it down. So we told the production company that we were no longer interested in being involved. The BBC expects to get its way, but because we threatened to walk away the BBC man was taken off the project – an unusual move. After that, Chrysalis got back total control and in the end made a really useful programme.

By 1999 we had built up a following and people were asking us to create some form of qualification that would endorse the style of work we were advocating. Thus we developed the Human Givens diploma course and launched it in April 2000. There are many highlights for course participants. One is that, in front of the students we film sessions with genuine patients and, when the patient has left, then play the film back to break down and explain the skills we used. At the end of the two-week intensive section there is a short written exam. We then required that those who passed the exam and wished to practice as an HG therapist must submit films of their work with patients so their competence could be independently assessed alongside their theoreti-cal understanding. Our long-term aim was to produce a nucleus of effective practitioners who could spread this much-improved approach to counselling and psychotherapy throughout the country – the manual we wrote for them has many times been described as the best in the field by people who have explored other psychotherapy courses.

Whilst working intensely to improve our teaching we made a number of breakthroughs. For example, before one of the talks Joe was due to give to the first diploma group we taught at the NHS Postgraduate Training Centre in Redhill, he was puzzling how he could explain why Cognitive Behavioural Therapy wasn't all it was cracked up to be. He hardly slept that night but in the morning he had the answer.

For years CBT training had been based on the idea that it's our thinking that affects our emotions. Therapists of this school would say that something happens to a person, which they call the activating agent (A), the individual then has beliefs and thoughts about it (B), and these beliefs have emotional consequences (C). The CBT idea is that, if you can help a person change their thinking style you can improve their emotional life. All kinds of tactics have been devised to do this. And it works for some people. But we knew the model was topsy-turvy and didn't work for most people we had come across who had previously been seen by CBT therapists.

For us, one of the most striking illustrations of how skewed the CBT model is came from two psychiatric nurses who attended a number of our seminars and worked in a big prison. They told us that the psychiatrist they worked under sent them on a course of CBT training he approved of and then instructed them that, after any violent incident among the inmates, they should ask those involved what thoughts were going through their mind before they punched someone. They did so but the answer they always got back was a variation of: 'I didn't think anything. I just hit him!' When they reported back to the psychiatrist, who was indoctrinated with CBT ideas, he just told the nurses that they must be at fault for not asking the question properly. It was only when we explained to them that the brain is a pattern-matching organ that they were able to see that the violent prisoners were right and their psychiatrist boss was wrong. The prisoners were accurately describing what happens when a pattern-match instantly triggers the fight-or flight response and, when a strong emotion is kicked off like that, thought has nothing to do with it.

This was what Joe explained on the first diploma course and I still remember the excitement in the room when he did so. We all knew it was a breakthrough moment. When things happen to people, the 'A' in cognitive therapy, the brain instantly begins pattern-matching the incoming information to instincts and learnt knowledge. The pattern the brain conjures up is then tagged with emotion and it's only then that we might start to think about what's going on. Thinking is a relatively slow process. So the true order of events is not ABC but APET. 'A' for the affecting agent from the environment (stuff happens). 'P' for pattern-matching. 'E' for emotional arousal, and 'T' for thought.

The cognitive scientist, Steven Pinker, when asked to explain how the brain works in five words, replied, 'Brain cells fire in patterns.' The importance of the brain's pattern matching processes as an idea proved of great help, not only when working as a psychotherapist and dealing with conditioning, depression, sub-threshold traumas, PTSD and addiction – but also when working on oneself. This understanding of the brain as a pattern-matching organ was what eventually led us to a larger organising idea, one that overcame the problem of how mind and matter interact, which is central to how the Universe manifests and why consciousness is central to everything that exists: the 'relaton' theory. But that is another story and you can read about it in *Godhead: The Brain's Big Bang*.

By 2006 other researchers had established that the cognitive element of CBT intended to modify thought was sometimes less effective than elements that focused on changing what people did. They showed that encouraging people to get their innate needs met by making new friends, changing jobs or taking up a new interest was more helpful than trying to get them to rework their ideas about themselves. So at least some academics were catching up with what, by that point, we had been teaching for ten years. They declared 'there was a worrying lack of empirical support for some of the fundamental tenets of CBT.'

Nevertheless, in the world of psychotherapy CBT steamrollered on. NICE 'guidelines' endorsed it and it was also in 2006 that the New Labour government, influenced by NICE and academics wedded to 'evidence based' theories, inaugurated the Improving Access to Psychological Therapies (IAPT) programme with CBT as the main intervention to be used. Its 'therapy by numbers' tick box approach suited the Whitehall target obsessed culture. But, like many of Blair's 'modernising' policies, IAPT proved an expensive disaster. Although the politicians and academic supporters of the scheme, and the managers who earned a living managing it, claimed it had a 40% success rate – that turned out to be an outright lie. The '4 out of 10 recovered' statistic applied only to the 12,000 or so who had actually finished their therapy: only 9% of those 130,000 who were originally assessed. A third of patients dropped out of the scheme after one session. Many others were deemed 'unsuitable for treatment' – whatever that means. It's no wonder that many critics have doubted the scientific credibility of the whole enterprise. We knew our outcomes were a lot better. However, no one with hands in the bottomless well of taxpayers' money set aside for CBT wanted us to have a look in: the fact that our approach to treating mental and emotional distress was demonstrably more effective was continually brushed aside by those holding the purse strings.

The extent of academic and political ignorance and corruption with regards to mental health in the UK is revealed when you contrast it to Sweden's experience. When Sweden made CBT the main plank of its mental health care system it spent 2 billion Swedish Krona training people to deliver it. But when they followed up with outcome research it was found that CBT 'had no effect whatsoever on the outcome of people disabled by depression and anxiety.' What is more, the treatment approach made a significant number of patient's symptoms worse (as any competent HG practitioner would predict). So, in 2012, the Swedes abandoned CBT. Lucky Swedes.

I have a theory as to why CBT is so often endorsed by so many establishment figures in the media: it puts the onus on the individual to get better, rather than doing something about the environment or the degenerate culture in which he or she lives. Which is convenient and tantamount to saying, 'It's your fault, not ours. You just have to become more resilient and change the way you think.'

By ensuring our seminar topics contained general information *and* original findings not available elsewhere that were derived from our own thinking and practical experience, we built up a strong core following. This meant that anyone who paid close attention would leave our courses with a more profound understanding of the subject than they would get from conventional so-called experts. They would also be better equipped to help people more effectively, not least because we gave their work a sound basis to build on: innate needs and resources and the concrete skills and protocols they could apply to help distressed people quickly.

For example, the seminars about the cycle of depression were the only public presentations on the topic that explained why depressed people always wake up tired and unmotivated and gave out information about the connection between dreaming and depression and how worrying over one or more emotional need not being met is always the prime cause of the condition. This made sense to practitioners and patients alike who could easily verify it from their personal experience.

The seminars about anxiety, as well as explaining what anxiety was and describing its prevalence, gave numerous tips for overcoming various disorders such as panic attacks, obsessive behaviour (OCD) and severe post-traumatic stress disorder (PTSD) symptoms. These were little known at the time but have now become mainstream. It also described disturbed reactions to sex and giving birth and added a detailed description of why the rewind technique for dealing with traumatic memories was so powerful.

The anger seminar not only explained why anger is a positive emotion that we need in certain situations to defend ourselves or our family – but how, when continually aroused inappropriately, it can become a chronic disorder and a serious threat to health: angry people die younger. We also described why there is an addictive element involved. You can see this in chronically angry individuals who aggressively present themselves as being *right* all the time and who make their way in the world by using anger to bully others.

The seminars about addiction now explain how an addiction forms and how this is the result of the brain's natural reward system for learning something new being hijacked. I remember when Joe announced this discovery during a brilliant talk to our first Human Givens Conference in York where he explained what this insight meant for improving the treatment of addictions, he got a standing ovation. The Human Givens protocol for treating addictions based on his insight is demonstrably highly effective.

Later we added a seminar that offered a new explanation for psychotic symptoms: that psychosis occurred when stress, anxiety and depression had disrupted the brain's ability to distinguish the difference between waking reality and the dream state. I had stumbled on this explanation when studying a filmed therapy session I did with a lovely and talented Welsh music teacher who had experienced a severe psychotic breakdown that had led her to attempt suicide. It suddenly came to me that when people are psychotic, they are in fact trapped in the REM state, a separate state of consciousness with dreamlike qualities. In other words, schizophrenia is waking reality processed through the dreaming brain. This neatly explained all the symptoms of psychosis. On having this explained to him at a presentation, one international expert on schizophrenia described it as the best model on the table for explaining its symptoms and encouraged us to pursue it. Initially we called the seminar, 'Patterns in the Brain' but later we changed it to, 'From Stress to Psychosis'.

We set up a punishing schedule for ourselves of lecturing, travelling around the country with seminars and workshops where the skills we advocate were practiced. This certainly helped spread our ideas and won the approval of tens of thousands. We were often doing three, four or five days lecturing at a time. When Professor Lewis Wolpert attended our depression day he told me over lunch that he would never have believed it was possible to lecture so intensely for a whole day, let alone several days on the trot. He said that whenever he gave an hour-long lecture, he had to take to his bed afterwards for a week to recover.

I think Joe and I worked so hard partly because it never occurred to us that there was any other way.

But despite all our effort it was difficult to break into the mainstream. For decades psychodynamic schools of therapy had dominated the field and therapists and organisations that trained them went on the attack. An example of the sort of situation we faced occurred when I was asked to speak at the Tavistock Centre in London, one of a series of nine evening talks they had been hosting weekly. Mine, on the HG approach to depression, was to be the last in the series. Apparently a London doctor had told the organisers that he wouldn't support their talks unless Joe or I were invited to give one of them so we could explain our approach. Since Joe couldn't go I went at the appointed time with Piers Bishop, a colleague of ours, who took along a box containing 60 of our *Breaking the Cycle of Depression* monographs to sell.

My presentation explained how, even in severe cases, it is usually possible to lift a depressed person's mood quickly using specific psychological techniques that we discovered were eminently teachable. I explained why humans are vulnerable to getting anxious and depressed when their innate emotional needs are not met and spoke about the connection between depression and dreaming. I also described how a strong emotion like depression acts as a lens that narrows down attention so that if you ask a depressed person about their childhood the lens will only let them see all the bad things that happened to them. So endlessly exploring the past does more harm than good – in the same way that constantly picking at a scab prevents a wound from healing. I included a couple of quick case histories. This was all well received by most of the audience. When I stepped down and at the end, I was surrounded by people telling me that I was the first person to offer a concrete explanation about the condition and offer sensible guidelines for its treatment. In just a few minutes Piers sold the entire box of monographs in what he described as 'a feeding frenzy'.

But my talk didn't please every attendee and I was asked to return the following week and sit on a panel with two psychoanalysts. So I went along again and began my presentation by summarising what I had said the previous week.

Then the first well known psychoanalyst stood up and told the audience that Michelangelo was a stupid man, 'Wasn't he stupid? Very, *very* stupid! ... He took twenty years to paint the Sistine Chapel when he could have employed a house painter...' gesturing at me, '...and done the work in a couple of days!'

He went on to say that it took about two years to get into deep rapport with a depressed person before one could deal with their *real* issues, which I took to mean before he could take them on the long and painful exploration so beloved of pseudo-therapists who travelled in the world at the expense of their long suffering, self-obsessed clients. I don't know what planet he was on but he certainly wasn't working in the real world.

The second person stood up and was also casually dismissive of the pragmatic HG approach and, in a patronising way began using incomprehensible psychobabble to describe a convoluted psychodynamic process: a 'journey' she took depressed people on. It sounded unbelievably complicated and time consuming so I said to her, 'That sounds fascinating, but how long does this process take?'

Raising her head and staring into the distance in a way that tried to imply great experience and deep wisdom, she drawled in her plumy voice, 'Oh yars…' She paused, turned to face me and said again, with a smug smile, 'Yars'. So I felt obliged to point out that, since it is known that about 80% of depressed people come out of depression on their own in between four and ten months without treatment of any kind, surely long-term therapy taking years was maintaining her clients in a depressed state – and that that would amount to a form of patient abuse!

There was a stunned silence at such directness but I was pleased to note that some in the audience showed their appreciation for my remark by clapping loudly.

Later that year, inspired by the abstract theoretical nonsense and associated craziness I had witnessed at the 'Tavi', we included a guarantee flash on the cover of our next prospectus: 'No Psychobabble!' It went down well with everybody except, of course, those fluent in psychobabble. This was too much for some in the field and so we were attacked for it.

People can be strange. For some reason, because at our lectures Joe and I explained the psychology behind how to help people in a caring sensitive way, some individuals assumed we must be vegetarians. When they found out we weren't, they stopped coming!

CHAPTER TEN

The next realm

LIKE many couples who work and live together, and with me being away on the road a lot of the time, Linda and I drifted far apart and we both knew it. We were making each other miserable. Nevertheless we planned a last family holiday together with Eleanor and Kimberley in the south of France. On the evening before setting off I was in the bedroom packing my bag for the trip when an unusual pain shot through my stomach – as if it was exploding in slow motion. I knew instantly something was seriously wrong but at first Linda, understandably, thought I was joking and took some persuading before phoning for an ambulance. The paramedics who arrived were brilliant. I was in such agony that it took them ages to carry me down stairs to the ambulance, and then they drove as smoothly as they could along the bumpy country roads to Eastbourne Hospital and relayed ahead that the patient they were bringing in was suffering sever abdominal pain and required urgent treatment.

The doctor who first examined me could have been a little more reassuring I thought: 'Oh dear!' she said, 'I don't like the look of this.'

It was immediately decided that an emergency operation was necessary and I was wheeled off to theatre. The last thing I heard as I was being given the general anaesthetic was the same doctor whispering to me that, 'When you come round you'll feel peculiar and probably be fitted with a colostomy bag.' I was trying to digest this information as I faded into oblivion.

Many hours later I awoke in intensive care with a ten-inch, stitched up wound down the centre of my stomach and tubes dripping stuff into my body and sucking stuff away. To my relief there was no colostomy bag. The nursing I received during the six days in intensive care was mostly brilliant. During that time I was told that my 'Meckel's diverticulum' had become infected and perforated. Like most people I had never heard of Dr Meckel or his diverticulum. But it was explained to me that a Meckel's diverticulum is a blind pouch approximately located at the lower end of the small intestine – a remnant of the yolk sac that nourished the early embryo. It contains all layers of the intestine and is located about two feet from the end of the small intestine. It is often about two inches in length and occurs in about 2% of the population - and in only 2 per cent of those does it perforate. I was unlucky – being one of the 2 per cent of the 2 per cent! In my case this perforation resulted in massive internal bleeding, severe inflammation around multiple organs, and peritonitis. The operation had apparently involved removing the infected pouch, sealing the resulting hole in the intestine and having a big clean up around my internal organs.

I must have looked awful because a few days after the operation a woman carrying a clipboard with boxes to tick came into my room to tell me she was my physiotherapist and needed me to answer a few questions. After confirming my name and address she asked, 'Do you use any artificial mobility enhancers?' Feeling a bit groggy after the operation and not being sure what she meant by the question I pondered over it and then came up with the answer I thought she was looking for.

'I drive a Volvo,' I said.

'No, no,' she replied, impatiently. 'Artificial mobility enhancers are things like Zimmer frames or walking sticks!'

'Well, why didn't you say so?'

I couldn't help wondering what idiot had designed a form with such obscurely phrased questions on it that any intelligent person in circumstances similar to mine would struggle to understand. I was also curious to know why I never saw the clipboard physiotherapist again. What was the point of her visit?

The one bit of care that wasn't so good – although I benefited from it in an unanticipated way – involved several near death experiences. I had a tube in my mouth that went all the way down into my stomach to keep it drained of fluid while it healed. I was told that under no circumstances was I to remove it. That night as I tried to sleep a problem developed. My throat filled with phlegm and, since I couldn't swallow or cough properly, it was sealing the passage around the tube so no air could pass down to my lungs. I was suffocating and couldn't speak to explain my predicament. I just kept passing out and beginning to die. The nurses told me later that, though they could see I was in considerable distress, they thought I was just complaining about having the tube in my mouth. When I became still they thought I had resigned myself to the discomfort. They didn't realise I couldn't breath and was suffocating to death.

However, something life-changing happened to me because of this. On 'dying' a calm came over me and to my utter surprise my mind entered a tranquil realm of sunlit trees and meadows. It was vivid – more real than anything I'd experienced since childhood. I immediately knew that, via the REM state, I had entered a dimension of reality that hitherto was unknown to me. It felt quite unlike a dream, lucid or otherwise, because I was also in contact with my ability to reason and knew what was happening. Then a kindly guide joined me to satisfy my curiosity about it. He took me around and explained in considerable detail how things worked there and how it differed from the material world. At one point, for example, we came to a clear flowing stream and were admiring trout slowly swimming among underwater plants. They made a beautiful sight, and my guide said, 'To navigate the water here these trout have an extra sense different than those on Earth.'

Then it occurred to me that because I was in the REM state everything I was experiencing – including *all* language, every word – was metaphorical. As soon as I thought this we found ourselves in a library of similitudes where columns of drawers rose into infinity. However high up a drawer was I could somehow open it. Each drawer had a word on its front face, and inside every one I opened were all the possible metaphorical relationships of that particular word: poetry more beautiful than I'd ever thought possible. The overwhelming feeling was that this was a supremely true and important metaphor in itself.

After a long period in this place my awareness was jerked back to the intensive care ward. By thrashing about I'd managed to move the tube enough to take in some air. I was still alive – just. But only a short time had elapsed, perhaps three or four minutes. Which was odd for I had been 'away' for a long time. Through the night, again and again, this happened: I would stop breathing, pass out and on each occasion return to this other world to meet my guide who continued showing me around.

I was so exhausted by the morning that, much to the consternation of the nurses, I removed the tube from my stomach myself in order to swallow and breath properly. Then the nurses apologised when they realised what had been going on.

A few hours later the tube was put back down, inserted with my conscious cooperation like I was a sword swallower. This time they made sure I could breath and although unpleasant, enduring the discomfort of the tube was no problem for me.

On reflecting over these experiences afterwards (there was plenty of time to do so during my weeks convalescing), several things occurred to me.

Firstly I became convinced that the REM state is involved in generating reality beyond the familiar one of normal dream content and daydreams. It was the portal into the realms of consciousness that exist beyond space and time that Shah had talked and written about.

To my great sadness I could not recall any of the poetry in my normal waking mind. Yet every time I passed back into that realm, more was always available for me engage with. This was not the same as when we forget our dreams so as not to muddle up waking reality with dreaming – although there is a connection to our dream life. It was similar to a lucid dream but not like any lucid dream I have had myself. The difference was that during it I could observe and think about the experience, *and its significance*. The experience left me with an inner conviction of the supreme universal importance of deep metaphorical pattern-matching, plus the knowledge that remembering the poetry was not what was important, only its immediate effect, something akin to wonder. The 'wonder' was that every metaphorical connection I grasped pointed to a reality beyond it. At a deep level I absorbed various patterns that had to wait for a time when they would be useful and could perhaps then be talked about.

Secondly, although it wasn't on my mind particularly, I gradually noticed that I was no longer afraid to die. This wasn't because I wanted to die any time soon (not that we have much choice in the timing of our final exit – and I still hope my end will not be as painful as my father's last few months), but because deep inside me something had changed. I knew for certain that death is not the end.

Later I scribbled a few notes about the experiences, but only one line stayed with me clearly: 'A war wet weapon is of greater use on the battlefield.' This was not a line of poetry as such, but more of a saying. I felt it had a deeper meaning and was important in some way, though it took me years before it resonated and suddenly became clear to me. I won't give the meaning away here because of another saying: 'He who would eat the kernel must first crack the nut.' After all, you might also like to eat the kernel by cracking the nut yourself.

They took me from the intensive care unit and into an open ward from where I phoned Joe in Ireland to tell him what had happened. To our mutual astonishment we discovered that at the same time I was rushed to hospital Joe was also – suffering in great pain from a huge trapped kidney stone.

＊ ＊ ＊ ＊ ＊

Soon, Eleanor went off to Reading University to study psychology and Kimberley was preparing to do a maths degree at Canterbury. By then Linda and I were living apart and she had someone else, which was a relief to both of us. I enjoyed being alone in the house some of the time, especially when I was absorbed in writing, but, as we all do, I also felt lonely and needed companionship and intimacy in my life. But after two long marriages it never occurred to me that I would find someone to enjoy such times with again.

My eldest daughter, Jane, had married a brilliant photographer, Toby, and they adopted a lovely little girl, Leanah. (Although my son Mark had never married, he had two sons of his own, Conrad and Jake.) Coming up to the spring bank holiday weekend Jane asked me what I was planning to do for the weekend. I told her I would be spending it alone and she suggested I phone up Véronique Chown who she knew had got divorced from her Asperger's husband. Jane felt from seeing me with Véronique at the HGI conference earlier that month that I liked her and enjoyed her sense of humour and positive outlook on life. 'Why not ask her out to lunch?' she said. So I did. It took more courage than anything else I've ever done but doing so opened a wonderful new chapter in my life.

Véronique and I began spending weekends together and then we went away to the south of France for a couple of weeks. I was soon welcomed into her family and large circle of friends. She has two children from her first marriage, Simon and Katherine. Simon is married to Lucy and they live in London with their children, Kit and Florence. Véronique's late mother was French from an ancient aristocratic line (her family tree includes two French Kings, Henry IV and V). Being in France with her was a treat as my schoolboy French wasn't up to much. Her father, Donald, was still alive. He was a retired engineer who reminded me of my Dad. He had designed and installed the lifts in the Post Office Tower and installed new lifts in many buildings in New York, including the Empire State Building. (For American readers a 'lift' is what we call an elevator.) He and I got on well after he gave me a good grilling when we first met to make sure I wasn't like her previous man who had made her ill with his crazy spendthrift behaviour.

Thus it came about that my childhood dream of visiting New Zealand, which dissolved when I met my first wife-to-be, Elizabeth, was finally realised with my third. We flew to South Island after a two-night stopover in Hong Kong, starting our trip by staying for three nights with friends, Don and Robin. They lived in the 'Garden City of Christchurch', a place where we both felt that, if we ever had to live in a city, we couldn't do better than settle there. Don and Robin took us to Akaroa, a delightful French settlement in the heart of an ancient volcano.

We then hired a Mercedes campervan and spent four weeks touring around and across that wild and beautiful island – with its one million or so inhabitants – such a contrast to our grossly overcrowded country. We visited Hanmer Springs hot water spa, then headed north for Kaikoura and then on to Queen Charlotte Sound, spending Christmas in remote Mistletoe Bay. We then continued up to the Abel Tasman National Park before travelling down the west coast to the Franz Josef and Fox Glaciers. We also took a small plane ride over the mountains and glaciers via Mount Cook. On we went through the Haast Pass to Wanaka and Arrowtown via the Cardrona Valley that was filled with millions of colourful wild lupins. From there we drove to Queenstown on Lake Wakatipu, and then down to Milford Sound.

Unfortunately, a year after we left New Zealand, a massive earthquake hit Christchurch and Akaroa. The quake killed 185 people, injured thousands and destroyed hundreds of beautiful buildings. Our good friends Helen, Don and Robin were in the main art gallery in Christchurch when it happened and were lucky to survive.

* * * * *

The rise of NICE and CBT had gradually changed the climate regarding psychotherapy and was inhibiting rigorous innovative thinking about treating mental and emotional distress, whilst the rates of metal illness across the population continued to rise. Therapists and counsellors were discouraged from thinking and experimenting for themselves and the numbers on our courses began to drop. People were increasingly forced to follow 'process', the hallmark of tyrannies everywhere. More and more often we were asked, 'Is the Human Givens approach NICE approved? Who accredits you? What's the evidence base for HG?' Because we could only answer, 'No one else can "accredit" us because people won't take the trouble to understand what we are doing to make us so effective', fewer and fewer managers wanted to pay their staff to train with us. They were, in effect, afraid to step out of line: a growing cultural trait in socialist countries like the UK has become under European Union domination.

I have travelled in nineteen different European countries and enjoyed the diversity and richness of life in each of them. In that sense I am pro European but one of my interests for a long time has been watching how the EU superstate project has developed and the impact it has had on our lives.

After the First World War, two friends who had held senior posts in the League of Nations, the Frenchman Jean Monnet and his British civil servant colleague Arthur Salter, created the blueprint for the project at the same time as communism took over Russia and Nazism was rising in Germany. A wonderful book about the history of the EU, *The Great Deception*, by Christopher Booker and Richard North, described how Monnet's and Salter's revolutionary plan panned out and led to a form of government that was '... designed to place the nation states which belonged to it under a *supranational* power, unaccountable to any electorate, ruling its citizens through the agency of each country's own national authorities. Although the nation states and their institutions of government remained outwardly intact, all these institutions, from heads of state and parliaments to civil services and judicial systems, in reality became increasingly subject to the decisions and laws of the new power that was above them all.'

In other words, the European Project was deliberately created to establish a vast bureaucratic tyranny to be run and exploited by unelected, unaccountable and irremovable elites.

Hitler's democratically elected paramilitary National Socialist Nazi Party was only in power for 13 years but, like the Soviet Union and the EU, also believed that their credo should dominate the whole of Europe. The centralised form of socialism Hitler tried imposing on Europeans by force however, resulted in war and the deaths of millions and ultimately failed. However, the supranational vision was subsequently achieved peacefully by the gradual formation of the European Union. The strategy used was that each country sovereignty should be hollowed out and centralised rule-making sneaked in as much as possible in a programme of ever closer union until all the member countries are subject to the EU Commission.

Just as the Nazi approach to imposing a tyranny failed, so did the communist one. It just took longer, which is why, by the time the Berlin wall came down, the habits of mind instilled by communist propaganda that had kept populations subservient had spread throughout much of Europe. But because in the west we were comparatively wealthy compared with Eastern Europeans, few noticed how subservient we were becoming.

The Nazis first set out the propaganda methodology that the EU adopted. Hitler wrote in *Mein Kampf* that, 'The chief function of propaganda is to convince the masses, whose slowness of understanding needs to be given time so they may absorb information; and only constant repetition will finally succeed in imprinting an idea on their mind.' This patronising and arrogant policy was adopted by the founding fathers of the EU to overcome any resistance to the slow power grab these unelected eurocrats intended.

Another quote often attributed to Hitler best describes what the EU has succeeded in doing: 'The best way to take control over a people and control them utterly is to take a little of their freedom at a time, to erode rights by a thousand tiny and almost imperceptible reductions. In this way, the people will not see those rights and freedoms being removed until past the point at which these changes cannot be reversed.' Bizarre as it may seem that is exactly what has happened to the people in Europe and the UK. A revolution has occurred and a new tyranny established.

This soft tyranny crept up on us. As Mark Leonard of the Centre for European Reform described it, 'Europe's power is easy to miss. Like an "invisible hand" it operates through the shell of traditional political structures. The British House of Commons, British law courts and British civil servants are still here, but they have become agents of the European Union, implementing European law. This is no accident. By creating common standards that are implemented through national institutions, Europe can take over countries without necessarily becoming a target for hostility.' As Franz Kafka said, 'Every revolution evaporates and leaves behind only the slime of a new bureaucracy.'

It is obvious to me and many older people that more and more of our citizens are now incapable of trusting their own judgement based on the evidence of their eyes and experience ... or of taking responsibility for educating themselves. Although our little college continued teaching anyone who appreciated what we were doing, the lack of curiosity among GPs, psychiatrists and people in general about why HG therapists get better results with patients than those treated with counselling, CBT or psychodynamically oriented therapy, confirmed what Shah had said about how we are conditioned to bow to authority figures.

In 1998, two years after Shah's death, his astonishing *Knowing How to Know* was published. A few words in the book summed up this particular aspect of behaviour really well. He wrote:

'A characteristic of almost all human societies is the general belief, hallowed by institutions and uncritically accepted, that something must be:

- convenient;
- plausible;
- believed;

- allowed by precedent;
- accepted as true;
- capable of 'proof' within confines laid down by self-appointed authorities or their successors;
- admitted by some established body of experts:

otherwise it is not allowed to be 'true'.

'The fact is, of course, as we can immediately see once we pause to analyse it: An idea, scheme, or almost anything else, really needs no other qualification than that it is true.'

Our culture is now so blind to veridical truth – and the population so servile – that the Human Givens approach, which is not difficult to understand and whose practical applications are so demonstrably valuable, has to struggle to be heard above the sheeplike clamour of people asking us, 'Who accredits you?'

In 2006, at the suggestion of Professor Alex McGlaughlin, who was Reader in Psychology and the Acting Dean at the School of Social Sciences at Nottingham Trent University (NTU), we decided to create an MA course in Human Givens Psychotherapy to overcome the accreditation issue that people kept on about. Alex, who was doing the HG Diploma, convinced us that if these ideas were secure in the world of academia they wouldn't be lost. The way to do it, he argued, was to create a degree course in Human Givens Psychotherapy and a lot of our students agreed. (Alex went on to write a brilliant introduction to our book, *An Idea in Practice: Using the Human Givens Approach*, which was shortlisted for the 'Mind Book of the Year' award in 2008.)

For the College, however, getting involved with a university proved a mistake. The university was not remotely interested in what we were teaching and only wanted to get more bums on seats and make sure we followed the protocols and procedures that, it turned out, are set down for master's degrees by the EU! Thus from my own experience it was confirmed that universities are no longer institutions where the main purpose is devoted to higher learning: they are bureaucracies run with an operating system that has the aim of raising money solely for the purpose of perpetuating themselves.

Financially it cost us far more than we were lead to believe it would and we couldn't pass on these extra costs to students (for example, the cost of re-marking poor essays) because we had sold the course at a fixed price. The university didn't want to fail anybody because it wouldn't look good: all must have prizes. Our involvement with NTU also wasted an enormous amount of time – endless dispiriting meetings, writing reports and extra management by our staff, including doing chores that the university was supposed to do but didn't, all of which took our attention away from running the College and selling its courses. From my point of view my enthusiasm for teaching drained away and I took my eye off the ball. That, plus our involvement with NTU, was the main reason Mindfields College collapsed in June 2009.

For me it was a big relief – a weight off my shoulders. I could relax and get on with writing *Godhead*. Or so I thought. Véronique and I went away to France to rest and enjoy some wild water swimming.

When I returned, and after what had happened had sunk in, I was badgered into keeping the teaching going by setting up shop again: Human Givens College was born.

* ** * *

Ten years after my near death experiences I experienced hospital life in the NHS again. There is nothing like a heart attack to remind one of how little time we all have on this earth and that we waste most of it. On a damp Tuesday afternoon in October 2012, fate decided that it was my turn to have one, perhaps so I could learn more about our innate physical needs and the aches and pains of old age.

This is what happened. I was down in Sussex at my office in Chalvington, writing a letter when a tight pain in my chest hit me out of the blue. At the time I had no idea what this paroxysm, clamminess and awful faint feeling was and staggered out to my car to find some Rennies, which I knew I had somewhere in my suitcase. My first thought, you see, was that I had a sudden case of really bad indigestion. On popping two of these indigestion tablets into my mouth the pain got worse. I felt so awful I slumped into the driver's seat and sat still, feeling ill, frustrated and decidedly uneasy. But after about ten minutes the pain stopped as suddenly as it had started and shortly after that I made my way back to my desk, feeling a bit wobbly at first, and got on with my work. Being a bloke I told no one and quickly became absorbed in various tasks and thought nothing more about it. As far as I was concerned the Rennies had worked.

That evening, in torrential driving rain, I made my way to Ditchling, had an early supper with an old school friend, Peter Luckin, and then drove back to our home in the Cotswolds arriving at about 11.00pm feeling shattered and worn out, but happy to switch off. I slept soundly.

Wednesday was just life as usual; work, walking and reading.

Thursday I took Véronique to Banbury station to catch a train to York to attend a supervision course. That night at about 2am I woke up with that same squeezing pain, only it was worse than before. I broke out into a cold sweat, felt nauseous and slowly felt my way downstairs where I collapsed in front of the dying fire attempting to treat myself with a cold laser machine and tried to keep calm. I began to face up to the fact that something was wrong with my heart. After half an hour or so, the pain subsided and I climbed slowly up the stairs and went back to bed. Sleep evaded me for a long while, kept at bay by worrying thoughts going round in my head.

I told no one.

Next day I felt fine again and went for a long walk. Saturday was good too, and Véronique returned mid-evening. In bed in the early hours after Véronique had fallen into a deep sleep the pain returned, though not quite so severe but bad enough to make me inwardly resolve to see my GP on the Monday. On Sunday morning I happened to mention to Véronique that I intended to visit the doctor next day and, not unnaturally, she wanted to know why. So I explained what had been happening. Although I objected and told her I didn't want any fuss, she called the doctor immediately and between them, within an hour, they had me admitted to Horton Hospital, where a blood test revealed that the pains were heart attacks.

During a heart attack apparently, heart muscle cells die and release proteins into the bloodstream and the blood test can detect them. The fact that I had higher than normal level of these proteins was proof of what had happened. I was asked if I had been doing anything physically strenuous when the first attack occurred and I said no, because I wasn't. (It was only later, after someone at the office reminded me, that I remembered that about an hour before the first attack I had quickly unloaded two pallets of heavy books into the store room and doing so had made me weak and breathless. At the time I just thought I was out of condition.) Nurses immediately injected me with a blood thinner and gave me a statin.

My advice now would be that should you suffer severe chest pains, call the doctor. Tell someone! Do not foolishly play down its seriousness to yourself as I did. A doctor at the hospital said that Véronique's action might well have saved my life because the next heart attack could have been fatal.

I was transferred by ambulance to the Heart Centre at John Radcliffe Hospital in Oxford for an angiogram, which revealed damaged arteries. They couldn't fit stents but kept me on a ward by myself for five days while they decided what to do. Then David Taggart, Professor of Cardiovascular Surgery, came to see me, introduced himself, and said that he and his team had studied the angiogram and the results of various tests and recommended I have a bypass operation and that I should go home and prepare myself. He also said I mustn't walk up steep hills or lift anything heavier than a kettle because that might kill me. He was as slim as a whippet and added that I ought to lose some weight as quickly as possible because I was obviously overweight and that is a prime cause of heart attacks. I asked him how I could do this and he replied, 'You're obviously an intelligent man. You don't need me to tell you how to lose weight, find out for yourself.' Taggart was not a man to mince his words!

* * * * *

As I look back I can see there were signs of things not being quite right with my heart. For example, one evening a few weeks earlier, I had arrived at Simon Fuller's place, the friendly B&B in Clifton we love to stay in when we are working in Bristol. The room I was allocated to was on the top floor of the five-story Georgian building. Declining Simon's offer to carry my suitcase for me I grabbed it and started to climb the stairs two at a time. When I reached the third floor I suddenly caught my foot on a stair and stumbled back into Simon who was following me. I insisted there was no harm done and continued a few more steps, now one at a time. Then it happened again and this time I crashed into the bannisters. Simon then decided to put me in a room on the third floor so I wouldn't have to climb any further. I was shaken quite a bit by having so nearly tumbled down the steep stairway. Was I just tired? Or was my heart not pumping hard enough to get me up the stairs?

Once alone I sat on my bed thinking how easily a simple thing like a stumble could change one's whole life; perhaps even kill me just when so many possibilities seemed to be opening up. I had my lovely wife, Véronique, a beautiful home that we had shaped together, and was living in a quintessentially peaceful part of the English countryside: all this I wanted to continue enjoying. I also had new challenges involving taking the Human Givens approach into business organisations, and had another book to write.

That night I had a dream that metaphorically encapsulated my ruminations. I was high up on a hill progressing along a difficult path from where I could occasionally glimpse an amazing view of a beautiful coastal town far below by the sea that seemed to represent perfection. Someone was with me and I offered to take a photograph of the view for them, using their camera, because they couldn't quite see it. Doing so, however, involved me leaning out from the path into a lot of vegetation that concealed a high cliff that I wasn't really aware of. But when I looked at the view through the camera I became aware that the edge of the cliff was crumbling away and I was beginning to fall to a certain death, all the time thinking that this meant I would no longer reach my destination: the beautiful scene ahead. Then I woke up sweating and discovered to my great relief that I was safe in bed and it was time to get up and go to work.

* * * * *

From the moment I entered the hospital I was given a cocktail of drugs and injected with a blood thinner at regular intervals. Some hours after Taggart's visit I was given a bag with boxes of tablets to take home with me together with a schedule of what to take and when. I took these pills as directed for six weeks until I received a letter giving me the date of the operation and saying I should stop taking them seven days before the operation. However, I stopped taking them as soon as I read the letter (even though this was ten days before the date they gave me). I did this because I could feel the drugs were dulling my brain and interfering with my memory, my ability to concentrate and depleting my energy levels. They also gave me a nasty rash. Within a couple of days off the medicines I felt much better and mentally sharper: my 'mojo' had returned to such a degree that everybody noticed: family, neighbours and colleagues. And my rash cleared up.

Whilst waiting for the operation I began reading about the side effects of the drugs I had been given, particularly statins and beta-blockers and was astonished at how severe they can be. I also read about losing weight. When Professor Taggart advised me to lose weight I was nearly fourteen and a half stone [203 lbs], a result I assumed of eating too much in restaurants as I travelled around the country teaching (plus a fondness for honey on toast at home). A few years earlier I had read *The Diet Delusion* by Gary Taubes that tells an astonishing story of just how much vested interests distort 'science' and create harmful public perceptions about what is good or bad for us, so I got hold of his book, *Why We Get Fat and What to do About It* and, with my wife's support, adjusted my diet. It turns out that what we are so often told is necessary for healthy living ain't necessarily so.

But now I was in the world of the NHS. This turned out to be a mixed blessing, thanks to its chaotic administration, as my letter to The Chief Executive of the Oxford University Hospitals NHS Trust illustrates:

31st November 2012

Dear Sir Jonathan Michael,

We have never met, but NHS No: 404-194-7235, (that's me) has a serious complaint. Please read this letter in full. (The Website of the Oxford University Hospitals NHS Trust invites us to 'get involved', so I am.)

The reason for writing (as well as trying to save taxpayers money) is to ensure that in the future some other poor unfortunate is not treated in the same way I was and thereby has to experience similar emotional distress and financial costs. (I do not take kindly to people who upset my, normally very resilient, wife to the point of tears – or who cause me to waste hard earned money.)

In early October this year I had three painful heart attacks and was rushed to the Horton General Hospital who sent me by ambulance to John Radcliffe for an angiogram, which confirmed the attacks were serious. I had to stay in for a few days to await the result of a discussion meeting. This was all done efficiently and the doctors and nurses I met were excellent. On the Friday morning the heart surgeon, Professor Taggart, came to see me after a meeting and said that he and his colleagues had unanimously concluded that I would benefit from having a triple bypass. I agreed to this, signed a consent form, and was told I would have to wait 'six to eight weeks', which was confirmed in writing, and could therefore go home, which I did. At that point I had complete trust in the hospital.

After a few weeks passed my wife began phoning the hospital to try and confirm a date – we are busy, productive people and had arrangements to make. Eventually she made contact with Dora Connolly who asked us by email if admission on the 28th and operation on the 29th would suit. We said yes it would. So far, so good.

In mid November I received a letter asking me to attend a preadmission appointment. It said to allow three hours so an X ray of my chest and ECG could also be done. After the X ray and ECG my wife and I made our way to the preadmission clinic and arrived on time: 12.30 pm. After over an hour waiting we queried and discovered that I was 'not on the list'. We showed the letter to the nurse and, when she saw it, agreed that we should have been. She was obviously frustrated that the information had not been passed through to her. She kindly stayed late and saw us anyway. (I am not complaining about any nurse or doctor I met.)

When we got back home there was a letter on the doormat from Louise Simms, Patient Access Administrator, saying she was pleased to inform me that a day had been arranged for my admission for surgery, Wednesday the 28th November, with the operation to take place the following day. There were instructions in the letter for what to bring from home etc. This was confirmation of the dates given by Dora Connolly. On that basis we booked (and paid for) a B&B near to the hospital so my wife could stay close by during the first few days, made a multitude of other arrangements, and duly turned up at the cardiothoracic ward where they were expecting me. I was put in an overflow ward (RAU) with other heart patients.

At about ten o'clock that night I was told by a bank nurse that she was very sorry but I did not seem to be 'on the list' for surgery the next day and that she couldn't understand why. As you can imagine, having spent weeks preparing myself mentally for the operation and its aftermath, I spent a frustrating and restless night not knowing if this was true or not. In the morning Professor Taggart, a busy man, took time out to find me and offer his profuse apologies on behalf of the hospital. He said this would most assuredly not have happened had he been in charge of his list but that the current system means that he isn't. He was therefore quite unaware that I was in the hospital until that morning. He promptly arranged a new date and gave instructions that under no circumstances must this be cancelled. (I am now to come in on the 12th of December and will be operated on the following day, without fail, though as yet I have no letter confirming this.)

Professors Taggart's obvious distress at what had happened, coupled with his honourable apology and prompt action, impressed me. To date, however, I have had no explanation or apology from the administrator at fault. Since psychological stress is known to be the principle cause of heart problems the way the Radcliffe dealt with me leads me to suspect that management is unaware that their job involves keeping heart patients as calm as possible. Perhaps they are badly in need of basic training about innate human needs, not just of patients but also of staff (since it is an innate need to feel we have volition and a reasonable degree of control over our life, including how we work).

I can tell by observation if an organisation or business has a healthy inner dynamic or not. When an organisation functions well it is like any flourishing living organism: all its systems work together in a healthy, meaningful way. A mature organic organisation is not easily taken in, it questions its own assumptions, is flexible and adaptable and the people in all departments take full responsibility for their work, pulling together in an organic way for the good of the whole. Its philosophy is that everyone's emotional needs should be met in balance because creating an environment where that is possible is what motivates people. One incompetent, unmotivated staff member at any level in an organisation damages the health of the whole.

I look forward to your response,

Yours sincerely,

Ivan Tyrrell

Sir Jonathan emailed me at 9 o'clock on the Sunday evening to apologise, which was pretty impressive. Other profuse apologies from various people lower in the hierarchy followed during that week. The local paper took my photo and gave the incident considerable space – a page in fact – under the heading, 'Hospital blunder delays operation'.

* * * * *

Two weeks later I was back in the John Radcliffe – and this time all went well. After the operation, which turned out to be not a triple but a quadruple by-pass, Professor Taggart came to discuss it and told me that my heart was in good shape, it was just the arteries that needed replacing. During our conversation he told me of another hospital management blunder. Apparently I could have been operated on a day earlier because his team was all set to start work when it was discovered that there was *nobody* on the list that day, even though many people were in the queue, so eight or nine people were paid a lot of money by us taxpayers to just sit around drinking coffee with nothing to do, except moan about the management that allows such things to happen.

In hospital I was given drugs again but felt too weak to protest. My attention was focused on recovery, getting home and becoming active as quickly as possible. Despite being extremely tired and weak (which I'm told is normal after a major op), as soon as I could, I started to walk around the wards once or twice a day and struck up conversations with other patients. Véronique spent as much time with me as she was allowed. I also continued reading books about the lifestyle causes of heart attacks and the side effects of drugs, particularly of the statins.

I was particularly impressed by Dr Malcolm Kendrick who wrote *The Great Cholesterol Con* for non-medical people like me, and

Dr Duane Graveline's books, *The Statin Damage Crisis* and *The Dark Side of Statins*.

I found out that it is not cholesterol that causes heart attacks but cortisol: the primary cause of the inflammation of the arteries. Cortisol is the hormone released in response to stress and a low level of blood glucocorticoids. Its primary functions are to increase blood sugar through gluconeogenesis; suppress the immune system; and aid in fat, protein and carbohydrate metabolism. Stress levels are raised, as we know, when innate *emotional* needs are not met fairly well. Another major factor that acts as a *physical* stressor and also produces cortisol is our unnatural modern diet, overloaded as it is with sugar producing carbs and processed foods. I had certainly had fifteen years of stress what with running the business, fulfilling a gruelling teaching schedule, the death of my parents and going through a break-up and divorce.

Graveline is a highly respected American physician, medical researcher and NASA astronaut. After being prescribed statins to reduce his cholesterol level, he developed transient global amnesia – he could not even recognize his family. His memory only slowly recovered after he stopped taking them. But when NASA physicians prescribed them again, at just half the dose, the amnesia returned, so Graveline came off them for good. He has since become an authoritative critic of them.

His research draws on the discoveries about the important role cholesterol plays in the body and in the metabolic pathways in the brain. It contributes vitally to the brain's proper functioning, including mediating the formation of new synapses. In his writings he refers to clinical trials and studies whose data show that statins have negligible impact on heart disease in primary patients (i.e. those who have not been diagnosed with cardiovascular disease) yet increase their mortality overall from all causes. Cholesterol is the precursor of vitamin D and all our steroid and sex hormones. It also acts as a vital component of the immune system and as a protective antioxidant in its own right.

The massive over-prescription of statins over the last 40 years was generated on the back of the 'diet-heart' hypothesis whose basic idea is that dietary saturated fat raises cholesterol levels, and these two substances somehow clog-up our arteries causing heart attacks. This notion is now thoroughly debunked by better science (as well as by common sense and experience). But it still clings on in our collective mind, partly, I think, because it generates vast fortunes for the pharmaceutical industry and has been uncritically accepted as true by most doctors. Many physicians still believe that cholesterol is a major cause of heart disease, despite the fact that people with high cholesterol tend to live longer and those with heart disease tend to have low levels of cholesterol. The food processing industry also benefitted as they were able, on the basis of this erroneous idea, to devise thousands of 'low cholesterol' products, margarines and spreads, to sell to the public from whom valuable information about the dangers of eating them was kept hidden.

I don't want to sound like a conspiracy theorist but when practices and products carry serious health risks it seems to me to be worth looking at the profits being made as the prime motive for manufacturers not doing something to correct the situation. Follow the money!

Having 'normal' or even 'low' cholesterol levels does not eliminate or even reduce the risk of heart attack or stroke. In fact, 75 per cent of heart attack victims have normal levels of cholesterol. In the hospital I was told mine was 'normal'. While statins do fairly reliably lower blood cholesterol, doing so brings no improvement in the risk of heart disease, or heart attack, and no reduced risk of death compared to controls that don't take it. This suggests that the cholesterol levels that statin drugs are purported to cure, have little or nothing to do with heart disease in the first place – something that is fortunately now realised by many in the medical profession.

Here's a quote from Dr. Myron Wentz about how essential to health cholesterol is: 'There is no part of the body where cholesterol does not play important roles in physiology and metabolism. Just because it is found in arterial plaques does not mean it is the cause of heart disease. Rather, cholesterol is there as a repair molecule, called on to mend damage caused by inflammation. Because you usually find firemen at the location of a fire does not mean that they started the fire. Indeed, there is mounting evidence that cholesterol is involved in preventing cardiovascular disease rather than in its development.'

Since statins were introduced as a wonder drug in the 80s, the incidence of heart attacks and strokes has not changed. If they worked the way the pharmaceutical studies claimed they did, the numbers of strokes and heart attacks should have fallen dramatically. They have not.

Whilst the lowering of cholesterol in a population does not reduce the rate of heart disease in it, the list of officially acknowledged statin side-effects has grown. Here are the main ones:

- Damage to the peripheral nervous system that can cause tingling, numbness, and prickling of the hands and feet, burning pain and paralysis.
- Muscle damage. Symptoms include severe muscle weakness, intense muscle aches and pains and disabling fatigue.
- Kidney damage. Over time, the breakdown of muscle tissue damaged by statins releases a protein called myoglobin into the bloodstream, which is filtered by the kidneys and eliminated from the body. Myoglobin degrades into substances that damage the kidneys and can be fatal.
- Heart failure. A healthy heart is dependent on a vital nutrient known as CoQ10, but statins deplete this. Statins inhibit the same enzyme used to manufacture both cholesterol and CoQ10, and this has been linked to the dramatic increase in heart failure seen since their introduction. In one research programme after taking the statin drug Lipitor for six months, 66 per cent of patients developed heart problems similar to those that can lead to heart failure, probably due to the side effect of statins depleting the body's store of CoQ10.
- Immune suppression. Statins can hinder the ability of the body's immune cells to kill pathogens and increase the production of cytokines, which trigger and sustain inflammation.
- Diabetes risk. Statins increase the risk of developing diabetes by up to 12 per cent.
- Reduced mental function. A deficiency of CoQ10 caused by statins can cause confusion, memory loss, and transit global amnesia (TGA) a terrifying, temporary but almost total disruption of short-term memory with a range of problems associated with accessing older memories.
- Increased cancer risk because they are a powerful immune suppressant.

A number of other problems have been linked to statins including cataracts, liver dysfunction, rashes, hair loss in women, upset stomach, headache or insomnia. And GPs have observed other side-effects such as irritability and 'generally feeling old' that are never mentioned in studies, yet are common.

Some innocent people are undoubtedly damaged and subjected to premature degenerative disease and death as a result of ingesting statins and I resolved not to be one of them.

On the sixth day I was discharged and for the first couple of weeks or so I felt uncomfortable and weak. There was pain to endure in my chest and the leg where a vein had been extracted for the transplant. I kept falling asleep and had to take Paracetamol a few times. It took a while before I really felt on the mend.

It was a bit grim in the week before Christmas and I visited my GP's surgery on Christmas Eve where I was examined to make sure the wounds were healing well and was encouraged to resume taking the statins and other medications, which I had stopped taking again as soon as I got home (except for one soluble aspirin daily, which is said to thin the blood and have the same anti-inflammatory effect on arteries that statins have). I began taking a vitamin D supplement daily to counter the lack of sunshine that winter, and was eating well again thanks to Véronique's care and wholesome cooking.

Six weeks after leaving the hospital I was back at the John Radcliffe for X rays, ECG and other tests before seeing Taggart for a check up. He told me that the X ray result was excellent and all the tests confirmed the operation was successful. Moreover, he said he could tell just by looking at me as soon as I walked in that I was very well indeed.

'How come?' I asked.

'It's your colour, your demeanour, the way you walk,' he said. 'You're obviously healthy.'

'That may be because I'm not taking any of the medication,' I said.

This did not go down well so I promptly shook his hand and thanked him for his skill and care. He said he would write to the pharmacist and ask her to discuss my medication with me. From that day on I've remained physically healthy without medication.

Doctors, I realised, are nowadays obsessed with dishing out 'meds' (there are even posters on the hospital walls with speech bubbles of TV celebrities saying, 'Don't forget your meds!'). They assume we are not normal if, by my age, we are not as a matter of course taking some medication or other. Now I'm not automatically against every drug treatment but I do think one should be careful about mixing drugs and not take ones whose side effects might be worse than the condition they are treating. One should also not regard drug company funded research with anything other than a huge pinch of salt. (The evidence for just how much salt you need to apply to the unscrupulous claims made by the pharmaceutical industry can be found in the brilliant book *Pharmageddon*, by Dr David Healy.)

After a setback like a non-fatal heart attack many people become anxious and begin to worry excessively. As we know, it is worrying that causes depression. And worrying about our inevitable demise doesn't make for a clear spirit. I take my inspiration from the words of Mark Twain: 'The fear of death follows from the fear of life. A man who lives fully is prepared to die at any time.'

The surreal events I experienced around my health setbacks do not stop at management madness in the NHS and the prescribing of statins and beta-blockers. Despite loading me up with medicines (and medicines to counteract the side effects of the medicines), two doctors separately suggested that I might get depressed during my convalescence and should be prepared to take antidepressants as well! No attempt was made to find out if I was worrying.

The intense near death experience I had a decade or more previously meant that, since then, I haven't feared dying and will submit readily when my time comes. I don't worry about it as I did when I was a child. In my teens, of course, I came to realise that not a single person can be confident that they will be alive a day hence. Whilst still believing I have things to do and enjoy on this earth, it is obvious that death doesn't wait to see if we've finished all our projects or had our fill of earthly enjoyments before it calls us back from whence we came.

Dying is the price we pay for the life we are given, in which, if we choose to do so, we can observe the wonders of creation. For me, losing my life force will be another transformational stage – and I accept that the transformation can go either way, for better or worse. Death will be like leaving a temporary home where much has become familiar and safe, and stepping through a previously unused door, the portal that is the REM state, into a largely unknown realm beyond space and time and where we can only take with us from life what we have wrought into our character.

However, ideally, like everyone else, I don't want to leave this world until I can submit myself entirely to the creative force that continuously brings the universe into being and can let go of attachments without regrets. In the meantime, every moment, I'm grateful to my wife and the doctors, surgeons and nurses and my family, colleagues and friends, for the continuing opportunity to marvel at Reality.

* * * * *

In November 1996 Joe and I were sitting in a Thai restaurant when we heard from Pat Williams that Idries Shah had died. On his gravestone are the words, 'Do not look at my outward shape but take what is in my hand.' What Shah gave for us to 'take' was not a personality to worship, not a cult to adhere to, nor emotional excitement that stops us thinking, but a huge collection of material that we could absorb if we were willing to make the effort to do so. This material has transformative power. In a mind relatively uncluttered it can take root and help clear out the superstitions, destructive habits, traumas and irrelevant expectations that imprison our essence and prevent our hearts from mirroring Reality. Only by being voided like this, and in the process of losing one imaginary self – reflected in the Sufi phrase 'To die before we die' – can we gain real self-knowledge. Then the opportunity of recognising that we are connected to universal consciousness arises.

Shah always emphasised in person and in his writings that the main barrier to our evolutionary progress is emotionalism and that, if we wish to evolve, we must learn to discriminate between different feelings. Strong emotions, he once said to me, are the bane of our existence, a burden we have to carry. It is strong feelings that prevent us from seeing beneath the surface of events to what is otherwise hidden. Only when enough of the population has learnt to carry this burden without being so easily overwhelmed by emotions will our species progress from our current level of primitivism.

For this to happen Shah had realized early in his life that the first step has to be educational: preparing the ground. To paraphrase the Wikipedia entry about him, he set about showing how Sufism was a universal form of wisdom that predated Islam, emphasizing that it was not static but always adapted itself to the given time, place and people to which it was applied. For Western people, he framed his teaching in modern psychological terms, just as earlier Sufis had framed theirs in terms acceptable to the cultures in which they lived – most notably Islamic cultures but also Hindu, Buddhist, Christian and others. Like those before him he made extensive use of traditional teaching stories and parables that contained multiple patterns of meaning designed to trigger insight and self-reflection in the reader.

I have only kept in contact with a handful of those who attended meetings at Langton or were in the London groups he supervised: Pat Williams, her husband David Pendlebury and Denise Winn mainly. And whenever I've met others who were there during those times we don't reminisce about them much because of the danger of sentimentalising that period, which would not be helpful to anyone. All everyone wants is for people to read, enjoy and learn from the material Shah left behind, which is easily available to read on the internet.

There is a metaphor that sums up for me how some individuals assimilated his influence: When a clove of garlic is added to a pot of different foods it gradually permeates the whole dish until it loses its own flavour, becoming part of the whole. The Sufi approach is likened to this. In those it touches it affects all aspects of their personality, imagination and behaviour. They are then more likely to freely give of themselves until they dissolve and merge with the whole culture, influencing it in subtle ways.

CHAPTER ELEVEN

The matter of knowledge

IDRIES SHAH died before Joe and I got going with our effort to improve the teaching of psychology and psychotherapy and sadly the opportunity to discuss with him what we were attempting to do had passed. Of course our therapeutic work was about stabilizing disturbed people, not spiritual self-development. However, when we began gathering our ideas together about time and the nature of consciousness and what mysticism is for, I would dearly have liked his input. One thing is for certain, without Shah's influence we would never have written *Godhead: The Brain's Big Bang*.

Shah once said that he could describe the true situation of humanity in a few words as near as it is possible to do so: 'The truth is straightforward enough, but it is so strange and unlikely that people would not believe me if I told them.' He made it clear that he had found it impossible to talk to people directly in straightforward language using scientific or psychological terms because the ideas are too challenging for most people. He had tried doing so and it didn't work, he had to approach people through entertainment: folk stories, tales of white haired old mystics in the mountains, secret societies or magical talismans and so on. That way the metaphorical patterns in the tales bypass resistance and begin to work in their minds until gradually they start to take effect. It is a more gradual process. Metaphors prime new internal templates for later realisation. 'If I were to just tell people the truth straight out – few would pay any attention,' he said.

One of the ideas in *Godhead* derives from the piece of truth – the fact – discovered by physicists that, at the quantum level, the smallest particles of matter everywhere are constantly disappearing, winking in and out of existence, and, each time they reappear, they are slightly changed. Joe and I asked ourselves, could this be connected to the truth that Shah was talking about? Is this a clue to the question of where we have come from and where we will return to, that Sufis urge us to reflect on?

It seems that, unless it is observed, an electron can't decide if it's a particle, a wave or both. This means that everything at the *macro* level in the Universe is in continual motion at the *micro* level: disappearing and reappearing according to the next possibility. And, since the macro and micro level coexist, that means that the whole Universe is oscillating in and out of existence in an eternal moment, and what we perceive as a solid reality is an illusion. But what is *not* an illusion is that we are observing the illusion!

One writer described the process like this: 'There is no temporal interval between the annihilation and the re-manifestation, so that one does not perceive an interruption between the two analogous and successive creations, and this existence appears homogenous... In so far as man is a possibility of manifestation but he does not see that which manifests him, he is pure absence; contrarily, in so far as he received his being from the perpetual irradiation of the Essence, he is.' The writer was Ibn al-Arabi, an Andalusian Sufi who was born in 1165 AD and known as 'The Greatest Master'.

In the fifteenth century another Sufi, Nur ad-Din Abd ar-Rahman Jami, wrote 'This universe is changed and renewed unceasingly at every moment and at every breath. Every instant one universe is annihilated and another resembling it is taking its place and the majority of men do not perceive this.'

In 1979 The Sufi Trust published part of *The Dabistan* of Moshin Fani (I painted the book jacket to Shah's instructions). The English translators called it *The Religion of the Sufis*. In it is the following passage: 'The real Being, under no condition of "a thing" and under no condition of "nothing" is called "essence, absolute being, objectivity" and it is manifesting itself in all existences, and under the condition of "a thing and nothing" is the form of the universe.'

A difficulty I had for many years was in recognising that so many of these inspired statements from the great Sufis of the past that were put before us by Shah were literally true. One has to persist in puzzling over them: perhaps for years before finding this out. The only way Joe and I could explain this universal oscillation was with the idea that there was a type of subjective matter existing side by side with all quantum particles keeping them linked together in what we called a 'universal relaton field'. We called the hypothesised subjective particles 'relatons' because they facilitate *relationships* between all forms of matter and give structure to it by carrying a field of possibilities, a type of force around each material particle that gives structure to relationships by recognising the possibilities available each moment for each particle. Relatons – subjective matter – we must have been in the Universe from the very first moment the Big Bang happened and accompanied every shard of primordial matter as the Universe expanded.

Each relaton field always develops and maintains relationships based on the best next possibility arising out of each oscillation.

Everything in the Universe is linked together through these fields.

We then noted that the action of relatons as a linking substance were referred to by others like Jami, who wrote:

'…the universe, together with all its parts, is nothing but a number of accidents, ever changing and being renewed at every breath and linked together in a single substance, and at each instant disappearing and being replaced by a similar set. In consequence of this rapid succession, the spectator is deceived into the belief that the universe is a permanent existence.'

If each particle making up the linking substance that generated the energy field that this Sufi spoke about was a 'relaton' and, since all relatons bring their knowledge with them, this field would have a form of awareness: it would know what was immediately happening in the material realm as it connected particles together so they could change form and evolve. And because all the fields in the Universe are connected: the Universe must be a conscious mind. Although all relatons at the beginning point of the Universe had an elementary object-consciousness, it would have been very dim at first because relatons would have been totally preoccupied with pattern-matching to matter. Now it is a supreme intelligence because it is pattern-matching to all the complexities of living things, including all forms of consciousness, and bringing them into being with each oscillation.

So consciousness was there from the start, unconfined, all-seeing, pervading everything. When human beings sensed that this 'mind' existed they gave it names such as 'God', 'Supreme Being' or 'Allah'.

This universal mind was declared by Muhammad to have revealed that, 'I was a hidden treasure, and I wished to be known, so I created a creation (mankind), then made Myself known to them, and they recognised Me.'

This universal mind can only see itself if a form of consciousness like us can materialise from within the eternal moment and look at what is continually being created. This requires that we, and everything that sustains us, must exist in time and thereby must die in order to return.

It occurs to me that this declaration of Allah/God/Supreme Being, however one refers to it, might explain something that has puzzled me since my art college days: why do we obsessively want to record passing moments in words or pictures? Why, in the presence of a beautiful scene, are so many of us driven to stop looking directly at it in the moment and take a photo or want to paint a painting instead? Perhaps this *urge* to preserve or make some sort of record of a moment, which so often seems instinctive, is an unconscious preparation for taking knowledge of this world back into the universal mind to add to its store of information and help to fulfil the universal mind's wish, '...to be known.' After all, since we are all one mind, when we die we all carry knowledge of this world back into the universal relaton field. It would follow that we must reveal more of the 'hidden treasure' every time we focus on its material expression: *and, if we live well, we can enrich it.*

When we had this relaton idea – that every material particle is accompanied by a subjective particle eternally searching for possible connections – it enabled us to make a case, in keeping with the laws of science, for evolution not having come about solely by chance. Instead, we suggest, it drew on totally interconnected knowledge, the patterns accumulated in the universal relaton field – a material and spiritual phenomenon of such scope and subtlety that human beings can only experience it momentarily in states of profound intuition. That some people have done so under certain circumstances is beyond doubt, as the above quotations illustrate. The following translation of the 12th century Persian telling of the classic tale of *Shirin and Farhad* included in a book by Ernest Scott, *The People of the Secret,* published by Shah's Octagon Press, clearly describes the same understanding.

'There is a strong propensity which dances through every atom, and attracts the minutest particle to some peculiar object; search this Universe from its base to its summit, from fire to air, from water to earth, from all below the moon to all above the celestial spheres, and thou will not find a corpuscle destitute of that natural attractability; the very point of the first thread in this apparently tangled skein is no other than such a principle of attraction, and all principles beside are void of a real basis; from such a propensity arises every motion perceived in heavenly or in terrestrial bodies; it is a disposition to be attracted which taught hard steel to rush from its place and rivet itself on the magnet; it is the same disposition which impels the light straw to attach itself firmly to amber; it is this quality which gives every substance in nature a tendency toward another, and an inclination forcibly directed to a determinate point.'

Ernest Scott was the pseudonym of a Scottish journalist, Edward Campbell. I designed the cover for *The People of the Secret* and commissioned an illustrator to airbrush the image I wanted on it: the earth with eight comets around it forming an octagon. When talking to Edward about the book I asked him how much influence Shah had on its content and he said that it was considerable and Shah supplied much of the quotations and sources for it.

What Joe and I inferred had happened was that, when the cosmological Big Bang occurred, not only was space-time shattered into the minuscule precursors of elementary and composite subatomic particles, but the universal relaton field was also shattered with it and every separate particle of primordial objective matter took with it a relaton connected to the relaton field. (In our idea, objective matter and subjective matter are always present together.) Each relaton – which, like any other particle, exists as a particle and a field – would be capable of making a perfect relationship with all other relatons and have an innate tendency to attract and join up with any of them in whatever ways presented themselves.

A perfect relationship is analogous to how two drops of water become one when juxtaposed. Once joined, the two drops cannot be differentiated: there is a common essence. In this way, as matter evolved more complex patterns, the accompanying relaton fields would also integrate in the eternal present: 'God', the universal mind, would become more knowledgeable about every inanimate and animate particle that existed. There are descriptions of the eternal present in Sufi writings such as *A Glossary Of Sufi Technical Terms* (Istilahat as-Sufiya) by Kamal ad-Din Abi al-Ghana'im 'Abd ar-Razaaq al-Qashani as-Samarkandi who died 1330AD. This was translated by Dr Nabil Safwat and revised and edited by David Pendlebury and published in 1991 by Octagon Press as *A Glossary Of Sufi Technical Terms*.

'The full expanse of the Divine Presence within which Eternity-without-beginning merges into Eternity-without-end. For that which has its being in both, both are represented as in the present time. Thus Eternity-without-beginning, Eternity-without-end and the present moment are all united within it. That is why it is called "mystical time", and the "source of time": for moments of time are simply patterns and alterations within it, by which its laws and forms are made manifest; while it endures exactly as it is, forever, endlessly – though it can combine with the subjective presence. As the Prophet said, "Your Lord has no morning and no evening."'

Talk of the Prophets, mystics and ancient knowledge doesn't impress Western scientists or intellectual types today. Nevertheless science has discovered that at a quantum level all matter in the Universe, including us, is continually being recreated: the entire Universe is oscillating in the eternal moment, as ancient and modern mystical writings describe. In a sense we are universe-hopping all the time to the next universal set of probability patterns, but totally unaware of it. This notion reconciles many questions surrounding the notion of free will, willpower and human destiny because, as the Universe completes itself with every oscillation, our essence is continually reintegrating back into the state of the Godhead. We, of course, know nothing about it because our soul and personality live in relative time in a 'slowed-down' universe, which is why we have a degree of free will (so the Godhead can ask questions of us). If this perpetual oscillation wasn't happening in the eternal moment, free will couldn't exist because we would all automatically integrate back to one – whoosh! – just that once, and that would be it.

The only way this truth can be *experienced* is by temporarily escaping the bonds of space and time, as mystics do. But, thanks to quantum science and the vast amount of information available in written form, this knowledge can at least now be *approached* through the intellect prior to experiencing it directly.

* * * * *

Simultaneously while Joe and I worked on *Godhead* we had to earn a living. Eventually we decided to appoint a board of trusted individuals to carry out the work expected of a membership organisation. From that founding moment the board started to address the question we were continually being asked by a significant minority of people wanting to do our training: who accredits the Human Givens approach? The new Labour government put an accrediting body in place and we were working towards accreditation with it when the government changed in 2010 and we had to start all over again with a new quango.

As I said, we become the slaves of those from whom we seek approval. At bottom this is why my heart sank when the HGI sought approval from the Professional Standards Authority (PSA), a quango that knows nothing about our work, does not consider therapeutic outcomes from different models of therapy, yet asks us to pay £12,000 just for the privilege of applying and having our 'processes' approved and £9,000 a year after that so that we can continue to say we are 'accredited'. (When asked why it was so expensive the quango represen-tative told us that we had to cover their office costs and salaries.)

As far as I can see, judging by the state of most hospitals, schools, the police and mental health services, there is no evidence that standards improve when government quangos are involved. Quangos are how ministers exercise patronage, extend their influence beyond their term of office, purloin legal powers over us that we taxpayers have not agreed to and evade responsibility for how they spend our money. Quangos are inherently undemocratic, expensive and conducive to over-extending government intrusion into the lives of citizens and businesses – and they make us pay through the nose for their endeavours.

Long ago I realized that healthy organisations are run with the minimal bureaucracy necessary for maximum efficiency and effectiveness. Those who run bureaucratic quangos do not produce wealth and so they have to live off those who do. (If quangos worked the country would have efficient, safe hospitals, a decrease in mental illness throughout the country, and effective education, transport and policing systems and so on.) Quangos feed off the efforts of those who do real work; or provide services that create added value and that customers are willing to pay for, either directly or through taxation.

It seems to me that the fee the quango charged to approve our organisation is a form of hidden taxation – a way of raising money to provide employment for non-productive white-collar workers who justify their existence by manufacturing red tape on an industrial scale, simultaneously making us more subservient. The cost of this, I think, just enlarges the mountain of debt that future generations will face.

Ever since HGI members pressed for PSA accreditation, however, members of the HGI board heroically struggled to understand the requirements we had to meet to prove our probity and gain this approval. This is in order to satisfy the demands of members that an outside, 'government approved' body should accredit us. It seems to me that, instead of being an independent body operating with a 'light touch', we are morphing into exactly the type of organisation we set out not to be – a fact that some others and I find dispiriting. We are becoming an administrative body in a way that splits our attention, undermining our prime purpose, just as universities were being undermined. Seeking accreditation involved several board members in thousands of hours of drudgery. We had to set up new committees for this and that, fill in forms and answer hundreds of questions – all in the name of 'protecting the public', which is what we were genuinely doing in the first place when we developed the HG approach.

Our original aim was to have a minimum sufficient regulation approach to what we do: to be pragmatic, independent, watch good therapy being done by others, encourage people to learn by immersing themselves in the experience of doing therapy, be inspired by the new psychological knowledge behind the HG approach, and to encourage people to study the ideas and examine their outcomes.

* * * * *

What I have realised as a result of working with the public and getting to know hundreds of people quite well is that Shah's description of the flaws in humanity are true: we do continually work against our best interests; we often can't see what's in front of our eyes. It's one thing to read about and declaim to all and sundry on our unbalanced, egotistical nature and quite another to really see these flaws in oneself, as we have to do if we are to make progress.

Near the beginning of this book I told of a pivotal event that led me to meet Idries Shah: a passage from *In Search of the Miraculous* where Ouspensky quoted Gurdjieff when he was talking about art. Here is another quote from that book that seems to sum up our times whilst explaining what Shah was doing and reminds us to be more aware of what is happening all around us:

'There are periods in the life of humanity, which generally coincide with the beginning of the fall of cultures and civilizations, when the masses irretrievably lose their reason and begin to destroy everything that has been created by centuries and millennia of culture. Such periods of mass-madness, often coinciding with geological cataclysms, climatic changes and similar phenomena of a planetary character, release a very great quantity of the matter of knowledge. This, in its turn, necessitates the work of collecting this matter of knowledge, which would otherwise be lost. Thus the work of collecting scattered matter of knowledge frequently coincides with the beginning of the destruction and fall of cultures and civilizations.'

* * * * *

It is evening as I write this and I feel the urge to briefly tell about my life now. Véronique and I live in Sibford Gower, an ancient Cotswold village close to a line of springs that feed into the River Stour and, ultimately, the River Severn. (Véronique has two children from her first marriage, Simon and Katherine. Simon is married to Lucy and they live in London with their children, Kit and Florence.) It was Véronique who found our house by the simple expedient of putting notes through the letterboxes of south facing properties she felt she could live in saying, 'If ever you want to sell your house, please phone this number ...'

Just as every person has a history, so does every place. Close by Sibford stand the mysterious Rollright Stones dating back to the Bronze Age. Since their construction thousands of years ago they have accumulated a wealth of myth and folklore around them. Modern day Druids hold eccentric ceremonies there and attempt to 'tune in' to the 'harmonics' of the place. Sibford itself began as an Iron Age settlement, was mentioned in the Domesday Book as being gifted by William the Conqueror to two Norman knights, then, for 300 years, it fell into the possession of Templar Knights. There are families in Sibford claiming descent from Templar refugees who in 1307 fled from the bloody persecutions of King Philip IV in France.

The area was not always peaceful. Five miles away is Edge Hill, site of the first pitched battle of the English Civil War in 1642. And a mile away from our house as the crow flies is the sinisterly named Traitors Ford where ambushes and summary executions occurred during that war. There were many other bloody skirmishes between Cavaliers and Roundheads nearby. Fortunately at the moment there is no open civil war in Britain.

In later years, George Fox, founder of the Quakers (The Society of Friends), preached in the village before the official persecution of his movement began in 1680. The Quaker influence is still here, which is probably why there is such a strong communal feel to the place: most people are warm, friendly and considerate. Within living memory if someone had a house that had become too large for them, they would swap it with a growing young family who needed more room – without money changing hands. The local Quaker school still provides a lunch every week for the elderly residents from the village and surrounding area, who are gathered by villagers to ensure companionship and to keep an eye on them. Véronique is one of the volunteers helping with this.

As soon as we moved to Sibford we were made welcome and the village wrapped itself around us. Within three weeks we were invited to three parties so we could be introduced to locals from round and about. It's a proper community full of varied characters each carrying a vast range of experiences. Many of them are now good friends. Locals often tell us how lucky we are to live here, which reminds me of Shah being amused by those who kept wanting him to agree with them that we were lucky to live in England because it was such a great country. But this part of the Cotswolds is undoubtedly a delightful area to live in and there are good people here, as there are everywhere of course.

There is little traffic so, in the surrounding lanes and countryside, children can roam as free as I could in the 40s and 50s. I also keep coming across examples of that endangered species: natives not continually tied to smartphones and who are willing to talk and enjoy one another's company without constantly giving in to the addiction of texting, Facebook or emailing – joy. There is time and space to read, reflect and write in peace, far away from traffic noise and what are to me the life-deadening sounds that emanate day and night from cities and urban sprawl.

The wind farm blight that has spread like a destructive canker over so much of the UK has not reached here and the bucolic atmosphere remains relatively unspoilt. The local pubs serve great food. Six working farms radiate out from the village. Farmers raise crops and animals and look after the rolling hills and valleys responsibly although, unfortunately, they are not allowed to cull the badgers that are spreading TB to cattle and caused a wonderful local organic dairy herd to be destroyed recently. It was rare treat to see a badger when I was a boy but, since they became a protected species, their numbers have increased to plague proportions and they have become a nuisance. There are hundreds of setts within a mile or two of the village. Because of overcrowding a third of badgers are diseased and, since they have no natural predators to reduce them they eat crops, hedgehogs and the eggs of ground nesting birds and have become a menace.

However the hunt rides and shoots still take place: in the shooting season friends drop by with a brace of pheasant for us. Farmer Bill round the corner provides us with wonderful honey from his hives. Gardening is a favourite pastime in the village, especially among much of the delightful Sibford Sisterhood (who were unfailingly generous in supporting us through our times of illness). Horses frequently add to the pleasure by generating one of my favourite sounds, that of clip-clopping hooves trotting down the lane. The wildlife, cloudscapes and sunsets can take your breath away, and there is no light pollution here, thanks to the villagers emphatically voting against street lamps being installed – so at night we see the stars sharp and clear.

I now work from home and have a new young team running the college. Joe is working successfully with Bart McEnroe in the business arena where so much stress and craziness is generated by caetextic behaviour. It was Bart who, after doing our diploma, recognised that it was innate emotional needs – the human givens – that motivate people. Companies and corporations are always looking for ways to do this and HG ideas can help them. Meanwhile I am working with the diplomat John Bell, Director of the Middle East and Mediterranean Programme at the Toledo International Centre for Peace, introducing HG ideas and skills into the diplomatic world via training programmes on long term approaches to tackling extremism, particularly as it affects conflict resolution in the world's trouble spots.

* * * * *

Joe and I wrote *Godhead: The Brain's Big Bang* because we couldn't find a book that satisfactorily explained the connection that we could see existed between creativity, mysticism and mental illness. It took seven years. Among other things the effort of writing it was a way of expressing our own responses to questions and observations raised by Idries Shah in his books and talks.

Shah wrote and spoke directly about how we have the possibility of developing a perception that can escape space and time. We asked ourselves, how would that work and attempted an answer. Shah also revealed stories from esoteric traditions that allude to the eternal moment and our illusory perception of time. One such is 'The Sultan who became an exile' found in *Tales of the Dervishes* where it is stressed that it is not whether this possibility to escape space and time and enter the eternal moment exists for us or not, but the significance of the happening if we do. If we are unprepared it is of no significance. So preparation is everything.

Another story in *The Commanding Self*, 'Revealing His True Nature', showed how, using hypnosis, a merchant was made to believe many years had passed during which he had experienced a completely different life, only to find that when he came out of trance only an hour had gone by and he was back where he started.

In *Godhead* we described why we thought that the ability to look at the cosmos and ask questions of it could only have arisen after we gained conscious access to the imaginative mind, the internal theatre in the REM state, about 40,000 years ago. It was that revelatory moment that started a few groups off on the quest to understand the deeper truth behind appearances. Some of these seekers eventually become aware by mystical knowledge of the 'all-knowing' universal mind that holds everything together in an eternal moment, continually oscillating between a state of nothingness containing all information and possibilities – what European mystics called 'the Godhead' and physicists call the vacuum, the lowest energy state possible that is nevertheless a seething turmoil of creation and annihilation – and the material reality we experience in what we like to call the real world that manifests from this state, based on what is possible for every particle in the Universe.

Shah often mentioned the problem of obsessionals getting in the way of people trying to do a job of work: in his case specifically, the work of preparing the ground for Sufi understanding.

In our work Joe and I came to realize that the essence of obsessive behaviour is being context blind and we could see that context blindness, what we called 'caetextia', was apparent throughout the autistic spectrum but was the most dominant manifestation of autistic behaviour at the highest functioning levels of the spectrum. Shah often stressed that we need to get a grip on our emotions rather than let them control us. One of the reasons for this is that we all become caetextic when we get highly emotional.

You can't always tell if someone is an obsessional immediately. For instance in the 1970s my family and I met a man at a lovely public swimming pool in California where we had gone to cool down. On the face of it he seemed normal enough but it turned out that he had an obsession – one he thought we would approve of.

This fellow realised that we were English from our accents and came over to chat. He told us that he loved our country and its history so much that he and his wife had been visiting England once or twice every year for decades. As we were getting ready to leave the pool he invited us to his home for afternoon tea. So we went. When we arrived we were shown into a huge living room.

After his wife served us tea and cake he seemed excited and asked us if we had noticed anything about the room. I couldn't help but see that along one wall and around the great fireplace were hundreds of little metal plaques of varying sizes with objects mounted on them. I pointed to them and asked, 'What are they?'

Obviously pleased that I'd spotted his collection he urged us to take a closer look. That was when we discovered that each plaque was mounted with a bit of stone, metal or wood and had an inscription naming the site in England where it had come from and a date. Each plaque carried an item chipped off the fabric of one of our national treasures! Stonehenge, Avebury, Tower of London, York Minster, Westminster Cathedral, Hadrian's Wall. As far as I could tell, without doing an inventory, he had bits of stone from all our major cathedrals and churches lovingly displayed alongside chips he had surreptitiously knocked from palaces, castles, country houses, famous pubs and iconic bridges. He even had splinters from Anne Hathaway's Cottage and old British ships like the Victory and Cutty Sark. He was a dedicated Anglophile but also a desecrator: a thief who stole little pieces of our historical fabric as trophies to display in his own country. The weird thing was that he thought we would be pleased to see this evidence of his love of English history and our homeland.

Nothing in this world is perfect. Everything decays: the most beautiful apple sooner or later becomes home for a worm. In a high valley hidden up in the Taurus Mountains Véronique and I visited a small summer camp of nomads. They were looking after their cows and goats grazing on flower-covered pastures. It was a peaceful scene made doubly magical by the gentle sound of goat bells and birdsong. We were entranced and strolled over the wide meadows towards some tall trees whose rustling leaves were shimmering in the sunlight. But up on a hillock was an incongruous wooden pavilion and, to our dismay, among the rocks and grass all around it were crushed beer cans, plastic containers and shards of glass from broken bottles. We later found out that the council of a local town some 30 kilometres away had thought it would be a good idea to get their young people up into these pristine meadows to appreciate the wild beauty of the place and grasp an idea of how their nomadic forefathers had lived. The carelessly scattered detritus we had seen was the result of these caetextic, council organised drunken coach parties.

* * * * *

We all manifest out of nothing. In an eternal moment the entire Universe oscillates between a state of nothingness that contains all information and from which we arise, to a state where everything is the material we see. This state of nothing that contains everything is our origin to which we all return. This manifestation out of nothing is called the arc of descent. But, this is a unitary phenomenon and there is also an arc of *ascent:* the route back to total integration of all information in the nothing state of 'oneness'.

The arc of descent and the arc of ascent are different manifestations of the same thing and represent a present moment so complex, inter-connected and vast – the entire Universe – that ordinary thought cannot encompass it. But, since this process has been witnessed by some human beings and they came to realise that the arc of descent and the arc of ascent hold the Universe together, it is possible to appreciate that, without striving for the truth beyond appearances and the reality beyond evil, there would be no existence for us. There is a special type of non-intellectual perception that can encompass 'Truth' and conscious-ness contributes to the continuing manifestation of the universe. This is so because every bit of matter is possessed of a level of consciousness, which is why and how it can and does form relationships with other types of matter. Without consciousness nothing would exist. Consciousness is integral to all matter.

* * * * *

For Sufis, Shah said, 'The world is a fashioning instrument that polishes mankind. They, by identification with the processes of continuous creation, are themselves fashioners of other complete men.' This means that Sufis are not, and can never be, what anyone else thinks they are. Not all Sufis are teachers but those that have that role concentrate on helping those that can to learn so that more of us can leave this place of bewitchment more easily, not grieving for it, not craving, but freely submitting to the requirements of reality.

The Idries Shah Foundation

You can find out more about the work of Idries Shah, which I urge you to do, by going to idriesshahfoundation.org

The Idries Shah Foundation exists to make sure his work remains available to the public throughout the world, to which end it has made his books available free to read online and published hard copies, which I personally prefer, are also available to purchase.

It also has a Facebook page that posts every day.

HG Books

Human Givens: A new approach to emotional health and clear thinking, Joe Griffin and Ivan Tyrrell

Godhead: The brain's big bang, Joe Griffin and Ivan Tyrrell

Dreaming Reality: How dreaming keeps us sane or can drive us mad, Joe Griffin and Ivan Tyrrell

Why we Dream: The definitive answer, Joe Griffin and Ivan Tyrrell

How to lift depression ... fast, Joe Griffin and Ivan Tyrrell

How to Master Anxiety, Joe Griffin and Ivan Tyrrell

Freedom from Addiction: The secret behind successful addiction busting Joe Griffin and Ivan Tyrrell

Release from Anger: Practical help for controlling unreasonable rage Joe Griffin and Ivan Tyrrell

An Idea in Practice: Using the human givens approach, Joe Griffin and Ivan Tyrrell (Eds)

The Origin of Dreams, Joe Griffin

The Survival Option, Ivan Tyrrell

Human Givens Journal, Editors Denise Winn and Ivan Tyrrell.

Books and the journal can be ordered from Human Givens Publishing Ltd, Chalvington. East Sussex, BN27 3TD, UK
Tel: +44 (0)1323 811662
Email: info@humngivens.com
Email: the-editor@humangivens.com
Or buy online at: www.humangivens.com

Acknowledgements

Grateful thanks are due to John Zada, Julia Welstead, Jane Tyrrell and my wife Véronique for reading the text, suggesting clarifications and proof reading. Jane particularly helped jog my memory.

My warm appreciation is offered for the stimulating companionship over the years of Joe Griffin, Pat Williams, Denise Winn, and my daughters Jane and Eleanor and the rest of the team at Human Givens College, not forgetting our wonderful tutors, students and the board members of the Human Givens Institute and the trustees of out charity the Human Given Foundation.

It goes without saying that the rest of my family, friends and associates who, in sum, are too numerous to mention without making these acknowledgements look ridiculously overblown, are also much appreciated.

The Human Givens Institute
www.hgi.org.uk

Human Givens Foundation
www.hgfoundation.com

Human Givens College
www.humangivenscollege.com